THE ART OF MEASUREMENT

ISBN 0-13-026174-2

Hewlett-Packard® Professional Books

OPERATING SYSTEMS

Fernandez	Configuring CDE: The Common Desktop Environment
Lund	Integrating UNIX® and PC Network Operating Systems
Madell	Disk and File Management Tasks on HP-UX
Poniatowski	HP-UX 11.x System Administration Handbook and Toolkit
Poniatowski	HP-UX 11.x System Administration "How To" Book, Second Edition
Poniatowski	HP NetServer Guide for Windows NT®
Poniatowski	HP-UX System Administration Handbook and Toolkit
Poniatowski	HP-UX 10.x System Administration "How To" Book
Poniatowski	Learning the HP-UX Operating System
Poniatowski	Windows NT® and HP-UX System Administrator's "How To" Book
Sauers, Weygant	HP-UX Tuning and Performance
Stone, Symons	UNIX® Fault Management
Weygant	Clusters for High Availability: A Primer of HP-UX Solutions
Yawn, Stachnick, Sellars	The Legacy Continues: Using the HP 3000 with HP-UX and Windows NT

ONLINE/INTERNET

Amor	The E-business (R)evolution
Greenberg, Lakeland	A Methodology for Developing and Deploying Internet and Intranet Solutions
Greenberg, Lakeland	Building Professional Web Sites with the Right Tools
Ketkar	Working with Netscape Server on HP-UX
Lee	The ISDN Consultant

NETWORKING/COMMUNICATIONS

Blommers	Practical Planning for Network Growth
Costa	Planning and Designing High Speed Networks
Lucke	Designing and Implementing Computer Workgroups
Pipkin	Halting the Hacker: A Practical Guide to Computer Security
Thornburgh	Fibre Channel for Mass Storage

ENTERPRISE

Blommers	Architecting Enterprise Solutions with UNIX Networking
Cook	Building Enterprise Information Architectures
Sperley	Enterprise Data Warehouse, Volume 1: Planning, Building, and Implementation

PROGRAMMING

Blinn	Portable Shell Programming
Caruso	Power Programming in HP OpenView
Chew	The Java™/C++ Cross-Reference Handbook
Grady	Practical Software Metrics for Project Management and Process Improvement
Grady	Successful Software Process Improvement
Lewis	The Art & Science of Smalltalk
Lichtenbelt, Crane, Naqvi	Introduction to Volume Rendering
Millquist	SNMPH
Mikkelsen, Pherigo	Practical Software Configuration Management
Norton, DiPasquale	Thread Time: The Multithreaded Programming Guide
Ryan	Distributed Object Technology: Concepts and Applications
Simmons	Software Measurement: A Visualization Toolkit

IMAGE PROCESSING

Crane	A Simplified Approach to Image Processing
Day	The Color Scanning Handbook
Gann	Desktop Scanners: Image Quality

OTHER TITLES OF INTEREST

Kane	PA-RISC 2.0 Architecture
Loomis	Object Databases in Practice
Mahoney	High-Mix Low-Volume Manufacturing

THE ART OF MEASUREMENT
Theory and Practice

RONALD W. POTTER

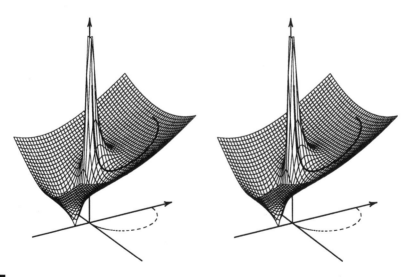

Prentice Hall PTR
Upper Saddle River, New Jersey 07458
www.phptr.com

Acquisitions editor: *Jill Pisoni*
Editorial assistant: *Linda Ramagnano*
Cover design: *Talar Agasyan*
Cover design director: *Jerry Votta*
Manufacturing manager: *Maura Goldstaub*
Marketing manager: *Lisa Konzelmann*
Projection coordinator: *Anne Trowbridge*
Compositor/Production services: *Pine Tree Composition, Inc.*

Prentice Hall books are widely used by corporations and government agencies for training, marketing, and resale.

The publisher offers discounts on this book when ordered in bulk quantities. For more information contact:

Corporate Sales Department
Phone: 800-382-3419
Fax: 201-236-7141
E-mail: corpsales@prenhall.com

Or write:

Prentice Hall PTR
Corp. Sales Dept.
One Lake Street
Upper Saddle River, New Jersey 07458

Printed in the United States of America
10 9 8 7 6 5 4 3 2 1

ISBN 0-13-026174-2

Prentice-Hall International (UK) Limited, *London*
Prentice-Hall of Australia Pty. Limited, *Sydney*
Prentice-Hall Canada Inc., *Toronto*
Prentice-Hall Hispanoamericana, S.A., *Mexico*
Prentice-Hall of India Private Limited, *New Delhi*
Prentice-Hall of Japan, Inc., *Tokyo*
Prentice-Hall (*Singapore*) Pte. Ltd., *Singapore*
Editora Prentice-Hall do Brasil, Ltda., *Rio de Janeiro*

Contents

Preface

This is a book about measuring and is consequently aimed at an audience interested in the *quantitative* aspects of the world around them. It is dedicated especially to those who feel they do not understand a physical system until they can fully *measure* its parameters, including the *statistics* on those parameters. The book is general in scope and does not attempt to cover particular fields of measurement in any detail. It is largely up to you, the reader, to adapt these ideas and techniques to your *own* particular area of interest.

Before the advent of microprocessors, a measurement generally involved *explicit* quantities such as distance or voltage, determined by reading a scale or a meter. Most early books about measuring techniques tended to emphasize the "best" methods for getting good results from this approach. There has always been a need to measure the characteristics of more complicated physical systems, but it was very difficult to do. Now that microprocessors are so ubiquitous, we have the ability to measure much more complicated systems, involving various *implicit* parameters, which are not directly accessible to a scale or meter. The new approach is to collect quantities of data from whatever points *are* physically accessible, and then to estimate the parameters of interest within the system that would *cause* this particular set of data. This estimation procedure is centered around a mathematical model of the physical system, in which there are "free" parameters. The measurement task is to estimate these parameter values such that the *observed* data "matches" the corresponding data from the *model*.

In addition, a measured parameter value expressed as a *single* number has little meaning and conveys only a *minuscule* amount of information when standing alone, unless many similar measurements have already been made, or unless a thorough error analysis of the measurement model has been completed. Is the number within 50% of the correct value, or is it within a part in a million? Is it perhaps a "wild" value that might occur only once out of many tries? Is it biased in one direction by some (unknown) amount? The probable *errors* in each measured parameter must be included as an *integral part* of the measurement, and all conditions and assumptions associated with the results must be clearly stated.

There are numerous, predominately theoretical, books on probability and statistics, Laplace and Fourier transforms, matrix algebra, and estimation procedures, which have little discussion of practical applications. Conversely, there are books that describe specific measurement tasks, but with minimal acknowledgment of the rationale or logical framework behind each one. What we *really* need is an approach that places *one* foot in the *theory* and the *other* foot in the *practice*. There are abundant practical measurement tasks that confront us, but the tools we need for these tasks reside in the *theory* of measuring. No one can be expected to do a professional quality job in *any* field without using the best available tools, applied in the proper manner.

In some respects this is a "how to . . ." book for people who make measurements, analogous to books that are available to the home handyman in endeavors like carpentry, plumbing, and wiring. There are well defined tasks to be performed, and there is a set of available tools to be used. The difference is that the tools here are mathematical procedures or *algorithms,* and the end products are numbers or *parameter estimates* in a mathematical model of the physical system of interest.

Although this is not meant to be an academic textbook on the subject, the treatment herein is more than superficial. This topic cannot be adequately discussed and explored without the help of mathematical concepts and relationships, since measuring is a *quantitative* activity. The required level of mathematical ability is somewhat difficult to define, but you will get the most out of the book if you have a background in such areas as *Fourier and Laplace transforms, matrix algebra, multidimensional vector spaces, probability theory, statistics,* and *estimation theory.* Even though some degree of technical expertise is a definite plus, nontechnical readers may *still* find the ideas interesting and understandable in a general way. You may simply skip the equations and read the *text.*

Many of the technical and mathematical "buzzwords" that appear herein are explained, although it is not possible to include a complete exposition on these subjects in a book of this size. We review some basic mathematical tools in Appendix A, and we include a Glossary in the back, where some of the words and concepts are briefly defined. If you run across a word or concept that is unfamiliar, then you might consider that as an invitation to investigate the subject more fully in *other* books.

The goals of this book are: First, to lay the groundwork for making *meaningful* measurements, by discussing the philosophy and abstract thinking that is required. The mindset or viewpoint of the measurer is *so* important that we emphasize the *philosophy* of measuring as a necessary starting point. Second, to address the many potential errors and error mechanisms that always seem to exist. It is sometimes very tedious to get decent results from a measurement because there are so many sources of error. The task of making a set of reliable measurements is primarily a task of system *error analysis.* Third, to review various theoretical procedures that are needed to do the "best" possible job in estimating the parameter values. At the end of the measuring process, we must decide where the measured parameter values actually *fall* within the range of all possible values, as well as on the degree of *confidence* we can place in these final values.

The first four chapters address the many broad theoretical and philosophical aspects of making good quantitative measurements, but it is equally important to illustrate the *practical side* of this activity. To this end, a few representative measurement examples are discussed throughout the first chapters, and are more fully explored in chapter 5. Four such examples have been selected, covering a broad spectrum of measurement applications. These are: (**1**) measuring the DC resistance of a battery or power supply, (**2**) estimating the loop gain of a closed-loop control system, (**3**) measuring the modal parameters of a vibrating mechanical structure, and (**4**) determining position coordinates on the Earth, using the Global Positioning System (a satellite navigation technique, abbreviated GPS). With these examples as guides, it should be possible for the reader to adapt these ideas and techniques to his or her own particular measurement project.

We should set the highest standards for each measurement task. The *quality* of measured parameters is just as important as the estimated *values* of the parameters themselves, and both of these depend on a quality measurement model. The consequences of incomplete, incorrect, or misunderstood measurements *can* be quite serious, and can also be *very costly.* Hopefully, after reading this book, you will be especially critical of measurements in general, whether made by yourself or by other people.

One of the graphical tools that we use rather freely in this book is the stereoscopic image pair, in which a separate image is drawn for each eye. By suitably combining these image pairs, you can see a three-dimensional view of an object or mathematical function. These images are more than just entertaining diversions, because they help convey ideas and concepts to our brain that might otherwise be hard to understand from flat drawings on paper. They enable us to actually *see* into a three-dimensional observation space, and to see one and two dimensional parameters spaces embedded in this three-space. For example, we can see two-dimensional joint probability density functions, and other two-dimensional surfaces as subspaces of a three-dimensional parent space. We can also see clouds of observation points around sets of parameter coordinates.

If you have not already trained your eyes to view these stereo images, you will be greatly rewarded when you master this technique. The object is to get each eye to look at (and focus on) *only* the image drawn for that eye. The left image is for the left eye and the right image is for the right eye. There are several ways to accomplish this task. One technique is to hold the paper relatively close to your face, while staring *through* the paper to infinity (by relaxing your eyes). Ignore poor focus in the beginning. You should see four images, comprising the two original images along with two more in between the originals. Concentrate on bringing the two interior images together by relaxing your eyes and imagine looking at the far wall of the room, through the paper. Once the images coalesce into one, slowly move the paper away from your face until it is easy to focus on the stereo figure. Some people like to hold a postcard or some larger opaque surface between their eyes, perpendicular to the paper. This seems to help decouple the eyes from one another. Don't worry about any sort of damage to your eye-tracking ability! The more practice, the easier this procedure becomes. If you get desperate, buy yourself a pair of stereo viewing glasses used for viewing pairs of aerial photographs. Good luck.

Introduction

Making measurements of physical quantities is an activity so commonplace we seldom think about the *complexity* of the process. After all, to measure a distance, you simply apply a ruler or tape measure and read off the result. A clock of appropriate design does a fine job of measuring and displaying elapsed time, and a thermometer indicates the temperature any time you glance at its scale. The two primary measurement tasks are to first construct a suitable "ruler" or *reference scale* for the quantity in question, and then to *compare* the unknown quantity being measured with the divisions on this scale.

Of course, repeated measurements of the same quantity are always somewhat *different.* As a user of this data, you may justifiably feel uncomfortable about these differences unless the *accuracy* of the measurement is determined or specified in some way. At least you would like to know the accuracy limits for some chosen percentage of the *time,* even though you may not know how good any *single* measurement might be. You would also like to know the extent of any "bias" that might lie hidden in your measured parameters. Does your thermometer always indicate a temperature that is 3 degrees too high? Is your ruler too short by 1%, so all of your distance estimates are too long by 1%? These are systematic errors, as opposed to random errors, but they are *still* errors that must be thoroughly understood.

You may also find that some of the physical quantities you need to measure are not explicitly *accessible* to your "rulers." For example, the values of the electrical elements *within* a network must often be deduced from data collected from a small number of *external* network nodes. Similarly, the effects of the many resonant frequencies and damping factors of a vibrating mechanical structure are generally mixed together in a complicated way when you observe the displacement of a point on the structure over time, and they must be *separated* by some means. Thus, you must consider *implicit* or *indirect* measurement methods for these cases.

Behind all of these basic measurement attributes is the assumption that the *thing to be measured* is well defined and understood by all who have an interest in the measurement task, or who might *use* the resulting parameter estimates. We always have a (conscious or unconscious) *mental model* of this "thing" we are attempting to measure, along with some idea of its place within some *larger* system. Unfortunately, it is possible for this mental model to be defective in a number of different ways. For example, it is easy to be wrong about the exact topology of an electrical network, or about the exact endpoints in a distance measurement, or about the exact geometry within which you are working. Your mental model of what you plan to measure may not only be rather *approximate,* but may also be different from that assumed by other interested people.

The book is centered around the following basic ideas and concepts:

1. **A measurement is an estimate of a parameter** in an abstract *mental model* that is supposed to represent reality. That is, if the model is excited in exactly the same way, and under the same conditions as its physical counterpart, then the results predicted by the model will match the results actually *observed* in the real world. The parameters built into the model are to be adjusted until the *best* fit is obtained between the actual observations and the observations predicted by the model. The word "model" does *not* imply the actual construction of a physical object, but rather a mathematical representation or description of the physical system, although block diagrams and flow charts are often used as intermediaries to help in visualizing the system topology. A model must be *quantitative* in nature, so its behavior, or output, can always be calculated from its various inputs and conditions.

2. **The model must be valid** for all cases of interest. The *quality* of a particular model can be judged by observing the fidelity of the output of the model compared to the real physical output, for a variety of *different* inputs. A major reason for having a model is to be able to accurately predict the output for any *combination* of input excitations and conditions. If the measured model parameters differ for different inputs, then the model must be incorrect.

3. **Every model is incomplete**. Some model parameters may actually represent *several* real parameters, either because that is deemed to be a suitable approximation, or because the correct model is not completely understood. There can be parameters that appear to be distinct and unrelated, but are actually parts of a *single* parameter. In this case, the parts cannot be measured separately unless additional data is collected to resolve the contribution of each part. Sometimes a particular parameter may not even be measurable, because its value has no apparent effect on the output of the model. Even the topology of the model may be wrong in some way. Since the model is only partially known, approximations are common.

4. **The accuracy of parameter estimates vary**. For any given set of raw observation data, some parameter values can generally be estimated with more accuracy and precision than others, because some parameters have more effect on the output of the model than others. In addition, some parameters may be affected by noise or interference more than others, depending on the locations of the various sources of contamination in the system and on the particular method or algorithm used in making the measurement. As mentioned above, some parameters may not even be *measurable* using only the available data. Each parameter in the model has its own special "personality," and each measurement algorithm has its own unique "signature," generally doing a better job on some parameters than on others.

5. **Implicit versus explicit parameters**. Some model parameters can be measured *explicitly,* like the distance between points, while others can only be *implied* because they are buried deeply in the model and are only visible via their effects on the output. The parameters describing the behavior of a closed-loop control system are good examples of implicit parameters, as are the elements in the equivalent circuit of a transistor.

   Another classification comprises parameters that are *self-evident* or *passive,* which do not require any source of excitation to measure, like time interval or pressure, in contrast with *hidden* or *active* parameters like viscosity or resonant frequency, which only become apparent when some sort of test excitation is applied.

6. **Estimation and optimization theory**. The values of *implicit* model parameters can only be estimated by *simultaneously* adjusting *all* parameter values until a best fit is obtained between the physical observations and the model predictions. It is generally *not* feasible to adjust *one* parameter at a time, because the parameters usually interact with one another (sometimes rather heavily). In this procedure, it is necessary to decide what "best" really means, and likewise to decide how to adjust all parameter values simultaneously so as to *converge* to this best fit in a fast and efficient manner (or even to converge *at all!*). Sometimes these techniques converge so slowly they are simply not practical.

7. **A measurement (or parameter estimate) is a random variable**, and hence comprises a *probability density function,* having a mean value, a variance (plus higher moments), and confidence intervals. This function describes the chance that a parameter value will fall within any specified range. The mean value may be biased, and the variance may *not* have been minimized. We use the concepts of *random variables, probability theory,* and *statistics* to study these effects.

8. **The quality of a measurement** (amount of *bias* and *variance*) depends both on the amount of noise in the original raw data set, *and* on the data reduction algorithm used. Thus, the properties and construction details of the estimation algorithm are quite important. Some algorithms may perform well, and others may perform poorly (or even be completely *wrong*). Unfortunately, it is often impossible to detect when a measurement is grossly incorrect by simply observing the results. For example, a bias will be invisible unless you happen to already *know* the correct

mean value. Bias errors are best detected and quantified by a mathematical analysis of the measurement model, *including* the data reduction algorithm.

9. **Data reduction algorithms are required.** In the *absence* of "noise" or unwanted perturbations, it is theoretically possible to calculate the values of n parameters from *exactly* n physical observations. However, unwanted perturbations are always present at some level, so these cause the parameter estimates to be effectively "random." As a result, it is nearly always necessary to make *more* than n observations in order to estimate the values of n parameters. Thus, a measurement nearly always involves some sort of *data reduction algorithm,* in which a mass of raw data is reduced to a few parameter values. This should be contrasted with various *data transformation algorithms* (like the Fourier transform, for example) that mold the data into a different *form* without reducing the information content of the data. A measurement is *not* just the collection of raw data, and *neither* is it the reversible transformation of this data into another format, but must generally involve a *reduction* in the amount of data to that corresponding to the number of model parameters.

   Having emphasized this point, there are indeed cases in which n observations *seem* to be used to estimate the values of n parameters. However, this is only feasible after the statistics of the parameter set have been established, either from many previous measurements or from measurement model calculations. A measurement is still a data reduction operation, but sometimes the bulk of the needed data can be collected and processed (or reduced) *ahead* of time, giving expected values for biases and variances, along with confidence intervals for each parameter, and perhaps including correlation coefficients relating the parameters to one another.

10. **A graphical interpretation of measuring.** We represent a set of n observations (where each observation is a real number) as a *single point* in an n-dimensional *abstract vector space* (called the *observation space*). Within this n-space, the measurement model, comprising m parameters, with all noise sources set to *zero,* will appear as a *subspace* of dimension m (implying that $m \leq n$). The model parameters form a coordinate system, so the location of any point *in* this *parameter subspace* is indexed by the set of m parameter values. The observation data will be perturbed by various noise sources in the model, so the *actual* observation point will seldom fall exactly *within* the parameter subspace. The estimation problem is to decide which point *in* the parameter subspace is the best representation of the *actual* observation point, wherever it is.

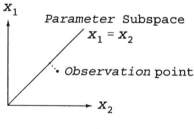

Observation Space

In the example above, we model a *constant* parameter value (meaning both observations x_1 and x_2 will be equal, except for noise). We choose the *perpendicular projection* of the observation point into the parameter subspace as our "best" parameter estimate, resulting in the *average* of the two observations.

This is called a *least-squares estimate* (which we will discuss in chapter 4). When the measurement model comprises a single constant parameter value, this perpendicular projection always produces the *average* of all of the observations, for *any* number of dimensions.

An estimation procedure is generally defined to be some sort of "best" projection of the *n*-dimensional observation point *into* the *m*-dimensional parameter subspace, from which all *m* of the estimated model parameter values can be obtained from the associated parameter coordinate system.

We should emphasize that we are talking about an *abstract* vector space, which is only a figment of our *imagination,* and has nothing to do with any *real* physical space. This abstract space is simply a *tool* we have invented that allows us to represent our measurement model, our parameter subspace, and our set of *n* noisy observations in a graphical manner. The theory of measuring is valid *without* this geometrical approach, but may be more difficult to understand.

The use of terms like input excitation and output observations seem to imply that all measurements must be made on "black boxes" having input and output connections. Often, it is at least *implied* that only *electrical* signals or waveforms are used. In practice, transducers are *indeed* often used to convert mechanical, acoustical, optical, or other quantities into electrical equivalents so they can be digitized and fed into a computer for processing (of course, this conversion operation introduces a *new* set of errors that must also be considered). However, these basic input/output concepts apply to *all* physical measurement situations, whether of an electrical nature or not, and whether the data is digitized into a computer or not. By way of illustration, the earliest use of these techniques was in measuring the orbital parameters of the *planets* and *asteroids* by Carl Friederich Gauss in the early 1800s. Gauss was instrumental in developing some of the most popular least-squares estimation techniques, while using *only* a set of hand-tabulated observations, along with paper and pencil.

This modeling idea must also include systems that *seem* to have *no inputs* at all, such as implied in the measurement of distance. In actuality, there are always *effective* inputs that perturb the output. For example, temperature and atmospheric pressure will generally affect *any* distance measurement, at least to some extent, no matter *how* the measurement is made.

Thus, inputs can be classified into two generic types: *intentional* (externally applied or known) and *interfering* (noisy or contaminating). Sometimes the interfering inputs can be partially observed, so it may be possible to reduce their effects on the output. Unfortunately, most of the time these inputs are largely unknown and can only be treated as a form of noise (which may or may *not* be random).

There is an important question of *semantics* that we must discuss, to avoid confusion in the reading of this book. The word "measurement" means different things to different people, and hence is somewhat loosely defined. Many books on estimation theory use the word *measurement* to describe what we prefer to call an *observation,* or perhaps *raw input/output data.* As a result, they may *not* equate a measurement with a *parameter estimate,* as we do in this book. Both of these data sets are considered to be *random* in nature, but a *measurement* is associated with a *parameter value* in a model, whereas an *observation* is associated with the *input and output data* collected from either the model or the physical system.

The definition of a measurement is primarily in the mind of the ultimate *end user* of the result. If you are this end user and are interested in designing analog-to-digital converters (which convert a voltage sample at some instant into a digital number for subsequent use in a computer), then your idea of a measurement may *indeed* be the digital value of that voltage. However, if you are interested in the frequency response function of some electrical or mechanical device, then *that* function is the thing to be measured, and the many voltage samples needed to obtain that frequency response function are simply considered to be raw data. If you are interested in the natural frequencies, damping factors, and/or modes of vibration of a mechanical structure, then *those* quantities comprise the measurement. The original voltage samples are considered to be raw data, while the frequency response functions are simply intermediate calculations. The end user always makes the final determination as to *what* is being measured.

Consequently, the best approach is to clearly distinguish the *original observations* (or raw data) from the eventual measured *parameter values* (or parameter estimates). Few end users are likely to be satisfied with measurements comprising only instantaneous samples of voltage. Even when this raw data actually *appears* to be the desired measured quantity, it is more likely that the *average value* of several samples of this raw data is actually preferred over a *single* sample. Notice that averaging is a *data reduction* process, which obtains the "best" estimate of something that is being modeled as a constant value, contaminated by noise.

Hopefully, the next few chapters will help to clarify these ideas. Making top quality measurements is always the goal, but this generally requires a considerable amount of thought, skill, and attention to detail. There are numerous trade-off decisions that must be made, because *perfect* measurements are not possible. It is always easier, quicker, and cheaper to cut corners, for example, by *assuming* no biases in the measurements, or *guessing* at the accuracy of each parameter estimate. However, the use of measurements of inferior quality can sometimes result in very serious consequences for the ultimate end user. This is especially disconcerting, because such users often have little choice but to accept these measurements at face value, on nothing more than *faith,* that they are accurate and complete. Help stamp out *mediocre* measurements whenever and wherever they occur!

1

A Philosophical Viewpoint

1.1 THE "ULTIMATE" MEASUREMENT

Let's begin with a *warmup* exercise for the imagination. Forget the reality of the world around you for a few moments and imagine you have been transported into some *new* world, with which you are completely unfamiliar. We will assume you are well versed in mathematics, physics, and the scientific method and are accustomed to making observations, postulating theories to fit the observations, and then testing these theories with new and different observations. You have been assigned the task of *characterizing* this new world in some way, so you can subsequently explain how it works to other people. Let's also assume you have plentiful resources at your disposal, so you can make all manner of observations and utilize unlimited computing power whenever needed. How might you try to accomplish this demanding task?

As a first step, you collect a vast amount of quantitative *data,* based on your *observations* of things that seem to be happening in this new world. Initially, things may seem to make little sense, but gradually patterns begin to emerge. Some conditions always appear to lead to the same results, and so become rather predictable. You might even go so far as to postulate a few tentative "laws of nature" that seem to prevail. You can then use these newly established "laws" to predict results you expect under some *new* set of conditions. Your tentative theories may fail at times, but often they will make reasonably correct predictions, and you will feel encouraged to continue observing and recording subsequent events that occur. There will always be *some* rogue observations that don't quite fit your theories, but of course that is not surprising, because you knew ahead of time your theories would not be perfect.

Let's digress for a moment. Geometries contain *invariant* quantities called *tensors,* which are independent of the coordinate system used in their representation. There are both *covariant* and *contravariant* tensors, distinguished by their equations of transformation between different coordinate systems. If you choose a *new* coordinate system, then each tensor will have *new* component *values,* but these new values can be determined from the *original* values, in conjunction with the transformation equations that *define* the new coordinate system (in terms of the old one), with absolutely *no* dependence on the attributes of the tensor itself. For example, you can express the location of a fixed point in a plane using either rectangular or polar coordinates. The corresponding coordinate *values* are, of necessity, *different,* reflecting the fact that the point is actually *fixed* in its physical location, but there exist two different, yet precisely related, ways to describe this location.

These tensors or invariants form the *foundation* of any geometry. For example, there is usually a metric tensor that describes the "distance" between any two points in the system. There may be a curvature tensor, a torsion tensor, and assorted other tensors that further describe the characteristics of the space. In the model of our *home* world, there are energy-momentum tensors, electromagnetic field tensors, and stress and strain tensors, among others, in addition to a metric tensor and a curvature tensor (which describes the effects of gravitational fields and acceleration).

There is also a fundamental question of the *dimensionality* of the space you are attempting to characterize. Is the space two-dimensional, three-dimensional, four-dimensional, or of *higher* dimensionality? How can you tell? People in our home world thought it was a three-dimensional place at one time, but after further observations they decided it was probably at least four-dimensional. They observed that the speed of light was an *invariant* with respect to transformations between coordinate systems that were moving at a *uniform velocity* relative to one another. The speed of light is a *scalar* quantity and is a tensor of order *zero.* However, a four-dimensional space is needed to account for this seemingly strange behavior, with *imaginary time* as the fourth coordinate.

After further study, people concluded this four-space was *curved* instead of flat, because that assumption seemed to best describe the behavior of events represented in *relatively accelerating* coordinate systems, and in the presence of *gravitational fields* associated with masses. These observations of our home world were made by a number of people, but it was largely Albert Einstein who constructed the theories of (special and general) relativity to explain these observations (circa 1905–1916). At the present time, considerable effort is being devoted to constructing some sort of *unified field theory,* which would explain all of the force fields we know about (gravitational, electromagnetic, and the weak and strong nuclear forces), along with all of the effects predicted by *quantum field theory,* in a single fundamental theory of "everything." Some of these theories require rather large dimensionalities (like ten, eleven, or twenty-six, for example!). We have *yet* to decide on the dimensionality of the space in which we live, or even to construct a comprehensive *model* of this space, even though we have countless observations on which to build.

Returning our attention to the task at hand, one of the techniques you *should* employ to characterize this new world is to establish a mental (or abstract) *model* that seems to adequately describe all of your physical observations, but to keep this model *separate* in your mind from what you perceive as physical *reality*. In other words, always maintain two *parallel* pictures or representations of the world. One picture comprises all of the *observations* that have been made of the physical world, and the other picture comprises a *mathematical (or geometrical) model,* designed to represent the way the world *seems* to work.

Since there are *invariants* in the physical world, such as the conservation of energy/momentum, the velocity of light, and the equivalence between gravitation and acceleration, it seems logical to use a mathematical model having a set of invariant tensors, and then to try to establish a *one-to-one* correspondence between the invariants in these two domains. Keep in mind that the only *connections* between these two domains are the observations of real physical events, in comparison to observations of corresponding events from the model. These *observations* from the two domains comprise the "glue" that couples the physical world with our *model* of the world.

The measurement task is to adjust the *parameters* in your mental model so it (at least approximately) predicts the *same* results you actually observe in the physical world, under "identical" conditions. Using the model, you can then make *new* predictions of things you expect to observe in the real world, under some *new* set of conditions, or with *new* input excitations. If you actually observe these results, then the validity of your model is strengthened. If your observations contradict the predictions of the model, then *modify* the model and try again (assuming your observations are indeed *correct*).

In this process, you never allow yourself to *equate* the mathematical model with physical reality, or vice versa. There is no reason to believe the physical world even *entails* any mathematical relationships, since *mathematics* is strictly a human invention. The only link between these two pictures of the world is via the observed versus the predicted outcome, for each test case you consider. The various rules, relationships, and mathematical quantities that exist in your model may or may not correspond to *anything* that exists in the physical world. Always remember your model of the world is an approximation and an abstraction. It is always in a state of *flux* because you continually upgrade the model as new observations accumulate.

This hypothetical task of measuring the parameters that describe some new world, is the "*mother* of all measurements," in comparison to which, *other* measurements seem relatively simple! In fact, *any* other measurement job, by definition, must comprise a *subset* of this world measurement task. However, the principles and procedures are the *same,* no matter what size the measurement assignment might appear to be. In each case, collect as much raw physical data as practical, and by some means, construct a good mental (meaning mathematical) model of the thing you are attempting to measure. With your mathematical skills, design an algorithm that will generate some sort of "best" estimates of the corresponding model *parameters,* such that the predicted output from your model closely *matches* the observed output from the physical system you are observing. Keep in mind that the definition of "*best*" is rather tenuous and will depend on your judgment to some extent. Measuring is something of an *art,* even though there are many aspects that can be described with mathematical precision.

1.2   THE MINDSET OF MEASURING

When you look at an ordinary rectangular table, you see an object with a width, a length, and an area. You could say, "The table is 3 feet wide and 6 feet long, with an area of 18 square feet." However, a more *apt* depiction is, "The table is being *modeled* as a *rectangle* having two *parameters,* width and length (from which the area can be calculated). The *best* parameter estimates, to date, are 3 feet for the width and 6 feet for the length." This latter description separates the physical object itself from the parameters in your mental picture of the object. In fact, nobody really knows the exact dimensions of the table, or that it is a *plane* object, or even a *rectangular* object. It is virtually impossible for the table to be *exactly* flat, and to have *exactly* parallel sides and square corners! On a molecular scale, the boundary of the table will comprise a rough irregular contour rather than a set of four straight lines. You simply *choose* a plane rectangular model because it seems like a good *working approximation* to the actual table shape. If that model proves to be deficient, then you stand ready to modify it, as needed.

It is natural to talk about the width, length, and area as *integral* parts of the physical table, because the table seems to actually *have* a width, length, and area, and they *seem* to be invariant with time. But the problem is, you have *no* way of knowing what the values of these quantities really *are,* nor that they actually *are* invariant with time. Your only option is to make repeated *observations* of the table dimensions, and then to estimate the most likely values of these rectangular parameters, perhaps by *averaging* the observations together. The table is always vibrating (because mechanical structures continually vibrate on *some* scale) and the dimensions of the table are always changing with temperature, atmospheric pressure, relative humidity, and so on. In addition, the resolution of your tape measure is limited, so you must use your best judgment for *each* reading of the tape. As a consequence of all of these variables, the observed table dimensions will be *different* every time you sample them.

Following our rule, we will maintain a clear mental separation between the *actual* dimensions of the table at any instant of time (which we intuitively feel must exist, but that we can never fully determine) and our best *estimates* (or *measurements*) of these dimensions, based on many repeated trials, using the model we have chosen. We never confuse the actual physical attributes of something with our mental model of those attributes. It might sometimes require a conscious effort to accept this idea, because most of us were never taught to make this distinction explicitly. One useful technique is to temporarily inhibit your senses (by closing your eyes, for example), so you are *only* aware of the model and are not distracted by any physical object. This separation rule permits you to simplify the measurement task by allowing *incomplete* or *approximate* models and to accommodate the *variations* you observe every time you repeat the measurement, without blaming your measuring instruments for faulty readings.

The concept is easier to comprehend when *hidden* or *implicit* model parameters are involved. For example, in the GPS (Global Positioning System) satellite navigation scheme, the desired user measurements are latitude, longitude, and altitude (referenced to the center of the Earth). You can calculate these quantities from the observed *differences* in arrival times between signals transmitted from at least four orbiting satellites, all having known positions relative to the Earth. In this example, the position coordinates of an observer are not necessarily associated with any local physical *object,* so it is very natural to think of them as *parameters* in a model of the Earth-satellite system.

1.3   MEASUREMENT QUALITY

If you are the end user of a measurement, you naturally expect results that are sufficiently accurate to use in *your* particular application. What does "sufficiently accurate" really mean? You are the user, so *you* must decide. In some cases, 10% errors might be tolerable, and in other cases you may require an error of only one part in 10^{12}. If you decide to purchase a plot of land for your new house, you would not be very happy if the owner decided to establish the property boundaries by *stepping* off the distances involved, and you would also be reluctant to pay a surveyor to measure these distances to the nearest *quarter wavelength* of the light from a helium-neon laser! You want these distances to the nearest centimeter and *neither* to the nearest meter *nor* to the nearest micron. The "best" measurement for your application may not always be the one with the most accuracy and precision. However, regardless of your accuracy requirements, you *do* want some indication that the measurement actually *meets* your specifications. In many respects, the actual measured *value* is somewhat secondary to an analysis of all of the possible *errors* that might perturb that value. A comprehensive *error analysis* is the best way to be reasonably sure the measurement quality is adequate for your needs.

If you repeat a measurement in exactly the same way a million times, you will get a million different answers. A histogram of these values, divided by the total number of measurements, gives an approximation to a *probability density function.* A measurement is not fully characterized until its probability density function is also determined, either by direct measurement or by calculation from a model. A *single* measured value can fall at any point within the abscissa range of the probability density function, but you have *no* way of knowing where it *actually* falls. The best you can do is to measure or calculate a probability (some number between zero and one) that the measurement falls between *limits* or boundaries of your choosing.

In addition to random variations, there are often many assumptions that have been made about conditions that might affect the measured result. For example, any measure of distance is affected by temperature and atmospheric pressure and is further affected by any errors that may be built into the reference scale you have chosen. Other errors are introduced by the method you use to *compare* the unknown distance with the reference scale. Sometimes the very *act* of measuring a quantity will alter its value. For example, the measurement of an electrical voltage will depend on the amount of current drawn by the measuring instrument through the output impedance of the network under test, as well as by the intrinsic accuracy of the instrument itself. These *non*-random errors are called *biases* in the parameter estimates. Bias errors, unlike random errors, cannot be reduced by averaging additional data.

A measurement is no better than the reference scale you use. In general, the reference scale will be in error by some *multiplicative scale factor,* and it may also be *offset* from the true zero point. A voltmeter may read 10 millivolts when the actual input voltage is zero, and it may read something like 1.01 plus 10 millivolts when the actual input is 1 volt. Its internal voltage reference may be a standard cell, a Zener diode, or simply a metal spring working against the force of the magnetic field generated by the flow of current through a calibrated resistor. These reference scales are usually functions of temperature, atmospheric pressure, humidity, and even elapsed time. The zero point offset is usually sensitive to similar effects, but might further depend on the balance between two small offset voltages, such as is often found in operational amplifiers.

In addition, the reference scale subdivisions are never exactly *uniform,* so these errors will be transferred directly to the quantity being measured. If the voltage scale is only linear to 1% of full scale, then any subsequent voltage measurements are limited to that precision. There are also random errors due to the limits imposed by various sources of electrical noise involved in the comparison between the unknown and the internal reference voltage. Even if the unknown voltage is exactly *constant* (which it cannot be), this internal comparator noise causes each measurement to be different.

You may have noticed that few measuring instruments (including distance scales) seem to come from the manufacturer with their errors fully characterized, or even with any *mention* of their accuracy at all. Perhaps they expect you—the user—to believe their instruments are perfect and thus always make accurate measurements under all conditions! Perhaps they think the average user would be unnecessarily confused by extra error information! More likely, it is simply deemed to be too expensive and time consuming for the manufacturer to characterize all of the possible errors that could be introduced by the equipment, especially if the end users are not *asking* for this information. Perhaps the responsibility for this state of affairs ultimately rests with the *uncritical* end user. We are all familiar with the slogan, "Let the *buyer* beware," but we might also add, "Let the *measurer* beware!" If you do not *ask* for accuracy information, then the manufacturer may not bother to provide it for you.

1.4   ATTRIBUTES OF THE MEASUREMENT MODEL

One of the most useful applications of a model of a physical system is in *simulating* the behavior of that system, to avoid the need to physically *construct* the system from component parts. Perhaps even more useful is the ability to *vary* some of the model parameters, to determine the effects of these variations on the system performance. In an actual physical system, you seldom have access to *all* of the parameters, and you are seldom able to vary all of them to fully characterize their effects.

These attributes of a general physical model also apply to the model of a measurement. Some parameters have more effect on the output observations than others. It is very possible some parameters have virtually *no* effect on the observed data. With a good model of the system and the measurement configuration, it is possible to calculate these characteristics. This is called a *sensitivity analysis* of a system. If some of the parameters change, then you can calculate the effects on the output of the model. You can also calculate the contributions of each error mechanism or noise source, allowing an *error schedule* to be constructed, showing which error mechanisms are most important and which ones can perhaps be effectively ignored. By inverting this procedure, you can obtain the sensitivity of each *parameter value* relative to each noise source in the model. Furthermore, a good model will allow you to "adjust" the measured values, if current conditions differ significantly from the conditions under which previous measurements were made.

This modeling procedure has at least *one* rather unexpected and generally unwanted aspect that needs to be disclosed and discussed. Once a model has been selected, any measurements that result from its use tend to enforce a "self-fulfilling prophecy," in the sense that measurements will be *forced* to fit the chosen model, often without giving any indication that the model might not be *correct*. For example, if you postulate that an AC voltage source is to be modeled as a *constant* DC voltage, then your measurement will indeed indicate a constant average value (of zero volts). You may not notice the voltage actually fluctuating around this average value in a sinusoidal manner, with an amplitude of 120 volts AC rms (root-mean-square). You get an accurate measure of the parameter you *asked* for, even though your model is completely wrong! In this particular case, an additional measurement of the *variance* of the voltage samples would show something was wrong, but that may not always be sufficient. For another example, suppose you assume there are five dominant modes of vibration in a mechanical structure (over some frequency range), when in fact there are *six*. Your estimation algorithm may not be "smart" enough to notice this problem, and the resulting measurements will be of little use to anyone, because you simply cannot represent the behavior of six *physical* modes with only five *component* modeling modes at your disposal. A good measurement design includes variance estimates and should also include techniques to show that the number of parameters and the topology of the model are essentially correct.

A similar thing can happen when your chosen estimation algorithm has a built-in *bias* mechanism. You will often have *no clue* that this error exists, even though the magnitude of this bias error can be large enough to *swamp* the parameter being measured. This is a common problem with certain control system measuring methods in which some of the system noise is *squared* and is therefore *not* eliminated by subsequent averaging. Again, the measurement may be completely *invalid,* but you may accept it as completely *correct* because you have no evidence to the contrary. You may inadvertently base some very important decisions on this bogus result. A thorough study of the measurement model, complete with all noise sources *and* the parameter estimation algorithm, is needed to spot potential bias problems of this sort.

The measurement model *must* include all of the significant sources of noise or interference that could have an effect on the result. There are generally several noise sources within the system under test, and there are always random contributions from the measuring instrument itself. The importance of each of these sources of contamination depends on the parameters being measured, as well as on the measurement or estimation algorithm used to reduce the data. Some parameters may be very difficult or impossible to estimate under relatively high noise conditions. Sometimes a different estimation algorithm will yield better results. Any given reduction algorithm will generally work better for some parameters than for others in the model.

One of the most difficult tasks is to choose the proper *topology* for the model. If key elements are missing or misconnected, the measured parameter values will generally be different each time the system is excited in a different way, in which case you really don't have a *valid* measurement at *all*. If *extra* parameters are included, the estimation algorithm may have trouble assigning values to *any* of the parameters, even the ones that are correctly *placed* in the model. Ironically, the measurement algorithm will usually have *less* trouble with these topological errors if there is a small amount of noise in the system. It is difficult or impossible to make good measurements on a system having the *wrong* topology when the raw data is extremely "clean." However, with sufficient noise, these topological errors can sometimes be accommodated surprisingly well.

Having outlined the measurement process and the *mindset* required to put the measurement into proper perspective, we will proceed to discuss each aspect in more detail in the chapters that follow and will show several examples to illustrate these concepts in a practical way. Keep in mind that a measurement has *some* aspects that are very precisely defined by mathematical relationships, but there are *other* aspects that are very much an art and require the skill and judgment of everybody involved in the measurement task. Don't let the *apparent precision* of the various mathematical procedures intimidate you or give you a false sense of measurement quality. Good judgment and common sense are indispensable commodities in *all* measurement activities.

BIBLIOGRAPHY ON OUR WORLD GEOMETRY

[1.1]   Davies, Paul, Editor, *The New Physics,* Cambridge Univ. Press, 1989. A very good review of the current state of physics, including relativity theory, quantum field theory, gravity, and a discussion of various "grand unified field theories," all written by expert authors in each specialty.

[1.2]   Einstein, Albert, *The Meaning of Relativity,* Princeton University Press, 1955. The words of the inventor of both special and general relativity.

[1.3]   Griffiths, David J. *Introduction to Quantum Mechanics,* Prentice-Hall, 1995. An up-to-date reference on this subject.

[1.4]   Hawking, Stephen, *A Brief History of Time,* Bantam, 1990. A nonmathematical book written by the man who first suggested the tunneling of particles (and hence energy and mass) out of black holes.

[1.5]   Misner, Charles W., Thorne, Kip S., and Wheeler, John Archibald, *Gravitation,* W. H. Freeman, 1973. This book covers more than you will ever want to know about gravity in great theoretical detail.

[1.6]   Pauli, W., *Theory of Relativity,* Pergamon Press, 1958. A good discussion of the theory of relativity.

[1.7]   Schiff, Leonard I., *Quantum Mechanics,* McGraw-Hill, 1955, A good textbook on quantum mechanics.

[1.8]   Synge, J. L., and Schild, A., *Tensor Calculus,* University of Toronto Press, 1952. This is an old but proven book on the theory of tensors.

[1.9]   Weinberg, Steven, *Dreams of a Final Theory,* Vintage Books (Random House), 1992. Weinberg won the 1979 Nobel prize for his deduction of the relationship between the weak nuclear force and the force of the electromagnetic field. He has written several other popular books on particle physics, gravitation, and the origin of the universe.

CHAPTER 2

The Measurement Model

2.1 THE OPTIMUM NUMBER OF PARAMETERS

The validity of a measurement rises and falls with the quality of the *model* you choose to represent a physical system. Yet, the choice or design of a suitable model is something of an art and depends on your detailed knowledge of the system and on your good judgment in selecting a suitable topology. A good model should be as simple and straightforward as possible, with the fewest number of parameters, and with a structure that allows all parameters to be estimated as directly as possible. Unfortunately, most physical systems are much too complicated to model in such an idealistic way, so there will be parameters that are either *not* included in the model or are incorrect in some way. You may know about some of these, and you may make a conscious decision to live with them, but there will likely be some parameters you know *little* about.

If you attempt to use *too few* parameters to represent the physical system, you will most likely find the model works poorly. You will obtain a different set of parameter values for *each* different applied input, so the model will not accurately predict the results for *arbitrary* inputs. A measurement based on this model would be of very limited value. As an example, consider a laser interferometer used to measure distance. The reference scale in this case is the wavelength of the laser light. Even if you know the light *frequency* very accurately, the wavelength varies with the velocity of light in *air*, which depends on the air temperature and the atmospheric pressure and humidity. If your model of this distance measurement does not include these variables, then you will get a decidedly different measure when any of these conditions change significantly.

This is a rather obvious example, but there are cases that are *not* so obvious. Consider the measurement of the modes of vibration of a thin, unconstrained circular plate. The lowest frequency of vibration corresponds to the first order *bending* mode around some axis through the plate. However, there are *two* such modes that are orthogonal, and hence do not interact with one another. If the bending of one mode occurs around a north-south axis, then the bending of the other mode will be around an east-west axis. Both modes will vibrate at the same frequency and have the same damping coefficient, but each will have a different *spatial* distribution. The input excitation point will dictate the relative strengths of each mode. If your model does not include two independent modes of vibration having the *same* frequencies, but rather assumes each mode has a different frequency, then your model for this measurement task will never work properly. Even worse, the resulting erroneous measurements might lead a user astray and result in the faulty design of a critical component in some structure.

Since the inclusion of too *few* parameters in a measurement model can cause such serious errors, it is natural for you to include *extra* parameters, so all of the important ones will be represented. If there are too many, then you might assume no harm will be done. Unfortunately, using too *many* parameters in a model is as bad as using too *few*. In most cases, you must estimate *all* parameter values *simultaneously*, in order to obtain an estimate of any one *particular* parameter. If you have too many unknowns, then you cannot solve the equations that describe the model in an unambiguous way. The solution generally involves a matrix, which becomes *singular* (and hence *not* invertible) when extra parameters are included. Actually, due to unavoidable sources of noise in the physical system, this matrix will be *poorly conditioned*, rather than singular. In this case, it can sometimes be inverted, but the results for *all* of the parameters will often be grossly wrong. As a rule, all of the parameters will either be relatively correct or else they will all be blatantly incorrect. You will seldom find a situation in which the important parameters are estimated accurately, while only the *minor* parameters are in error.

This dilemma really has no satisfactory solution. This is a place were you must rely on a certain amount of *art* in an otherwise mathematical procedure. Probably the best strategy is to start with extra parameters, attempt a solution, and then gradually reduce the number of parameters until the system matrix becomes better conditioned (there is a mathematical way to measure the *condition number* of a matrix). This often happens rather abruptly, so you can sometimes tell the *best* number of parameters to use by this indicator (this is the same procedure you would use to determine the *rank* of a matrix). Unfortunately, if the system noise is relatively large, the condition number may *not* change so abruptly, and it may be nearly impossible to tell when the optimum number of parameters has been found. It is rather ironic that when too *many* parameters are specified, the parameter estimates tend to be better when a small amount of noise is present than when the data are very "clean." This happens because the noise will tend to mask the singular nature of the system matrix, sometimes allowing an inverse of the matrix to be calculated.

2.2   VARIOUS PARAMETER ATTRIBUTES

Even if you have determined the correct *number* of parameters and are able to solve the estimation equations, you will generally find that some parameters in the model are estimated with better accuracy than others. If the effect of a particular parameter on the output of the system is very *small*, then it will be difficult to obtain an accurate estimate of *that* parameter value. Taken to the limit, if a parameter really has *no* effect on the output under any input conditions, then that parameter must be *invisible* and should be removed from the model. However, you may only need to excite the system differently to register a response from an otherwise hidden or invisible parameter, so proceed with *caution* when discarding parameters.

Another possibility is for one parameter to have *nearly* the same effect on the output as another parameter. In this situation, it is very difficult to decide on the output contribution from each individual parameter, resulting in a poorly conditioned system matrix. Unfortunately, the accuracy of *all* parameters may be reduced, including those that have a dominant effect on the output. This is similar to the case where you assume too many parameters in the model, although in *this* situation it may be possible for you to improve the estimates of these similar parameters by choosing a different input excitation, or a different monitoring point.

Sometimes there are certain model parameters whose values are *independent* of the other parameters in a system. Parameters in this class can be estimated without concern for the others, and this property greatly simplifies the measurement task. For example, the temperature coefficient of a parameter can usually be measured independently of the parameter value itself. Sometimes a physical system comprises subsystems that do not interact in any significant way. It is usually much easier to measure the values of two independent models with n parameters each, than to simultaneously measure the values of $2n$ parameters that mutually interact. One of the techniques in building a measurement model is to relegate all independent subsystems to separate models and to consider the measurement in question as two or more independent measurements.

Of course, the *topology* of the model is just as important as the number and nature of its parameters. Generally, you will understand the physical system sufficiently well, so the major elements and their interconnections are fairly clear. At worst, a few well-designed tests may be required to clarify a few aspects of the model. The real problem becomes apparent when some of the more secondary elements of the system must be modeled. For example, the low-frequency equivalent circuit of a transistor is well known and you can readily measure the elements of this circuit. However, when high frequencies are involved, there are a host of so called "parasitic" elements, like stray capacitances and lead inductances, that you must include in the model to get anything resembling a usable representation. There can be a large number of these parasitic elements, and it may be virtually impossible to separate their effects so you can measure them individually. The usual approach is to use something called "engineering judgment" (there is the *art*, again) and to incorporate a few parameters in the *proper* places in the equivalent circuit, with the hope that these parameters will adequately represent the more complicated physical network.

One rather troubling by-product of this approximation procedure is the possibility that the measured values will be physically impossible (*unrealizable*), or at least implausible. For example, a measured parasitic capacitor or inductor might turn out to be negative or to be unreasonably large or small in value. These abnormal element values might be successful in predicting the behavior of the model in an adequate *mathematical* manner, but it is readily apparent that they are not correct, and that the model topology is likewise incorrect to *some* extent. As a user, you would likely be singularly unimpressed with these excuses for measurements, and you would probably want to reconsider the model involving these elements. A *good* model will not only make accurate output predictions, but will also appear to *logically* represent the physical components of a system.

It is time to apply some of these modeling ideas to a few practical examples. In the following four sections we will discuss: (1) measuring the DC output resistance of a battery or power supply, (2) measuring the loop response of a closed-loop control system, (3) measuring the modal parameters of a vibrating mechanical structure, and (4) measuring position coordinates using the GPS satellite navigation system. We will only carry these examples far enough in *this* chapter to derive the measurement model, and we will continue with the remaining discussion of these examples in later chapters.

2.3   EXAMPLE: DC BATTERY RESISTANCE

We begin with what appears to be a simple task. Imagine you want to measure the *output resistance* of a battery or DC power supply. What measurement model will you choose for this job? By restricting your attention to only the *DC* resistance, you can simplify the model considerably by eliminating all reactive elements, like capacitors and inductors. The most logical model is probably an *ideal* battery element (having *zero* resistance), in series with an *ideal* resistor, as shown in Figure 2–1. You could try to generalize this model to comprise a distributed combination of smaller batteries and resistors, but it is possible to show such configurations are equivalent to Figure 2–1.

Even if you choose the simple model of Figure 2–1, there are still more questions. Does the ideal battery voltage or the ideal series resistor depend on load current or temperature, or perhaps on some additional factor? What are the various possible sources of noise? We know resistors generate thermal noise, but the ideal battery voltage might also

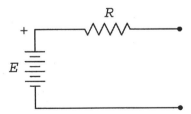

Figure 2–1   Simple Battery Model

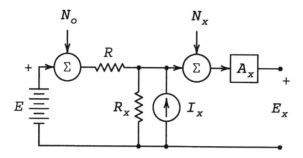

Figure 2–2 DC Measurement Model

fluctuate slightly. We know our measuring instrument will introduce some noise, as well as some error, since the calibration of the instrument will never be perfect. Figure 2–2 shows a more complete measurement model and includes some of these error mechanisms. For this example we will assume a circuit having linear and time invariant elements, and we will ignore temperature effects. Any noise due to battery voltage fluctuations or due to thermal effects from R is modeled as N_o. Any noise in the voltmeter used to measure E_x is represented by N_x, and the voltmeter calibration error is modeled by A_x. R_x is a battery load resistor, and this element can also include the input impedance of the voltmeter. I_x is a test current generator. Incremental changes in either R_x or I_x (or both) can be used to supply the test excitation. For this example, we will assume the voltmeter has no significant offset or bias error.

The equation describing this model is:

$$E_x = A_x \left[(E + I_x R + N_o) \frac{R_x}{R + R_x} + N_x \right] \tag{2.1}$$

There are a number of ways to obtain an estimate of R, or of both R and E, by using different values of R_x and/or I_x, while observing E_x. Since both N_o and N_x are random quantities, it follows that E_x will also be a random variable. Since estimates of R or E utilize samples of E_x, it also follows that *these* estimates (or measurements) will be random variables, as well (see chapter 3 for a more complete discussion of random variables).

Notice that R appears in both the numerator and the denominator of this expression. This indicates that we have a *nonlinear equation* in R, and that the measuring algorithm will also be nonlinear. We always *hope* for linear equations because they can be solved in *closed form* using matrix algebra, with little difficulty. The solution to a nonlinear equation generally involves some sort of *iterative* approach, where you must first *guess* the solution and then iterate toward a more accurate solution in successive steps. This procedure *may* or may *not* converge to a final stable result, and you often have little control over the number of iterations needed to reach the required accuracy.

We will describe the remaining steps in the measurement process in Section 5.2 of chapter 5. We are content with a discussion of only the *model* in this chapter. However, notice the measurement model is not just the diagram in Figure 2–2, but includes the mathematical representation given by Eq. 2.1. We see that even one of the simplest measurement tasks is not quite as simple as it might appear at first glance.

2.4   EXAMPLE: CONTROL SYSTEM LOOP GAIN

A more typical measurement might be to characterize the loop dynamics of a *closed-loop control system.* Figure 2–3 shows a typical block diagram, along with some of the possible noise sources you might find in such a system. Generally, all of the elements shown in the diagram are functions of frequency or of the Laplace variable s and comprise both a magnitude and a phase angle at each frequency (these are called complex numbers).

A control system is defined to be *linear* if the output of the *sum* of two inputs is the same as the sum of the outputs for *each* input applied separately. As a rule, the loop parameters are also constant with respect to time. Unfortunately, most control systems are at least somewhat nonlinear, and some types also have time dependent elements. In our current example, we will restrict our attention to *linear* and *time invariant* systems to keep things as simple as possible.

The frequency characteristics of a component in the loop are often represented by the Laplace transform of the time behavior of that component (which is called the *transfer function* for that component). The Laplace transform is represented either by the quotient of two polynomials in s (called a rational fraction), or by its partial fraction equivalent

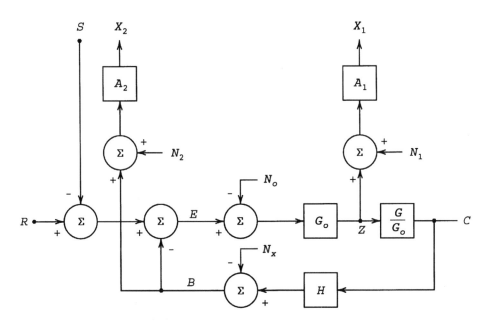

Figure 2–3   A Typical Control System

(see Appendix A). The roots of the numerator polynomial are called the *zeros* of the function, and the roots of the denominator polynomial are called the *poles* (because the function goes to ± infinity at these points). The time behavior of each component is the sum of a set of complex exponential functions, each of which corresponds to one of the poles of the transfer function. The partial fraction form is the Laplace transform of this sum of complex exponentials.

There are numerous textbooks that define and discuss the Laplace transform, for those who may not be familiar with this representation, but one of the most useful properties is that multiplication by s in the Laplace domain is equivalent to differentiation with respect to time in the time domain. A second very useful property is that the output of a linear system is the product of the input excitation and the system transfer function in the Laplace domain, whereas in the time domain the output is obtained by *convolving* the input with the *impulse response* of the system. Multiplication is generally easier than convolution (which requires the evaluation of a time domain integral). We briefly review the Laplace transform in Appendix A and discuss some of the associated technical terms in the Glossary.

In Figure 2–3, we have appended the leftmost summing junction so we can insert a test signal S into the input path. R is the normal reference voltage for the loop and represents the signal we *expect* the loop to track, under normal operating conditions. The loop dynamic behavior is determined by the product GH. Ideally, Z should represent the error signal from the primary summing junction, but in practice there is often some transfer function (shown as G_o) in the path, before Z can be physically probed. The two noise sources N_o and N_x represent all of the noise in the loop. Two such sources are needed in this case, although sometimes one is sufficient. B represents the signal to be controlled, meaning that the loop is expected to force B to be as nearly identical to R as possible. The actual output of the control system is C. The calibration errors and noise contributions of the measuring instrument are modeled as A_1, A_2, N_1, and N_2, while X_1 and X_2 are the actual signals utilized by the measuring instrument.

The measurement task is to observe signals (voltage or current time waveforms) at two selected points in the control system and then deduce the transfer function parameters of the entire loop from these observed time waveforms. In most cases, you must perform these measurements with the loop *closed,* because the system may not be stable with the loop open. Moreover, it is sometimes necessary to make these measurements with the control loop operating in a normal manner, so typical control signals may be present, while you insert a separate *external* test signal into the loop. The normal control signals will generally act to contaminate the test signal, while at the same time the test signal will tend to disrupt the normal operation of the loop, at least to some extent. Hopefully, you can find a compromise in which both signals can coexist without overly affecting either process.

It may be tempting to use the *normal* control loop waveforms to make this measurement (instead of inserting an external test signal), but unfortunately, *that* signal usually cannot be guaranteed to supply *power* at all frequencies of interest. If an input frequency component is missing (or if its power is too low to be usable), then there is no way to make a good loop gain measurement at that frequency.

There are numerous ways to measure a control system, depending on the available test signals (random noise, a swept sinusoid, or a chirp, for example) and on the *algorithm* used to reduce the data to a set of parameter estimates. You can sum an external test excitation S with the reference signal R, as shown in Figure 2–3, or you can inject it into the loop by summing at any other convenient point around the loop. In the first case, there are at least *five* combinations of *pairs* of signals that can be used to implement five different measurement methods. In the second case, there are at least three combinations of signal pairs, giving a total of at least eight possible measurement configurations.

In addition, we can select several algorithms for processing the data we collect from these monitoring points to produce estimates of the loop gain parameters. Each choice of signal pair and data reduction algorithm works differently. Some methods work best when the loop gain is *large*, while others do best for *small* loop gain values. Some methods involve the *difference* between two relatively large signals and are therefore sensitive to small errors in the *balance* between the two channels of the measuring instrument. Some methods are more sensitive to noise in the loop or noise in the measuring instrument than other methods. Some methods are more prone to producing *biased* results than others, due to a variety of different mechanisms. It is difficult to pick *one* best technique that works well under all conditions, although the example we discuss in this book *is* one of the better approaches in most cases. In general, you must examine each method in some detail to decide on its merits and shortcomings, but a complete study of that sort is beyond the scope of this book.

It is very important for control loops to be *stable* during normal operation and *not* be on the verge of breaking into continuous oscillations. Unstable control systems can easily destroy some very critical equipment, and *that* can be both costly and sometimes dangerous. It is likewise crucial that the loop stability margins be measured accurately, along with the various natural frequencies and their corresponding damping coefficients. We also want to know the amount of *error* we can expect on each measured parameter in the system.

Control systems are generally fairly difficult to measure accurately, but they are representative of the sorts of measurements we must make in the real world. Such systems are often noisy and nonlinear. In addition, the actual number of significant parameters is often unknown, and some of the known parameters are more difficult to measure than others.

Our task in this chapter is to develop a suitable measurement *model* for the control system block diagram shown in Figure 2–3. The mathematical modeling of this system involves two equations, one for each input to the measuring instrument, and these are:

$$X_1 = (S' + N_x) \frac{A_1 G_o}{1 + W} + A_1 N_1 \tag{2.2}$$

$$X_2 = S' \frac{A_2 W}{1 + W} - N_x \frac{A_2}{1 + W} + A_2 N_2 \tag{2.3}$$

where

$$S' = R - S - N_o \qquad (2.4)$$

$$W = GH \qquad (2.5)$$

The measurement model is not complete until we have designed a suitable *algorithm* to reduce the raw data obtained via X_1 and X_2 to a set of parameter values that describe the loop, represented by W. However, for this example we will postpone this part of the modeling process until section 3.4 of chapter 3, where we discuss the properties of random variables. We complete our discussion of control loop measurements in section 5.3 of chapter 5.

2.5   EXAMPLE: MODES OF VIBRATION

You can describe the *modes* of vibration of a continuous mechanical structure by a set of partial differential equations in conjunction with an appropriate set of boundary conditions. However, for computing purposes, it is usually better to approximate such systems by a *lumped equivalent model,* valid within some frequency range of interest. Then, you can represent the system by a matrix, whose elements are either frequency response functions or transfer functions (in the Laplace domain). In this form, the modes of vibration are represented by vectors that are the *homogeneous solutions* (solutions with no external applied force) to the system equations.

If you use a lumped element mechanical model, you can calculate the behavior of the structure by writing a force balance equation at each *node* in the model. Each such node comprises a *mass* element connected to other adjacent nodes via *stiffness* and/or *damping* elements. Any applied force will be exactly balanced by the sum of mass reaction forces (mass times acceleration), spring reaction forces (stiffness times displacement), and damping reaction forces (viscosity times velocity). The resulting displacement of each node is obtained by the simultaneous solution of these equations.

We begin by showing the equations for a very general lumped mechanical model. We write *force balance equations* in all coordinate directions for *each* mass element, and if rotation is allowed or included we write *torque balance equations* in each plane of rotation around each mass element (using the proper moments of inertia for each rotation axis). For an *r*-dimensional space, there are r force balance equations and $r(r-1)/2$ torque balance equations (which is the number of r coordinates taken two at a time, defining all of the possible planes of rotation) at each mass point. This gives a total of $nr(r+1)/2$ equations for n nodes.

We define the r coordinates in the system as x_j for $1 \le j \le r$. We index the n nodes (or mass elements) by ℓ, where $1 \le \ell \le n$. For the present example, we will ignore rotation effects, so we only write the $n \times r$ force balance equations, as follows:

$$m_\ell \ddot{x}_{j\ell} + \sum_{p(\ne \ell)=1}^{n} \frac{x_{j\ell} - x_{jp}}{d_{\ell p}} g_{\ell p} = f_{j\ell} \qquad (2.6)$$

where

$$g_{\ell p} = c_{\ell p}\dot{d}_{\ell p} + k_{\ell p}\left(d_{\ell p} - \bar{d}_{\ell p}\right) \tag{2.7}$$

is the damping plus stiffness force between nodes ℓ and p, and

$$d_{\ell p} = \sqrt{\sum_{q=1}^{r}\left(x_{q\ell} - x_{qp}\right)^2} \tag{2.8}$$

is the distance between nodes ℓ and p. The external applied force, if any, at node ℓ in coordinate direction j is $f_{j\ell}$. A positive value of $g_{\ell p}$ pulls nodes ℓ and p together, corresponding either to the case when $d_{\ell p} > \bar{d}_{\ell p}$, or to the case when $d_{\ell p}$ is increasing with time. The portion of this force acting along the jth coordinate is determined by the corresponding direction cosine expression $(x_{j\ell} - x_{jp})/d_{\ell p}$. The distance denoted by $\bar{d}_{\ell p}$ is the *quiescent* distance between the two nodes when the stiffness force due to the spring is zero. The two parameters $k_{\ell p}$ and $c_{\ell p}$ are the respective stiffness and damping coefficients of the elements between these two nodes.

One of the problems with these system equations is that they are nonlinear in the displacement components, partly because these components appear in the denominator of each direction cosine term, and partly because each $d_{\ell p}$ distance is inherently nonlinear due to the root-mean-square operation in Eq. 2.8 above. To avoid this problem, it is customary to assume the motion of each node is very small compared to the distances between nodes, thereby keeping the direction cosines relatively constant and allowing the use of linear forms for the distances between nodes. The resulting linear approximations to the system equations become:

$$m_{\ell}\Delta\ddot{x}_{j\ell} + \sum_{p(\neq\ell)=1}^{n} \frac{\bar{x}_{j\ell} - \bar{x}_{jp}}{\bar{d}_{\ell p}} \sum_{q=1}^{r} \frac{\bar{x}_{q\ell} - \bar{x}_{qp}}{\bar{d}_{\ell p}} g_{\ell pq} = f_{j\ell} \tag{2.9}$$

$$g_{\ell pq} = c_{\ell p}\left(\Delta\dot{x}_{q\ell} - \Delta\dot{x}_{qp}\right) + k_{\ell p}\left(\Delta x_{q\ell} - \Delta x_{qp}\right) \tag{2.10}$$

where $g_{\ell pq}$ is the force on the mass at node ℓ from dampers and springs connecting nodes ℓ and p, along the coordinate q. The overbars indicate quiescent average values when all spring forces are zero, and the overdots indicate time domain differentiation. The Δx quantities are differences between the actual x values and their quiescent average values.

There are two sets of direction cosines in Eq. 2.9. The *inner* set (indexed by q) describes the portion of the differential displacement (and velocity) between two nodes *along* each coordinate axis that contributes a force *collinear* with the spring and damper connecting those two nodes, and the *outer* set (indexed by j) describes the portion of the *resulting* collinear force that excites the mass elements at each node *along* each coordinate axis.

For linear systems, you can use the Laplace transform to convert time domain differentiation into multiplication by the Laplace variable s in the Laplace domain. Thus, a mass reaction force in Laplace form is represented by $m(s^2X)$, where m is the element mass, and s^2X is the acceleration of the mass in the direction of the applied force (here, X is the displacement vector). Similarly, the damping reaction force is $c(sX)$, where c is the viscosity attached to the mass (and sX is the velocity of the mass), and the stiffness reaction force is given by kX, where k is the stiffness attached to m. We take the Laplace transform of Eq. 2.9, giving:

$$m_\ell s^2 X_{j\ell} + \sum_{p(\neq \ell)=1}^{n} \frac{\overline{x}_{j\ell} - \overline{x}_{jp}}{\overline{d}_{\ell p}} \sum_{q=1}^{r} \frac{\overline{x}_{q\ell} - \overline{x}_{qp}}{\overline{d}_{\ell p}} (sc_{\ell p} + k_{\ell p})(X_{q\ell} - X_{qp}) = F_{j\ell} \quad (2.11)$$

where X is the Laplace transform of the displacement Δx, F is the Laplace transform of the driving force f, and s is the Laplace variable. In this linear form, we can arrange the various terms into a matrix-vector equation of the form:

$$BX = F \qquad (2.12)$$

where each element of B, called the *system matrix*, is of the form $(ms^2 + cs + k)$. If there are n nodes in the lumped model, then both F and X will have n elements, and B will have $n \times n$ elements. See Appendix A for a brief discussion of matrix algebra.

   If we can *invert* this equation, we can then express the displacement X in terms of the applied force F as:

$$X = B^{-1}F = HF, \text{ where } H = B^{-1} \qquad (2.13)$$

We can invert the system matrix B as long as all of its rows are *linearly independent* (likewise for its columns). This means the n rows (or columns) completely span an abstract n-dimensional space within which all force and displacement vectors for our system must reside. However, the elements of B are functions of s, and there are certain values of s for which at least one of the rows (or columns) becomes a linear combination of the others, resulting in a system *subspace* having only $n - 1$ dimensions. Sometimes this happens to more than one row or column for the same value of s. Under these conditions, B cannot be inverted, at least in the usual sense. The determinant of B becomes zero, and there is now at least one vector that lies outside of, and *orthogonal* to, the system subspace. These outside vectors are called *modal* (or *bimodal*) *vectors*. Modal vectors are the displacement vectors that are obtained under free vibration conditions, in which the applied force $F = 0$. The collection of these vectors is called the *homogeneous solution* to the system Eq. 2.12.

   How can there be a displacement vector when there is *no* driving force? You must exercise your imagination! There is *indeed* a mathematical solution for this case, involving the sum of a set of *characteristic functions* having *arbitrary* coefficients or strengths. These functions are defined by the boundary conditions (or constraints) on the system in question. However, these characteristic functions are not *excited* until either an external force vector is applied or until some initial conditions are imposed on the motion vectors (displacement, velocity, or acceleration). When this happens, the coefficients on these functions are no longer arbitrary, but take on whatever values necessary to satisfy these applied forces and initial conditions.

   We will use the mathematical solutions involving these characteristic functions to build a *model* of this mechanical system, even though these functions cannot be excited without a driving force. Then we will be able to see ways to measure the resulting model parameters, using an external driving force *after all*. This is a good example of *hidden* parameters that are not apparent to an observer until the system is excited in some way. Modal vectors u are therefore defined to be the solutions of:

$$Bu = 0 \qquad (2.14)$$

This is called the *homogeneous equation* for the structure. We also define *bimodal vectors* v (which differ from modal vectors when the system matrix is *asymmetric*) as the solutions of:

$$B^t v = 0 \qquad (2.15)$$

Ordinarily, to solve equations like 2.12 for X, you simply multiply both sides of the equation by the inverse of B, as we indicate in Eq. 2.13 above. However, when you try this technique on Eqs. 2.14 and 2.15, you seem to get $u = 0$ and $v = 0$, which are not very *useful* answers! Fortunately, there is another way.

In the Laplace formulation, det B (the determinant of B) is a polynomial in s, and therefore this polynomial appears in the denominator of *each* element of H. The roots of this polynomial are the "poles" of the system. It is *only* possible to *define* nonzero modal vectors at the poles of the system. You avoid infinite elements in BH (at the poles) by using modal vectors (or sums of modal vectors) as the *columns* of H, so when you premultiply H by B, the resulting zero *vector* products exactly *cancel* the denominator zeros introduced by det B. Likewise, the *rows* of H must be transposed *bimodal* vectors, or sums of transposed bimodal vectors.

Thus, the part of H associated with a simple pole at s_o (called H_o) must be of the form $uv^t / (s - s_o)$, where v^t denotes the transpose of the bimodal vector v. The product uv^t is called an *outer vector product,* and results in an $n \times n$ square matrix with a *rank of unity* (in contrast to the *inner* vector product $v^t u$, which is a *scalar* quantity). For *symmetric* system matrices, we have $v = u$. The complete transfer matrix H comprises the *sum* of all n of these *unit rank* modal matrices associated with *each* of the n pole values.

Sometimes you will find two or more modal vectors that have the *same* pole value. For example, H_o may look like $(u_1 v_1{}^t + u_2 v_2{}^t) / (s - s_o)$. This is called a *repeated mode* and corresponds to two *independent* displacement vectors having the same pole value. You will find this case in a freely suspended square or circular plate, where each of the two orthogonal directions of vibration have the same natural frequency and damping values, but have different *spatial* distributions, and hence different modal vectors.

Another possibility is an element of H having a *double pole* of the form $u_2 v_2{}^t / (s - s_o)^2$. If this occurs, there will *also* be a *single* pole at s_o (with u_2 *still* as a modal vector), but there will be a *second* modal vector u_1 *also* associated with this pole. Thus, for a pole of multiplicity two, there are two associated modal vectors. This occurs when two *coupled* substructures share the same pole value. The energy from the mode in *one* substructure ·feeds into the *other* substructure, and the *composite* transfer function is that of two single pole structures in *cascade*. Double poles also occur on the negative real axis in the s-plane when a resonance is *critically damped*.

You can always adjust the second modal vector (u_1) of a double pole to be *orthogonal* to the first one (u_2), although its resulting *amplitude* will always be precisely related to the first vector. In any case, there is a two-dimensional vector *subspace* associated with a pole of multiplicity two, defined by the associated pair of modal vectors u_1 and u_2. The general form of the transfer matrix associated with this double pole is:

$$H_o(s) = \frac{(u_1 v_2^t + u_2 v_1^t)(s - s_o) + u_2 v_2^t}{(s - s_o)^2} \tag{2.16}$$

If we premultiply this by B, we see an obvious first order zero at $s = s_o$ because, by definition, Bu_2 has a first order zero at this point. However, the presence of a *second order zero* is not so obvious. It can *only* occur if the numerator coefficients in the remainder (after $s - s_o$ is removed by division) are adjusted to have an *additional* first order zero at this point. Another way of getting the same result is to require the first derivative of the *numerator* of $B(s)H_o(s)$ with respect to s be zero at $s = s_o$. This condition is actually the basis for the determination of the vector u_1, which ensures that a numerator zero of multiplicity two will *indeed* exist at s_o, to thereby *cancel* the second order denominator term.

Notice you can always replace u_1 by $u_1 + au_2$ for arbitrary values of any scalar a, since Bu_2 has a first order zero at the pole. Thus, even though u_1 is orthogonal to u_2, and the *amplitude* of u_1 is defined by the *amplitude* of u_2, you can always add an arbitrary multiple of u_2 to u_1, without changing any of the equations. To deduce u_1 from the (generally composite) coefficient of the unit multiplicity numerator, you must first remove all of u_2 in a least-squares sense (leaving the residual u_1, orthogonal to u_2).

You can use the same generic formulation for higher multiplicity poles, as well. We simply require the first $p - 1$ derivatives of the *numerator* of $B(s)H(s)$ be zero (in addition to the original numerator) at a pole of multiplicity p. This will define a total of p modal vectors (and hence a p-dimensional *subspace*) for that pole, so the numerator of $B(s)H(s)$ will have a pth order zero at the pole. Any of these modal vectors can also include arbitrary amounts of any of the other modal vectors which are associated with poles of *higher multiplicity* (for that pole value). This allows for independent coefficients on the terms of all multiplicities. You can recover each separate modal vector by sequentially removing each *higher* multiplicity vector from all *lower* multiplicity vectors in a least-squares sense, starting with the vector of highest multiplicity.

The final measurement model for the transfer matrix of a vibrating mechanical structure (including multiple poles and asymmetric matrices) is given in *partial fraction* form as:

$$H(s) = \sum_{j=1}^{n} \sum_{k=1}^{p_j} \frac{a_{jk}}{(s - s_j)^k} \tag{2.17}$$

where the residue matrix is:

$$a_{jk} = \sum_{\ell=0}^{p_j - k} u_{k+\ell} v_{p_j - \ell}^t \tag{2.18}$$

The poles are located at s_j with corresponding multiplicities p_j and residues a_{jk}. Strictly speaking, the residue of a pole is defined as *only* the a_{j1} component, but in this book, we will use the term in a *wider* sense to include the numerators of *all* multiplicities. Sums of the outer products of the modal and transposed bimodal vectors make up these residues, keeping in mind that each vector can include *arbitrary multiples* of all vectors of higher multiplicity for *that* pole value, and the scaling of both u_{p_j} and v_{p_j} is completely arbitrary. In this form, the transfer matrix is not *totally* defined because of these arbitrary modal and bimodal vector amplitudes. You can always establish the proper amplitudes either mathematically via $HB = I$ (away from the pole), or by the actual measurement of the elements of the transfer matrix. We can write Eqs. 2.17 and 2.18 in matrix form as:

$$H(s) = \Theta \Lambda^{-1}(s)\Psi \tag{2.19}$$

where the *columns* of Θ are the modal vectors and the *rows* of Ψ are the transposed bimodal vectors (both of which are independent of s). $\Lambda^{-1}(s)$ is a *quasi-diagonal matrix* comprising the poles of the system. For unit multiplicity poles, the corresponding component of Λ^{-1} will be *on* the primary diagonal, while for multiple poles there will be a *block* of $p \times p$ components centered on the diagonal, where p is the pole multiplicity. We give an example below, taken from chapter 5.

$$\Lambda^{-1}(s) = \begin{bmatrix} \dfrac{1}{s} & 0 & 0 & 0 & 0 & 0 & 0 \\[2mm] 0 & 0 & \dfrac{1}{s-s_1} & 0 & 0 & 0 & 0 \\[2mm] 0 & \dfrac{1}{s-s_1} & \dfrac{1}{(s-s_1)^2} & 0 & 0 & 0 & 0 \\[2mm] 0 & 0 & 0 & \dfrac{1}{s-s_2} & 0 & 0 & 0 \\[2mm] 0 & 0 & 0 & 0 & 0 & \dfrac{1}{s-s_1^*} & 0 \\[2mm] 0 & 0 & 0 & 0 & \dfrac{1}{s-s_1^*} & \dfrac{1}{(s-s_1^*)^2} & 0 \\[2mm] 0 & 0 & 0 & 0 & 0 & 0 & \dfrac{1}{s-s_2^*} \end{bmatrix} \tag{2.20}$$

In this matrix, the upper left element represents a *single* pole at the origin, which corresponds to what is called a "rigid body mode" because the vibration frequency is zero. Next, we have a 2×2 block representing a *double* pole at s_1. These multiple pole blocks are *lower-right triangular matrices,* with the primary *cross*-diagonal elements comprising *unit* multiplicity poles, and with subsequent secondary (parallel) cross-diagonal elements comprising progressively higher multiplicity poles, until the *highest* multiplicity pole occurs in the lower right corner of the block, *on* the primary diagonal. The matrix inverses of blocks of this type are called *Jordan blocks,* for those readers who are heavily into matrix theory. Next we have a *single* pole at s_2, and then we have the elements for the *complex conjugates* of these poles.

The arrangement of these elements is arbitrary, depending on the desired order of the modal and bimodal vectors in Θ and Ψ. The only requirements are that each vector be matched with its proper pole value (and multiplicity) and that the determinant of that block be correct. In most textbooks, Jordan blocks are shown rotated 90° (and hence are asymmetric), but this rotation angle is rather arbitrary. We have chosen to define $\Lambda^{-1}(s)$ as a symmetric matrix and to relegate any asymmetry in the system to differences between Θ and Ψ^t.

It is interesting (and a little ironic) that the inverse of B can be represented by the very parameters that cause B to be *singular*, namely the poles and the modal and bimodal vectors. The inverse of B is still not defined at these poles, but the matrix product $BH = HB = I$ is *always* valid everywhere in the s-plane, even *at* the poles, and for any multiplicity. Another related, but nevertheless interesting, feature is that the displacement vector X is equal to HF, and yet the columns of the numerator of H (modal vectors) are the displacement vectors when the applied force vector F goes to *zero* (this is possible at the poles because the elements of H simultaneously go to infinity due to det B). There are no contradictions here, but these relationships are still intriguing.

This form suggests a method we can use to measure both the poles and modal vectors of H, at least for mechanical structures that are not *too* heavily *damped* (this modal representation does not work well for structures like sandbags, although it would still be theoretically valid *if* the forces between the sand particles were *linear* relative to the motions of each particle).

The idea is to estimate the *frequency responses* between several points on the structure and then to use the Laplace domain modal model, shown above as Eq. 2.17, for the *transfer matrix*. It is a well known theorem in complex variable theory that if two analytic functions can be matched along any finite line segment (or among all derivatives at any point), then these functions will match *everywhere* in the complex plane (this is called the *principle of analytic continuation*). Hence, if the parameters in Eq. 2.17 can be adjusted so the values for H along the frequency axis (corresponding to $s = i2\pi f$, where $i = \sqrt{-1}$ and f is the frequency in cycles per second or Hertz) "match" the *measured* frequency responses, then the resulting parameter values will represent the desired estimates or measurements of these s-domain poles and residues.

Consider the poles and residues in the s-domain as a compact sort of *code* that fully represents an *entire* frequency response function along the frequency axis, as well as the corresponding transfer function throughout the complex plane. No matter how many samples of this frequency response function you might collect, this same small set of s-plane parameters completely describes that function (excluding any noise on the data, of course). The Laplace domain formulation is actually a *shorthand* way of describing the relationship between an otherwise large and complicated collection of input and output time domain samples you observe from a linear system. You can only observe these s-domain functions along the *imaginary* (or frequency) axis, but you can always *calculate* the function at any other desired point in the plane.

This modal representation of a transfer function has at least one very important advantage. The complete measurement of a *general* transfer function matrix requires the measurement of $n \times n$ matrix elements over the frequency range of interest, whereas the modal approach only requires the measurement of n individual elements. You can see the reason for this attribute in Eq. 2.17. You can find *all* of the pole values from *each* element of H, since the determinant of B appears as the denominator in each of these elements. In addition, *all* modal (or bimodal) vectors likewise appear in *each column* (or *row*) of H (at least in *most* cases), and you can determine each individual vector by its effect on the shape of the frequency response near its corresponding pole. This reduction in the data collection task by a factor of n can be extremely important in many practical measurement situations, especially when the poles occur at low frequencies or are spaced close together. To resolve poles of this kind, you must collect data over long time intervals, which *can* make the data acquisition process expensive.

There are many potential sources of error in this model, as might be expected in a measurement of this complexity. The representation of a *continuous* mechanical system by a *lumped* model is an approximation. The calculation of the various frequency response functions from data collected by exciting the structure with some external source, and then observing its resulting motion, is full of error possibilities. There will be various sources of noise that contaminate the observations, and there are often nonlinearities in the mechanical system to contend with. It is also very difficult to decide on the proper *number* of poles to use in the Laplace transform representation. There are always higher frequency poles (and modes of vibration) that you cannot separately resolve, so you must represent them in some composite way. You may find *repeated* poles (and modes) and sometimes *multiple* poles (and modes) that share the same numerical pole values, but have different modal vector components. You should design both the measurement model and the measurement strategy to include these cases. In addition, you may be driving the structure in a way that fails to excite one or more important modes.

We see there is at least one modal *vector* associated with each and every *pole*. As with many measurement tasks, you must usually measure the values of *all* of the poles, simultaneously with *all* of the modal vector components, in order to obtain any measurement of *individual* parameters at all. This involves the solutions to many *simultaneous nonlinear equations,* which can be a formidable task. There are ways to simplify this procedure to some extent, and we will return to this measurement problem in chapter 5. For now, recognize that the *model* for this modal measurement is the matrix-vector Eq. 2.12, with parameters embedded in the matrix inverse form of Eq. 2.17, whose elements are *transfer functions* of the structure in the Laplace variable s.

2.6   EXAMPLE: GPS NAVIGATION SYSTEM

In the GPS navigation system, a set of Earth-orbiting satellites simultaneously transmit coded radio signals that contain the orbital elements for each satellite, along with the time of day from an onboard clock, and a unique pseudorandom noise sequence that can be used by a receiver to estimate the *differences* in arrival times of the signals received from each satellite *pair*. There are nominally twenty-four GPS satellites in twelve-hour circular orbits approximately 12,413 miles above the Earth's surface (16,371 miles from the

Earth's center). These are arranged so at least four satellites can be seen simultaneously from any point on the Earth.

Using only the three differences in travel time to the receiver from four satellites, you can solve a single quadratic equation in conjunction with a pair of linear equations to obtain the three coordinates (latitude, longitude, and altitude above the Earth's centroid) of the receiver. Alternatively, an iterative solution can be obtained if you have a good starting point, and if you can tolerate the time it takes to iterate to an accurate result.

You can usually resolve the two ambiguous solutions based on physical arguments (for example, you may know the receiver is on the surface of the Earth, or is near your last position, etc.) If necessary, you can use a fifth satellite to resolve this question. If you know your *altitude*, then you can determine your latitude and longitude using only three satellites, and the corresponding *pair* of time differences.

In practice, the travel *time* differences determined by the receiver are converted into differences in *distances* to the satellites by multiplying by the velocity of propagation of radio waves through the Earth's atmosphere. The remainder of the measurement problem is a mathematical calculation based on the known geometry of the satellite group and on the estimated distance differences between them and the observer.

Imagine a pair of GPS satellites placed a *unit* distance apart and centered along the *x*-axis of a rectangular coordinate system. Surfaces corresponding to constant differences in distance to each satellite are called *hyperboloids*, or hyperbolas of revolution. An example of a hyperbola is the curve produced by intersecting a cone with a plane parallel to the cone central axis. Figure 2–4 shows cross-sections of several of these hyperboloids, corresponding to a set of distance differences denoted by *D*. In this figure, the two satellite transmitters are located along the *x*-axis at points $x = -.5$ and $x = .5$, and any receiver recording a distance difference *D* must lie *somewhere* on the corresponding hyperboloidal surface. Notice the *signs* of *x* and *D* are always the same. The *y*-axis represents a *degenerate* hyperboloid (the *yz*-plane) obtained when $D = 0$. The hyperboloids also degenerate into straight line segments when $D = \pm 1$, and these lie along the *x*-axis, beginning at each transmitter and extending to infinity. The equation for these hyperboloidal surfaces is:

$$x^2 - \frac{D^2}{1 - D^2}(y^2 + z^2) = \frac{D^2}{4} \tag{2.21}$$

where *x* carries the same sign as *D*. Each surface cuts the *x*-axis at $x = D/2$. For large coordinate values (far from both transmitters), each hyperboloid asymptotically approaches the surface of a cone, whose apex is at the origin, and whose slope relative to the *x*-axis is $\sqrt{1 - D^2}/D$.

Although Figure 2–4 is based on transmitters spaced a *unit* distance apart along the *x*-axis, it is a simple matter to rescale the transmitter spacing and to translate and rotate the coordinate axes in any way desired. The basic hyperboloidal shape will be scaled, translated, and rotated in a corresponding manner.

We will use a rectangular coordinate system (x,y,z) in this example, although it is straightforward to convert to and from polar coordinates whenever necessary. It is easier to solve the navigation equations using rectangular coordinates, even though the user probably expects polar coordinates from the receiver.

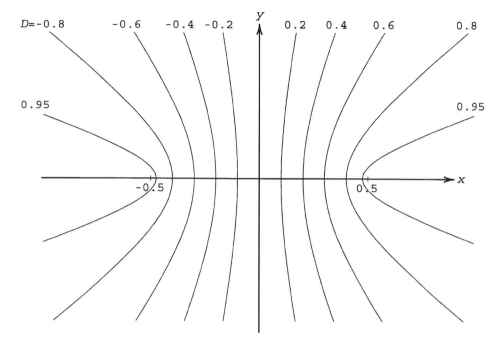

Figure 2–4   Hyperbolas of Constant Distance Difference, D

Now, imagine a *third* satellite in the system. There will be a *second* hyperboloid associated with this third transmitter, in conjunction with the one from the *original* pair. Except for a few special cases, these two hyperboloids will intersect in space, producing a *space curve*. When a *fourth* satellite is added, the resulting *third* hyperboloid will generally intersect this space curve at *two points*. The rectangular coordinates of these two possible solution points can be obtained by solving a quadratic equation. Only *one* of these solutions will be correct, so you may need to develop a strategy for eliminating the spurious solution.

The details of this *closed form* solution are given in Appendix B, for those who might be interested. The derivation is simple in principle, but involves a rather large number of algebraic terms in the calculation. To summarize the procedure, there are three equations, corresponding to the three differences in distance between *pairs* of transmitters. One of these equations can be subtracted from the other two to get a pair of *linear equations*, from which two of the three receiver coordinates can be written as linear functions of the *third* coordinate. Then, a *quadratic* equation in this third coordinate is obtained by substituting these relations into one of the three *original* difference equations. Once a pair of solutions for one coordinate are obtained, the aforementioned pair of linear equations will give the remaining two coordinates of each solution.

In this model, there will undoubtedly be small errors in the expected positions of the satellites, and the propagation velocity of the radio waves will depend on atmospheric conditions to some extent, so these will cause errors in the distance differences. Another major error source is the noise in the receiver, both due to thermal noise and to additional noise mechanisms in the transistors used to amplify the received signal. You can minimize the receiver noise by repeating the measurement many times, but this may not work well due to the relative *motion* between the satellites and the observers position.

In addition, some degree of uncertainty will always be introduced by *rounding* errors in the many computations required to obtain the solution. Unless you use *double precision* numbers (say 53 mantissa bits) in the processor, rounding errors can be significant. There are certain regions of space in which any errors in the time differences will be greatly magnified. In general, any position near a straight line connecting any two satellites, that is *not* between the satellites (called a baseline extension) will be relatively inaccurate, because one hyperboloid will be approaching the degenerate form of a straight line and will be very sensitive to small errors in the time difference. Fortunately, in the GPS system, the satellites are essentially on a spherical surface well above the Earth, so these baseline extensions are seldom a problem. A more serious configuration is when the satellites are in a *plane rectangular* arrangement. For this case, there is *no* available position information in a direction perpendicular to the plane of the transmitters, in either of two possible planes that bisect the *opposite* sides of the transmitter rectangle. You can avoid these degenerate cases by simply choosing another satellite for the measurement.

Currently, the GPS system has an accuracy of 60 to 100 meters, with the potential for a 4:1 improvement in the next few years. There is a popular variation on the basic scheme called *differential GPS,* in which the receiver is calibrated on local markers whose positions are accurately known. The errors in measuring these markers are subtracted from any subsequent position measurements in a local region (80 to 160 km) around each marker. In this manner, the position accuracy can be improved to about 1.5 meters. There are other techniques that can be used to further enhance position accuracy, but for somewhat specialized applications.

In addition to measuring position, you may also require a navigation system to measure the *velocity* (both magnitude and direction) of the observer, and this is even *more* sensitive to the many error sources than is a position determination. You may also want your model to include *acceleration* estimation methods, for some applications. Techniques for adding these features are discussed in section 5.5 of chapter 5.

We have not attempted to draw block diagrams of the measurement models for these last two examples, because such diagrams would not significantly improve our understanding of the systems in question. However, as a consequence, the locations of the various sources of noise or other disturbances that degrade the accuracy of the parameter measurements may not be completely clear. We will simply add noise terms into the system equations to provide the *same* perturbations on the mathematical variables that would occur on those *corresponding* signals in the physical world.

2.7   SUMMARY

Selecting the "best" measurement model is very important. It forms the foundation for all of the subsequent steps in the measurement procedure, and the results will not be useful to anybody if there are significant errors in the model. However, constructing a good model is somewhat of an *art* and requires considerable knowledge about the physical system under study. The model cannot be too *simple* and it cannot be too *complicated*. It will generally be incomplete, and somewhat inaccurate, so *good judgment* is required to decide if it is still adequate for the needs of the final *user* of the measured results. The model is always a mathematical equation or set of equations, allowing us to calculate the output from some prescribed input excitation at any time. It must include all significant noise sources, and all important conditions under which the model is *valid*. It must also include all details of the parameter estimation algorithm.

In the following chapters, we will consider techniques for estimating the parameters of our model in some optimum or "best" way, using a limited set of observations of the physical system in question. We will also consider ways to describe the accuracy or precision of these estimates, so the *end user* can decide if the measurement is indeed suitable for his or her needs.

BIBLIOGRAPHY ON MODELING EXAMPLES

[2:1]   Brown, James Ward, and Churchill, Ruel V. *Complex Variables and Applications,* 6th ed., McGraw-Hill, 1996. This classic reference was first published in 1948 and is still going strong.

[2:2]   Dorf, Richard C., *Modern Control Systems,* Addison-Wesley, 1980. There are numerous reference books on control systems, and most of them discuss the Laplace transform. This is a popular reference on both topics.

[2:3]   Gantmacher, F. R., *The Theory of Matrices,* Volumes I and II, Chelsea Publishing Co., 1960. A very good reference on all aspects of matrix theory.

[2:4]   Golub, Gene H., and Van Loan, Charles F., *Matrix Computations,* The Johns Hopkins University Press, 1983. This is another very good reference on matrix theory.

[2:5]   Grumman Aircraft Corp., *Final Report, System 621B, User Equipment Definition and Experiment Program, Phase I.* GAC No. 621B-FR1. Los Angeles: Space and Missile Systems Organization, Dec., 1970. This documents the original derivation of the closed form solutions to the GPS navigation equations.

[2:6]   Knopp, Konrad, *Theory of Functions, Part I,* Dover Publications, 1945. This is one of the early books on the theory of complex variables.

[2:7]   Potter, R., "A General Theory of Modal Analysis for Linear Systems," *The Shock and Vibration Digest,* Nov. 1975. This reference includes more detail in the derivation of the modal equations for vibrating mechanical structures.

[2:8]   Potter, Ron, and Olsen, Norm, "Modal Analysis for the Connoisseur," *Sound and Vibration,* Jan. 1988, pp. 18–25. This is a paper emphasizing multiple poles and asymmetric matrices, and shows an actual physical measurement of a double pole on a mechanical structure. Unfortunately, the publisher interchanged the graphics portions of Figures 16 and 18.

[2:9]   Roberts, G. E., and Kaufman, H., *Table of Laplace Transforms,* W. B. Saunders Co., 1966. This is an excellent collection of Laplace transform pairs, including many higher functions.

3

Measurements as Random Variables

3.1 PROLOGUE ON UNCERTAINTY

Someone (*possibly* a voluble politician!) once said, "I *never* make a definite statement." Of course, that person was a liar since *that* statement itself is a definite statement! How about, "The probability is very *low* that I ever make a definite statement"? The idea that things are definite, well defined, and unambiguous is deeply ingrained in our minds and our culture. We may be willing to admit that our observations or perceptions are imperfect at times, but we tend to think we are observing "real" things or events; with a little more care we could do a much better job, and we *could* actually describe these things or events as accurately as we wish.

This bubble of faith was burst in the early part of the twentieth century when observations of small particle behavior led to the concepts and theory of quantum mechanics and to the resulting *uncertainty principle*. However, even without this basic uncertainty between the positions and momenta of small particles, there is still an *uncertainty mechanism* at work on a *macro*-level in everything we do! Nearly every time we perform an experiment, make an observation, or repeat a task, we get *different* results! Admittedly, the results may *look* similar, but at some level there will be differences. Even if you repeatedly attempt to count the number of beans in a jar (which you *know* to be some invariant integer), you will *still* sometimes get different answers.

There are always unknown or uncontrollable sources of "noise," interference, or error that creep into any experiment, observation, and task, and that change the results every time you attempt these activities. These perturbations may be *within* the system under consideration, or they may be introduced when you try to make *observations* of the system. Now, if your raw observations of a physical system are always different, then your repeated estimates (or measurements) of the parameters of the *model* for that system will *also* be different. You should memorize this simple mantra: "Every measurement I make (under the same conditions) is somewhat *different* and therefore somewhat *incorrect*."

Having emphasized this idea of incorrect measurements, we should expand our perspective. At *some level* of error, the end user of the measurements will be *satisfied* with the results. What is more, this user may have little interest in paying a premium price for greatly improved accuracy. Thus, the task in making measurements is to determine the expectations of the *end user* of this information and then to match *that* with the accuracy of the results. We know perfection is impossible, but we also know it is neither necessary nor even desirable! The worst situation is not *knowing* the quality of our measurements.

The real question is: How do we explain and quantify the accuracy of our measurements to the end user in some meaningful and useful way? For example, we could say all measured quantities are accurate to within ±1% of their correct values. However, that seems like a very *definite* statement, and the user might reasonably ask how you *know* that tolerance level will *never* be exceeded.

In fact, it is seldom possible to set rigid error tolerances on a measurement. A more realistic procedure is to define a *confidence "level"* for each measurement and then to determine the corresponding *confidence "interval"* for that parameter value. For example, we might specify that our measured quantities lie within the *interval* of ±1% of the correct value, say 95% of the time (a confidence *level* chosen by the *user*). This tells the user the specified accuracy level is *not* a hard limit, but may occasionally be violated (on the average of 5% of the time, or once out of every twenty tries).

Unfortunately, you will immediately recognize there is *still* some uncertainty in this accuracy description. The 95% confidence level must be somewhat in error because it is also a measured quantity! There is really no end to this process. It is not generally possible to *completely* specify these measurement errors, at least in real physical applications (it is sometimes possible to place hard limits on *mathematical* quantities that are used in simulating real systems, but not on the physical quantities themselves). In the real world, there are always large perturbations that occasionally occur (call them *catastrophic* events) that nobody can predict. A single cosmic ray (a high energy particle from space) might pass through a critical transistor in the system in question and induce an error in its operation. Or, perhaps something malfunctions due to overheating. At some point, the Earth will be hit by another giant asteroid or comet, and *that* event will certainly introduce some unexpected (and possibly *catastrophic*) errors into your measurements!

In this chapter, we will introduce some of the concepts and "buzzwords" of *probability theory,* and we will apply these ideas to our measured model parameters, with the goal of quantifying our measurement errors in some reasonable manner.

3.2   INTRODUCTION TO PROBABILITY THEORY

Imagine collecting a few million voltmeter readings from a 13 volt DC battery (which is *nominally* called a 12 volt battery!) into the memory of your computer. We already expect each reading to be *different*, assuming the resolution of the voltmeter is adequate to *show* these differences. If we assume we have not materially affected the charge on the battery during the measurement session, then we expect the many readings to cluster around the correct voltage, but we also expect some *spreading* to occur around this value. How can we assign *numbers* to describe and represent this behavior?

Select some number of intervals, say 1000, along the voltage axis so as to include all of the voltmeter readings from the measuring session. *Round* each reading to the nearest voltage *interval* (sometimes called a "bin"), and then add a single *unit count* to the contents of a memory cell you have chosen to represent that bin. The result is called a *histogram* of all of the voltmeter readings. Next, divide the integer count in each bin by the *total number* of voltmeter readings in the histogram to obtain the proportion of the total readings that fall into each bin. This normalizes the histogram so its "area" is unity. This is an approximation to the *probability density function (PDF)* of the voltmeter readings. It's an approximation because each voltage bin has a *finite* rather than an *infinitesimal* width, and the number stored in each bin (the approximate magnitude of the density function) is quantized by the *finite* number of readings that actually fell into that bin. For example, if only one count occurred in a bin, *that* would be a rather inaccurate measure of the probability density function for that particular voltage interval.

For the record, we assume the random process producing these readings is both *stationary* and *ergodic*. By way of review, we always assume that a large (infinite) *ensemble* of examples of a given process exist *simultaneously* (or in parallel), and all the statistical parameters are determined at *each point in time*, from this ensemble. A *stationary process* is one whose "ensemble" statistical parameters (mean values, variances, correlation coefficients, probability density functions, confidence intervals, etc.) *do not vary* with time. An *ergodic process* is one whose ensemble statistical parameters are not only *stationary*, but are the same as those obtained from any *one* member of the ensemble taken along the *time* axis (in other words, *ensemble* statistics are the same as *time domain* statistics for an ergodic process).

If we actually *knew* the PDF of these voltage readings, then we could accurately predict confidence *intervals* for any selected confidence *level*. Unfortunately, we never have this knowledge with complete certainty because this PDF must be measured, and remember, measured quantities are always somewhat different! One useful option is to *calculate* the PDF based on an *assumed model* of the suspected noise sources. *If* our noise model is correct, and *if* our model of the physical system is correct, then we expect our calculated PDF to likewise be correct. We can "match" the measured PDF approximation to this mathematical model, to gain some confidence that we have *indeed* chosen the correct noise model.

It is very common to assume the PDF for every measurement is of Gaussian form (defined by Eq. 3.1), because this is a particularly easy form to use, and because it *is* often the *correct* form to use. It is also sometimes called a "normal" distribution, or a "bell-shaped" curve. However, there are times when the PDF is *not* Gaussian, so you must be careful about such assumptions. For example, the sum of the squares of voltages (a measure of power), *each* having a Gaussian PDF, has a *chi-squared* PDF, which exists only for *positive* abscissa values. In digital or quantized systems, we have discrete or discontinuous PDFs comprising sums of *delta functions*. Sometimes our PDFs have rectangular, triangular, or exponential shapes.

The general expression for a Gaussian PDF is:

$$p_x(x) = \frac{1}{\sqrt{2\pi}\,\sigma_x}\,e^{-\frac{1}{2\sigma_x^2}(x-\mu_x)^2} \tag{3.1}$$

where μ_x is called the *mean value*, and σ_x is called the *standard deviation* of the random variable x (or, alternately, of the PDF of x). By definition, the area under a PDF is always unity, which therefore determines the amplitude scaling of the function. The mean value is the first *moment*, which locates the "center" of the PDF along the abscissa, and the *standard deviation* is a measure of the "width" or "spreading" of the PDF around the mean value.

The shape of this Gaussian PDF is shown in Figure 3–1. In our measurements on the 13 volt battery, the mean value μ_x corresponds to 13 volts, and the spread of the PDF around that mean value, given by the standard deviation σ_x, represents the (somewhat exaggerated) *uncertainty* in the measurement, due to both battery and voltmeter noise and to random errors in reading the voltmeter.

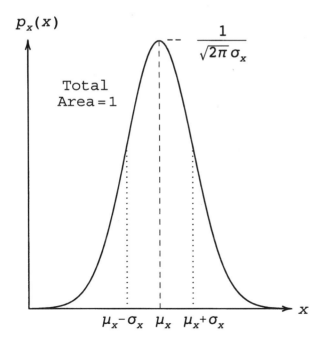

Figure 3–1 Gaussian Probability Density

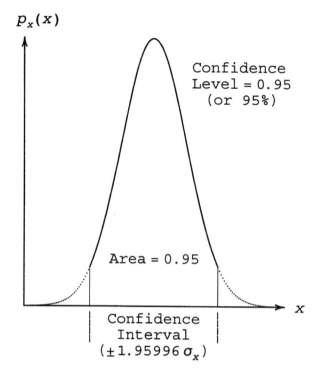

$p_x(x)$

Confidence
Level = 0.95
(or 95%)

Area = 0.95

x

Confidence
Interval
$(\pm 1.95996\,\sigma_x)$

Figure 3–2 Gaussian Probability Density

Figure 3–2 shows the *same* Gaussian PDF but illustrates the concept of a *confidence interval* along the abscissa (or *x*-axis), corresponding to a specified *confidence level*. In this example, the confidence *level* is specified to be 0.95 (or 95%), so the confidence *interval* is adjusted until the area under the PDF is likewise 0.95, leaving the remaining area distributed under the two "tails" of the function. In this case, the confidence interval along the *x*-axis is $\pm 1.95996\,\sigma_x$ and is defined to be *symmetrical* about the mean value, but that is *not* a general requirement. In some cases this interval might be strictly on *one* side of the PDF.

The *mode* of a PDF is the highest point on the function and represents the most likely abscissa value to be observed. For symmetrical PDFs, this is also the mean value. For asymmetrical shapes the mode will be different than the mean. The mean value μ_x is the first moment of the PDF about the origin and is also the result of *averaging* an infinite number of *independent x* readings together.

Another useful parameter of a PDF is the *median*, which is the abscissa value that divides the area under the PDF in *half*. Thus, the probability of getting a reading *above* the median is the same as the probability of getting a reading *below* the median, namely 0.5. Again, for symmetrical shapes, both the median and the mode are equal to the mean, but for asymmetrical shapes they will generally be different. The mean, median, and mode represent three different "educated guesses" as to the location of any single voltmeter reading, relative to the PDF. You have *no* way of knowing where *any* single reading actually falls.

The probability of the reading falling *within* any particular abscissa *interval* is given by the area under the PDF over that interval. The total area is unity (by definition) because it is certain the reading will fall *somewhere* under the PDF. Conversely, for continuous variables, the probability that a particular abscissa *value* will occur is *zero*, corresponding to the area over an interval having zero width (this is *not* always true for discrete or quantized variables; see section 3.6).

This probability density function (or normalized histogram) represents our *best* (a priori) judgment about the behavior of our measurements of the DC battery voltage. That is, from previous experience in measuring battery voltages, and from our model of the noise mechanisms inherent in this battery-voltmeter system, we decide ahead of time the PDF has an approximate Gaussian shape, and we try to anticipate the standard deviation σ_x of this shape. Then we take a *single* voltmeter reading of the battery voltage and try to predict from this postulated PDF what the probable error might be in this single measurement.

Notice the many uncertainties in this procedure. *First*, we don't know (for sure) that the PDF is actually Gaussian in shape; *second*, we don't know the standard deviation of this distribution with a great deal of accuracy; *third*, we don't know where the mean is located along the abscissa; and *fourth*, we don't know where our single voltmeter reading falls within this distribution. All we really know is there is a *95% probability* that the reading is within the $\pm 1.95996\ \sigma_x$ confidence interval around the true mean, $x = \mu_x$, *if* the PDF is *indeed* Gaussian. One time in twenty tries (on average), the voltmeter reading will be *outside* of this confidence interval, by an unknown amount, and for the other nineteen tries (on average) it will fall somewhere *within* this confidence interval. However, you cannot know into *which* of these two categories any particular *single* voltmeter reading belongs.

Of course, if this level of performance is not adequate for your needs, you can always alter the specified confidence level, say to 0.99 and then calculate the corresponding *new* confidence interval (which would be $\pm 2.57583\ \sigma_x$ for this Gaussian case). Now, your single voltmeter reading will (on average) fall within this *new* confidence interval 99 times out of every 100 tries.

Another alternative is to take more than one voltmeter reading, and then to use some sort of *estimation algorithm* (such as *averaging* readings together) to decide on the *best* answer for the battery voltage. However, this composite result is still a random variable and still has a PDF with a mean value, a standard deviation, and confidence intervals for any chosen confidence level, so some of the measurement uncertainty is *still* present, although it *is* reduced (by the square root of the number of readings averaged together).

Keep in mind that our knowledge of the "tails" of the PDF is generally poor, because it takes an increasingly large amount of data (and time) to measure this part of the PDF far from the center of the distribution. This means the accuracy of the confidence interval deteriorates as we squeeze the confidence level closer to unity. In addition, the Gaussian PDF never goes to *zero*, but continues over an infinite abscissa range, in contrast to our parameters, whose values are always *finite*. Many of the PDFs we study have similar unrealistic forms of behavior in the *tail* regions, but they may still be useful in practice, just as long as we are aware of these idiosyncrasies.

Some people have suggested that *catastrophic failures* of physical devices are simply manifestations of PDF tails that extend to very large abscissa values. This could be true, but there are doubts about this interpretation. Catastrophic failures are more likely caused by *nonlinearities* in physical systems that *may* occur even for moderate parameter values and have very little to do with large random noise events. This viewpoint is in line with recent studies of *chaos theory,* in which *minute* perturbations of the states of some nonlinear systems can lead to wildly different system behavior. Unfortunately, this very argument implies that our attempts to measure these low probability regions of the PDF will be heavily influenced by such occasional events. We have discovered yet another uncertainty in our measurements. Progressively *higher* confidence *levels* may result in progressively *lower accuracy* on the confidence *intervals*, due to our limited knowledge about the tails of these PDFs.

3.3   PROBABILITY THEORY—EXTENDED

The concept of a probability density function (PDF) can be readily extended to several random variables by means of a *joint* PDF, and from *that* the effects of any of the variables can be "removed" by integrating the joint PDF over the entire range of those variables, producing a *marginal* PDF. A joint PDF can be constructed in the same way as before, by building a *multi-dimensional* histogram of readings of two or more random quantities that occur *simultaneously.* For example, suppose you construct a three-dimensional histogram of the latitude, longitude, and altitude coordinates obtained from millions of readings of your *fixed* position using a GPS satellite navigation receiver. These millions of readings will form a "cloud" of points around your location in a three-dimensional space, where each coordinate corresponds to one of the three random variables, latitude, longitude, and altitude. A *three-dimensional* probability density function is obtained by normalizing the *histogram* constructed from this cloud of points, by the total number of observed points, as the number of these points approaches infinity. This three-dimensional joint PDF covers all possible combinations of values among the three random variables. Its shape indicates the amount of *variance* in each variable and the degree of *correlation* between the variables, while the *offset* between *its* mean and the *true* mean indicates the *bias error* in each variable.

If all of the random variables are *independent* of one another, then the joint PDF will be the product of the PDFs for each of the individual variables. This is actually the *definition* of independence among random quantities. Random variables that are *not* independent will usually comprise a part that *is* independent and a part that is *not.* For example, if $x_2 = x_1 + x_0$, it is obvious x_2 cannot be completely independent of x_1, even *if x_0 is* completely independent of x_1. Random variables that are completely *dependent* are strict functions of either themselves or of other random variables, so the dimensionality of the resulting joint PDF for this case is generally *less* than you would otherwise expect.

We see the *dimensionality* of a joint PDF can be reduced, either by integrating over one or more of the random variables to obtain a *marginal* PDF, or by imposing some functional relationship between one or more of the random variables.

An example might help to clarify this marginal PDF idea. Using the satellite position measurement discussed above, suppose you already know your altitude relative to the center of the earth. The three-dimensional joint PDF of your estimated position looks like a *cloud* around your true location and extends both *above* and *below* your actual known altitude. Since you are not interested in the altitude part of this cloud, you can integrate this joint PDF over the entire range of the *altitude* variable, thereby eliminating *that* variable and getting a *two-dimensional marginal PDF* in latitude and longitude only. This new marginal PDF looks like a (two-dimensional) *disc*, confined to your known altitude. The probability associated with each *area element* on this disc will be the *sum* of the probabilities represented by the set of *original* points that *project perpendicularly* into *that* area element.

This is, admittedly, a degenerate case where the altitude is not actually a function of either latitude or longitude, but is instead a constant. However, the same procedure could be used if you were confined to the *sloping surface* of a mountainside. For this case, you could introduce a new set of coordinates that are *rotated* to make the *new* "altitude" coordinate perpendicular to the mountain surface, then integrate the joint PDF, as before, over all possible values of this new altitude. The remaining two coordinates of the resulting marginal PDF over the mountain surface could then be transformed *back* to the original latitude/longitude system. The resulting two-dimensional marginal PDF would now look like a *sloping disc* parallel to the mountain surface, but would still be a function of only latitude and longitude. Thus, for *n* random variables, a *marginal* PDF is a *subspace* (having a dimensionality less than *n*) of the *n*-dimensional space occupied by the *joint* PDF.

Another option would be to simply integrate the original joint PDF over the *true* altitude coordinate, *without* rotating the coordinate system parallel to the mountain surface. If the altitude variations were *independent* of the latitude and longitude variations, then this technique would be satisfactory, but these quantities are usually related in some way, so the *best* estimation procedure will generally be more complicated. The merits of different approaches of this sort are discussed more fully in the next chapter.

It is always possible to integrate the PDF over the entire range of any of the variables to eliminate *that* variable's effect on the resulting density function. For example, a one-dimensional PDF can be obtained for *any one* variable by integrating the joint PDF over *all other* variables. Then, the mean value and standard deviation for *that one* random variable can be determined. However, keep in mind these results are "average" values obtained while allowing all of the other random variables to move *throughout* their total ranges, so this *may* or may *not* be useful information.

Figure 3–3 shows a stereoscopic view of a two-dimensional joint Gaussian PDF $p_{xy}(x,y)$ for independent random variables x and y, along with the two marginal PDFs $p_x(x)$ and $p_y(y)$, each having a mean value that is offset from the origin. The view is *from* the third quadrant, looking *into* the first quadrant.

One of the most useful applications of the joint PDF is in the calculation of the PDF for a *newly defined* random variable that is some *function* of a set of original random vari-

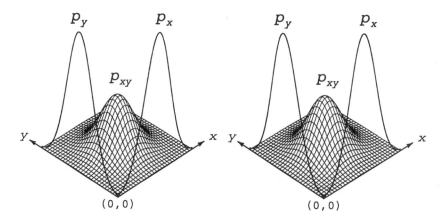

Figure 3–3 Two-Dimensional Joint and Marginal Gaussian PDFs

ables. For example, suppose we wish to define a new random variable y as the *sum* of two *independent* random variables, say x_1 and x_2. What will the PDF of y look like? We simply form a two-dimensional *joint* PDF by multiplying the two one-dimensional PDFs for x_1 and x_2 together. Then, we solve for any *one* of the original variables in terms of y using the (newly defined) functional relation between y and the other variables. We substitute this expression into the joint PDF, and then integrate over all remaining original variables, leaving a marginal PDF that is *only* a function of y. For clarity, let's go through the mathematics of this procedure.

We define the PDFs of x_1 and x_2 to be $p_1(x_1)$ and $p_2(x_2)$, respectively. The joint PDF will then be:

$$p_{12}(x_1,x_2) = p_1(x_1)p_2(x_2) \tag{3.2}$$

Our new random variable is defined to be:

$$y = x_1 + x_2 \tag{3.3}$$

We replace x_2 by $y - x_1$ and integrate Eq. 3.2 over x_1, giving:

$$p_y(y) = \int_{-\infty}^{\infty} p_1(x_1)p_2(y - x_1)dx_1 \tag{3.4}$$

You may recognize this expression as the *convolution* between the two original PDFs. We will let the reader show that when any two PDFs are convolved together, the mean value of the result is the *sum* of the original mean values, and the variance (which is the square of the standard deviation) of the result is the *sum* of the original variances. By induction, the PDF for the sum of n independent random variables is obtained by convolving the n individual PDFs together, giving a mean value and a variance that are each *sums* of the n original set of mean values and variances, no matter what the *shapes* of the original PDFs might be.

The convolution of Gaussian PDFs with one another always produces another Gaussian PDF, for which the mean value and standard deviation can be easily calculated using the above rules. Thus, we can define y as the sum of n independent Gaussian random variables, each with its own mean value and standard deviation, as:

$$y = \sum_{i=1}^{n} x_i \text{, where} \tag{3.5}$$

$$p_i(x_i) = \frac{1}{\sqrt{2\pi}\,\sigma_i} e^{-\frac{1}{2\sigma_i^2}(x_i - \mu_i)^2} \tag{3.6}$$

When these n PDFs are all convolved together, we get

$$p_y(y) = \frac{1}{\sqrt{2\pi}\,\sigma_y} e^{-\frac{1}{2\sigma_y^2}(y - \mu_y)^2} \tag{3.7}$$

where

$$\mu_y = \sum_{i=1}^{n} \mu_i \tag{3.8}$$

$$\sigma_y^2 = \sum_{i=1}^{n} \sigma_i^2 \tag{3.9}$$

When a random variable is scaled by some value, say n, the amplitude of its PDF must be *inversely* scaled by the same amount to maintain a unit area. So, if z is a scaled version of y, we have:

$$p_z(z) = |n| p_y(nz) \text{ , where } z = \frac{y}{n} \tag{3.10}$$

Using Eq. 3.5 for y, we recognize the random variable z as the *average* of n independent random variables, and using Eq. 3.7 in conjunction with Eq. 3.10 we can write the PDF for z as:

$$p_z(z) = \frac{1}{\sqrt{2\pi}\,\sigma_z} e^{-\frac{1}{2\sigma_z^2}(z - \mu_z)^2} \text{ , where} \tag{3.11}$$

$$\mu_z = \frac{\mu_y}{n} = \frac{1}{n} \sum_{i=1}^{n} \mu_i \tag{3.12}$$

$$\sigma_z^2 = \frac{\sigma_y^2}{n^2} = \frac{1}{n}\left[\frac{1}{n}\sum_{i=1}^{n}\sigma_i^2\right] \tag{3.13}$$

As you would expect, the mean value of the average of n independent random variables μ_z is simply the average of the individual mean values, as indicated in Eq. 3.12. However, the variance of the average of n random variables is only $1/n$ times the average of the individual variances, as indicated in Eq. 3.13. The corresponding *standard deviation* is reduced by the *square root* of n. This reduction in standard deviation (and variance) is the main reason for averaging random variables together. Note, however, this reduction is only by the square root of n, so it takes four times the number of averages to reduce the width of the PDF by a factor of two.

Sometimes we need to determine the PDF of a *new* random variable that is some *function* of *another* random variable. For example, we might want the PDF of the *square* of a Gaussian random variable, since this would represent the power in a noisy signal having a Gaussian *voltage* PDF. Assume x is the original Gaussian random variable, having zero mean value and a standard deviation of σ_x. Define a new random variable $u = x^2$. We desire the PDF of u along with its mean value and standard deviation. We must first invert this definition of u to get $x = \pm\sqrt{u}$. Then we can substitute this into the PDF for x. In order to maintain unit area, we must also multiply by $|dx/du| = 1/(2\sqrt{u})$. There are two solutions to this inversion (the two signs allow *one* positive value of u to include contributions from *both* positive *and* negative values of x), so we must *add* the contributions from each solution. The result is:

$$p_u(u) = \sum_{1,2} p_x(x)\left|\frac{dx}{du}\right| = \frac{1}{\sqrt{2\pi u}\,\sigma_x}e^{-\frac{u}{2\sigma_x^2}} \quad, \text{ for } u \geq 0 \tag{3.14}$$

The mean value of u is σ_x^2 and its variance is $2\sigma_x^4$. This is called a *central chi-squared PDF* with *one degree of freedom*.

We illustrate this concept in Figure 3–4 below. The functional relation between the old x and the new u random variables, $u = x^2$, is plotted as a dashed line in the xu-plane. The joint PDF p_{xu} for x and u is a *space curve* above this dashed contour, since there is only one independent variable. We generally think of a joint PDF as being a function of two or more variables, but here is an exception. The original Gaussian PDF for x is shown as a dotted shape above the x-axis, and the resulting PDF for u (chi-squared with one degree of freedom) is shown as a dotted line above the u-axis. The differences in amplitude among these three PDFs is dictated by the requirement of unit area under each curve when integrated relative to the independent variable for *that* curve. Note the two branches of the joint PDF, corresponding to positive and negative values of x, which *both* contribute (in an additive manner) to the resulting PDF of u.

We often want to *average n* of these squared random variables together to reduce the variance. The PDF for the *sum* of n such random variables is called *central chi-squared* with *n degrees of freedom* and is given by

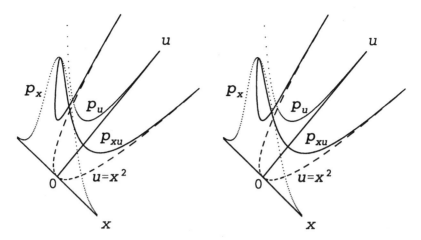

Figure 3–4 PDF of the Square of a Gaussian Random Variable

$$p_v(v) = \frac{v^{\frac{n}{2}-1}}{2^{\frac{n}{2}}\, \Gamma\!\left(\frac{n}{2}\right)\sigma_x^n}\, e^{-\frac{v}{2\sigma_x^2}} \;,\quad \text{for } v \geq 0 \tag{3.15}$$

where

$$v = \sum_{i=1}^{n} x_i^2 \tag{3.16}$$

and each x_i has zero mean value and a standard deviation of σ_x. We can calculate this PDF by means of the *characteristic function* and the Fourier transform, which we will discuss shortly (see Eq. 3.23). The mean value of v is $n\sigma_x^2$, and the variance is $2n\sigma_x^4$. For $n = 1$, we get the PDF in Eq. 3.14, with its corresponding values for mean and variance. $\Gamma(m)$ is called the *gamma function*. For reference, $\Gamma(1/2) = \sqrt{\pi}$, $\Gamma(1) = 1$, and there is a useful recursion relation, $\Gamma(m+1) = m\Gamma(m)$.

For the *average* of the squares of Gaussian random variables, we use the form of Eq. 3.10, except with $w = v/n$, so the PDF of w becomes:

$$p_w(w) = \frac{\left(\frac{n}{2}\right)^{\frac{n}{2}} w^{\frac{n}{2}-1}}{\Gamma\!\left(\frac{n}{2}\right)\sigma_x^n}\, e^{-\frac{nw}{2\sigma_x^2}} \;,\quad \text{for } w \geq 0 \tag{3.17}$$

The resulting mean value of w is σ_x^2, and the variance is $2\sigma_x^4/n$, so averaging *again* reduces the standard deviation by $\sqrt{n}$. We will call Eq. 3.17 the *normalized central chi-squared PDF* with n degrees of freedom, in contrast to Eq. 3.15. Notice the mean value of

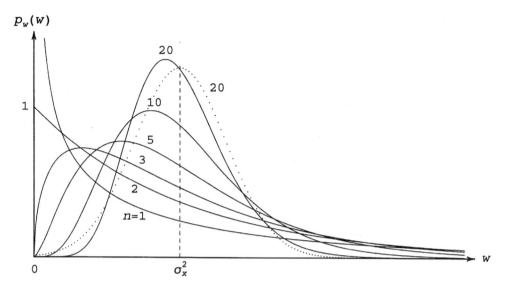

Figure 3–5   Normalized Chi-Squared PDFs (n degrees of freedom)

w is independent of n. Several of these normalized chi-squared density functions are plotted in Figure 3–5.

As n increases to large values, this PDF approaches a Gaussian shape centered at σ_x^2 with a variance of $2\sigma_x^4/n$. This is illustrated by the dotted curve in Figure 3–5 for $n = 20$. This is a very general property of most PDFs of sums of random variables, *independent* of the shape of the original PDF.

There is a *Central Limit Theorem* that states that the PDF of the *sum* of n independent random variables approaches a Gaussian shape (or has a Gaussian envelope when the random variable is quantized) as n approaches infinity, for a large class of original PDF shapes. We will not give a *proof* of the Central Limit Theorem, but we can make some *plausibility* arguments. The Gaussian shape has two related properties: (1) *convolutions* of Gaussian shapes yield Gaussian shapes, and (2) *products* of Gaussian shapes (centered at the same place) yield Gaussian shapes. Other functions can have *one* of these two properties, but not *both*. These two properties are related because the Fourier transform of a Gaussian shape *also* yields a Gaussian shape (or at least a Gaussian envelope, ignoring any phase angles). There are *other* functions whose Fourier transform *pairs* have the *same* functional form, but these forms are *not* invariant under repeated convolutions or multiplications with themselves.

The Central Limit Theorem can be visualized to operate in either of two different ways, corresponding to repeated *convolutions* or to repeated *multiplications*. To visualize the *first* way, imagine a *non*-Gaussian PDF being convolved with a Gaussian PDF. Decompose the non-Gaussian PDF into the *sum* of a Gaussian part (having unit area) and a residual *non*-Gaussian part (having zero area). When these two parts are subsequently convolved with another Gaussian PDF, the two Gaussian parts convolve together to yield a new Gaussian PDF, while the Gaussian convolution with the *non*-Gaussian residue produces a new shape (still with zero area) that is *reduced* in amplitude by some amount (because the Gaussian kernel includes portions of *both* positive *and* negative values of the non-Gaussian component). Eventually, after many such convolutions, the Gaussian component of the original PDF will remain, but the *non*-Gaussian residual will become progressively attenuated.

To visualize the *second* approach, imagine a *non*-Gaussian shape having a maximum amplitude of unity at the origin. Decompose this into the *sum* of a unit amplitude Gaussian shape and a residual non-Gaussian shape (which will therefore have a value of zero at the origin). The multiplication of the Gaussian component by another similar Gaussian shape (having unit amplitude at the origin) will produce another unit amplitude Gaussian shape, but multiplication with the *non*-Gaussian residual will *reduce* the magnitude of this residual everywhere (except at the origin, where the value is zero *anyway*), because the Gaussian multiplier is *less than unity* everywhere except at the origin. Eventually, after many such multiplications, the Gaussian component of the original shape will remain, but the *non*-Gaussian residual will become progressively attenuated.

The *expected value* of a function $f(x)$ of a random variable x is defined by the integral

$$E\left[f(x)\right] = \int_{-\infty}^{\infty} f(x)p_x(x)dx \tag{3.18}$$

where $p_x(x)$ is the PDF of x. For each value of x, the value of $f(x)$ is weighted by the probability $p_x(x)$ that *that* value of x will occur, and then all of these weighted values are summed together.

As an example, the *m*th moment of a PDF is the expected value of $f(x) = x^m$, written as:

$$E\left[x^m\right] = \int_{-\infty}^{\infty} x^m p_x(x)dx \tag{3.19}$$

The 0*th* moment is the area under the PDF, which is always unity by definition (note that $E[1] = 1$). The 1*st* moment is the *mean value* of the random variable x. The *variance* is the second moment minus the square of the first moment, and the *standard deviation* is the square root of the variance. As you can see from Eq. 3.19, it is possible to calculate any number of moments for the PDF, although some of these may be redundant or zero. The Gaussian PDF can be described completely by using only the first and second moments (all other moments are either zero or functions of the first two). In some cases, the third or fourth moments can be useful, but there is seldom any need for higher moments.

Central moments are obtained when x is replaced by $x - \mu_x$ (in which the mean value is subtracted from x) in Eq. 3.19. For example, the variance is the second *central* moment, and is a measure of the noise power in our battery voltage example. The *third* central moment (divided by the cube of the standard deviation) is a measure of the *skewness* (or lack of symmetry) of the PDF around the mean value, and the *fourth* central moment (divided by the square of the variance, minus three) is a measure of the *kurtosis* or *flatness* of the distribution, compared to a Gaussian PDF (for which *both* the skewness and kurtosis are zero).

When $f(x) = e^{i\omega x}$, we obtain the *characteristic function* for the PDF, written as:

$$\Phi_x(\omega) = E[e^{i\omega x}] = \int_{-\infty}^{\infty} e^{i\omega x} p_x(x) dx \qquad (3.20)$$

This can be recognized as the *inverse Fourier transform* of the PDF. The characteristic function of the *sum* of several independent random variables is the *product* of their individual characteristic functions, since a basic property of the Fourier transform is that the *convolution* of functions in *one* domain represents the *multiplication* of the *transforms* of those functions in the *transform* domain.

If we differentiate $\Phi_x(\omega)$ (with respect to ω) m times, and then evaluate this result at the origin ($\omega = 0$), we get i^m times the mth moment of the PDF of x. That is:

$$D^{(m)} \Phi_x(\omega)|_{\omega=0} = i^m E[x^m] \qquad (3.21)$$

where $D^{(m)}$ represents the mth derivative operator (with respect to ω in this case). The characteristic function (via the properties of the Fourier transform) can be very useful in making otherwise difficult calculations of the properties of many PDFs. Here are two examples of characteristic functions. For a Gaussian PDF (given by Eq. 3.1) we have:

$$\Phi_x(\omega) = e^{i\mu_x\omega - \frac{1}{2}\sigma_x^2\omega^2} \qquad (3.22)$$

which itself has a Gaussian *envelope* in the variable ω, with a second central moment of $1/\sigma_x^2$. Thus, as the PDF of x gets *wider*, the characteristic function in ω gets *narrower*.

For a central chi-squared PDF with n degrees of freedom we have:

$$\Phi_v(\omega) = \frac{1}{(1 - i2\sigma_x^2\omega)^{\frac{n}{2}}} \qquad (3.23)$$

In all cases, the units of ω are the *reciprocal* of the units of the original random variable. Also, the *amplitude* of all characteristic functions at the origin ($\omega = 0$) is unity, because the *area* under the corresponding PDF is unity.

It is also straightforward to define the expected value of a function of *two or more* random variables. We multiply the function in question by the *joint* PDF and then integrate over the full range of all variables. For the case of two random variables we have:

$$E[f(x,y)] = \int_{-\infty}^{\infty}\int_{-\infty}^{\infty} f(x,y)p_{xy}(x,y)\, dx\, dy \qquad (3.24)$$

where $p_{xy}(x,y)$ is the joint PDF of x and y. An especially useful case is when $f(x, y) = (x - \mu_x)(y - \mu_y)$, where μ_x and μ_y are the mean values, respectively, of x and y, written as:

$$E[(x - \mu_x)(y - \mu_y)] = \int_{-\infty}^{\infty}\int_{-\infty}^{\infty} (x - \mu_x)(y - \mu_y)p_{xy}(x,y)\, dx\, dy \qquad (3.25)$$

The *correlation coefficient* ρ_{xy} between random variables x and y is defined to be:

$$\rho_{xy} = \frac{E\left[\,(x - \mu_x)\,(y - \mu_y)\,\right]}{\sigma_x\,\sigma_y} \tag{3.26}$$

If x and y are identical, this expected value is simply the variance, so the correlation coefficient is *unity*. If x and y are *linearly independent*, then the expected value is zero, so the correlation coefficient is *zero*. This is a way to describe any *linear* relationship that might exist between two random variables. However, it is possible for the correlation between two random variables to be zero, even when the two variables are completely dependent. For example, if $u = x^2$, the correlation coefficient ρ_{xu} between x and u will be zero, even though u is *completely determined* by x. We can see this by noting from Figure 3–4 that the joint PDF between x and u is an *even* function of x, while the product $(x - \mu_x)\,(u - \mu_u)$ is an *odd* function of x, relative to the mean value of x. Thus, the integral in Eq. 3.25 will be zero over the full range of x. In this example, we are correlating a *first*-order random variable x with a *second*-order random variable $u = x^2$, and there is no *linear* dependence between these two quantities.

We next discuss the important topic of *conditional PDFs*. Let's assume we have an n-dimensional joint PDF where the random variables are *not* necessarily independent. We cannot represent the joint PDF as the product of the individual PDFs unless the random variables *are* independent. However, there is a *factorization method* we can use very effectively. The n-dimensional joint PDF can be expressed as the product of an m-dimensional *conditional* PDF and an $(n-m)$-dimensional *joint* PDF (where $m < n$). This conditional PDF factor is simply the original joint PDF with some of the random variables assigned *fixed values*, but divided by the joint PDF of these "fixed" values to force the volume under the conditional PDF to be unity.

Let's define an m-dimensional vector X whose components x_k are the random variables in the conditional PDF, along with an $(n-m)$-dimensional vector Y whose components y_j are the "variables" that are fixed. We define the conditional PDF by means of:

$$p_{XY}(X, Y) = p_{X|Y}(X|Y)\,p_Y(Y) \tag{3.27}$$

where the left side is the *joint* PDF among all X and Y variables, and the right side is the product of the *conditional* PDF of the components of X, while holding the components of Y fixed, times the *joint* PDF of the components of Y alone. Thus, we can write the conditional PDF (of X, holding Y constant) as:

$$p_{X|Y}(X|Y) = \frac{p_{XY}(X, Y)}{p_Y(Y)} \tag{3.28}$$

If we integrate Eq. 3.27 separately with respect to X and Y, we get the following two properties of the conditional PDF:

$$\int_{-\infty}^{\infty} p_{X|Y}(X|Y)\,dX = 1 \tag{3.29}$$

$$\int_{-\infty}^{\infty} p_{X|Y}(X|Y) p_Y(Y) \, dY = p_X(X) \tag{3.30}$$

where the integrals are actually multiple integrals over all of the components of the vector of integration.

Thus, the m-volume under the conditional PDF is unity when integrated over the m random components of X, for *all* values of the fixed components of Y, as indicated in Eq. 3.29. If the integration is performed over the components of Y (now allowed to *vary*), we get the joint PDF for the components of X, as indicated in Eq. 3.30. The same results are obtained if X and Y are interchanged, and the consequential identity from Eq. 3.27 is called *Bayes theorem*.

We should also mention the *cumulative probability distribution* (*CPD*), obtained by integrating any PDF from $-\infty$ to some point of interest along the abscissa. The value of the CPD is zero when the upper integration limit is $-\infty$, and unity when the upper integration limit is $+\infty$. CPDs can be multidimensional, and they can be defined for joint, marginal, or conditional PDFs.

3.4   EXAMPLE: A NOISY MEASUREMENT

In Figure 2–3 of chapter 2, we illustrated a model for a typical control system, and we described the behavior of this system by Eqs. 2.2 through 2.5. These equations are repeated below as Eqs. 3.31 through 3.34 for easy reference. Our ultimate goal is to measure the parameters defining the loop gain W (using the two signals X_1 and X_2), along with either the PDFs or at least the mean values and variances of these parameters. If there were *no* noise sources in the model, we could simply divide X_2 by X_1, giving $X_2/X_1 = (A_2 W)/(A_1 G_o)$ $= \hat{W}$. We use a *caret* symbol above a quantity to denote an estimate of that quantity. There is a *scaling* error of $A_2/(A_1 G_o)$ in this estimate (which could be removed by proper calibration of the measuring instrument), but otherwise this technique works reasonably well as long as X_1 has an adequate amplitude at *all* frequencies of interest.

$$X_1 = \frac{A_1 G_o}{1 + W}(S' + N_X) + A_1 N_1 \tag{3.31}$$

$$X_2 = S' \frac{A_2 W}{1 + W} - N_x \frac{A_2}{1 + W} + A_2 N_2 \tag{3.32}$$

where

$$S' = R - S - N_o \tag{3.33}$$

$$W = GH \tag{3.34}$$

If a sufficiently short transient time waveform is used as a test signal, then the spectrum of X_1 can satisfy this requirement of reasonable amplitude at all frequencies. However, such short time transients must have a relatively large peak amplitude, in order to inject sufficient *power* into the control loop to generate a measurable response. This often excites nonlinearities in the system, which in turn *can* lead to the generation of *spurious new* frequencies that introduce errors in the measurement. However, in many practical situations a short time transient works well, and is often the easiest waveform to generate.

Another possibility is to use a *swept sinusoid* or *chirp*, in which the amplitude of the test signal is held constant while the frequency is swept through the range of interest. There is still the problem of injecting sufficient power into the system at *each* frequency, since each frequency is only excited for a short period of time during the sweep. However, the nonlinearities *may* not be as significant for this type of signal (depending on their nature). A variation on the constant amplitude sweep is the *variable* amplitude sweep, where the input amplitude is adjusted to hold the *output* amplitude approximately constant. This may also help reduce the contributions from at least some of the nonlinearities.

With any of these methods, the effects of noise can be reduced by repeating the measurement many times, and averaging the results together. You may find systematic errors (called *biases*) in the ultimate values of $\hat{W}$ due to various mechanisms, and the variance on the final measurement may not be *minimal*, but you can at least predict these effects in advance from the measurement model.

The best input excitation signal for *many* applications is *random noise*. The power spectrum of any *single* random noise record usually has "holes" where the power is very low, but by averaging the results from many different noise records, these holes get filled to give an input spectrum having a reasonable amount of power at *all* frequencies of interest. The spurious frequencies introduced by system nonlinearities also tend to average to zero, because the phase angle of each "spur" will be randomly different for each input noise record.

However, if *random noise* is used as the system input, we cannot simply divide X_2 by X_1 because there will sometimes be holes in the spectrum of the denominator X_1, which may result in large quotient errors at these frequencies. If the input noise PDF is Gaussian (with zero mean value), it is possible to show the variance of this simple quotient is infinite (the PDF for this quotient is called a *Cauchy density*). We need a method of averaging the *numerator* spectra together and the *denominator* spectra together, *before* the division operation, so any possible denominator holes will be filled *before* division. We will proceed to investigate this general method and to derive the resulting estimates of the loop gain parameters, along with their statistics.

In order to average these pairs of spectra together, we need to *first* multiply each spectrum by some signal that has roughly the opposite *phase* at each frequency, so we can effectively eliminate phase angles, and thus avoid signal cancellations that would otherwise occur. We could choose the *complex conjugate* of the external input excitation signal S', but this might require a third channel on the measuring instrument. We prefer to construct a suitable signal from the two inputs X_1 and X_2, if possible. We could choose the conjugate of X_1 for this signal, but we notice the *sum* of X_1 and X_2 comprises a much smaller contribution from the noise source N_x, as well as a much larger contribution from S' (at least when W is large), than X_1 does alone. From Eqs. 3.31 and 3.32 we get the sum of these two signals as:

$$X_1 + X_2 = S' \frac{A_1 G_o + A_2 W}{1 + W} + N_x \frac{A_1 G_o - A_2}{1 + W} + A_1 N_1 + A_2 N_2 \quad (3.35)$$

To calibrate the measuring instrument properly, we would set $A_1 G_o = A_2$. If we do this, the contribution from the noise source N_x is completely eliminated, and Eq. 3.35 becomes $X_1 + X_2 = A_2 S' + A_1 N_1 + A_2 N_2$.

We now need to form the products $X_2 (X_1^* + X_2^*)$ for the numerator, and $X_1 (X_1^* + X_2^*)$ for the denominator. Then we can average several of these *quadratic* spectra together (*separately* for the numerator and the denominator) to reduce noise contributions and to fill any holes that might otherwise occur along the frequency axis. We will use an *overbar* to denote this *ensemble average*. So, instead of using X_2/X_1 to estimate the loop gain W, we use:

$$\hat{W} = \frac{\overline{X_2 X_1^*} + \overline{|X_2|^2}}{\overline{|X_1|^2} + \overline{X_1 X_2^*}} \quad (3.36)$$

There are twelve terms in the numerator and twelve terms in the denominator of this expression, involving averages of the various cross-products between the input excitation S' and the three noise sources N_1, N_2, and N_x. If we assume the cross-products of *one* noise source with another are negligibly small, we can eliminate many of the terms, keeping *only* those products that involve S'. If we further assume the terms involving S' times a noise component are much smaller than the one involving S' times its *own* conjugate, we can use the approximation $1/(1+\epsilon) \approx 1 - \epsilon$ for small values of ϵ to replace the division operation. We finally get the following approximation for the estimated value of W:

$$\hat{W} = \frac{A_2 W}{A_1 G_o} \left[1 - \frac{1 + W}{W} \frac{\overline{N_x S'^*}}{\sigma^2} + \frac{1 + W}{W} \frac{\overline{N_2 S'^*}}{\sigma^2} - \frac{1 + W}{G_o} \frac{\overline{N_1 S'^*}}{\sigma^2} \right] \quad (3.37)$$

where

$$\sigma^2 = \sigma_S^2 + \sigma_R^2 + \sigma_o^2 \quad (3.38)$$

and σ_S^2, σ_R^2, and σ_o^2 are the variances (or power) of the three signals S, R, and N_o, respectively, making σ^2 the variance or power of the *composite* input S'. Note that when $|W|$ is small, the noise contributions from N_x and N_2 are magnified by $1/|W|$, and when $|W|$ is large, the contribution from N_1 is magnified by $|W|$.

These quantities (except for the variances) are *complex numbers* at each frequency of interest. We generally assume the noise power is equally divided between the *real* and the *imaginary* parts of a complex spectrum, because all phase angles are equally likely in most cases. Thus, the variance on the real part and the variance on the imaginary part will *each* be half of the *total* variance.

Each of the three noise terms in Eq. 3.37 is the *average* of the *product* of two random variables. If we assume all of these random variables have zero mean Gaussian PDFs, then we can calculate the PDF of each product, using the methods discussed in the previous section of this chapter. Let's assume $u = x_1 x_2$ is the product of two independent

Gaussian random variables x_1 and x_2 having zero mean values, and with variances σ_1^2 and σ_2^2, respectively. We use the general integral relation:

$$\int_0^\infty e^{-\frac{1}{2}(u^2 x^2 + v^2 x^{-2})} \frac{dx}{x} = K_o(|uv|) \tag{3.39}$$

to obtain the PDF of u, resulting in:

$$p_u(u) = \frac{1}{\pi \sigma_1 \sigma_2} K_o\left(\frac{|u|}{\sigma_1 \sigma_2}\right) \tag{3.40}$$

where K_o is the *zero* order *modified Bessel function* of the *second* kind. The mean value of this PDF is zero, since it is an *even* function of u. By means of the Fourier transform relation:

$$\frac{1}{[1 + \omega^2]^{\frac{n}{2}}} = \frac{1}{\sqrt{\pi}\,\Gamma\left(\frac{n}{2}\right)} \int_{-\infty}^\infty \left|\frac{x}{2}\right|^{\frac{n-1}{2}} K_{\frac{n-1}{2}}(|x|)\, e^{i\omega x}\, dx \tag{3.41}$$

we can write the corresponding characteristic function for $n = 1$ as:

$$\Phi_u(\omega) = \frac{1}{\sqrt{1 + (\sigma_1 \sigma_2 \omega)^2}} \tag{3.42}$$

The variance of u is $\sigma_1^2 \sigma_2^2$, or the product of the variances of x_1 and x_2. Actually, we can see some of these results even without calculating the PDF or characteristic function. Since x_1 and x_2 are independent random variables with zero mean values, we know the correlation coefficient is zero, so $E[x_1 x_2] = 0 = E[u]$, which is the mean value of u. The variance of u is similarly given by $\sigma_u^2 = E[x_1^2 x_2^2] = E[x_1^2]\,E[x_2^2] = \sigma_1^2 \sigma_2^2$. We can verify this variance by calculating the negative of the second derivative of the characteristic function with respect to ω, evaluated at $\omega = 0$, as we indicated in Eq. 3.21.

The random variables due to noise in Eq. 3.37 are *averages* of the products of pairs of independent Gaussian variables, so we know the resulting mean value of this average remains zero, while the variance is reduced by n (for n averages). The characteristic function for this *average of products* is the product of the characteristic functions for *each* pair of Gaussian products, with the variance reduced by n because of the averaging procedure, so we can immediately write the *composite* characteristic function as:

$$\Phi_w(\omega) = \frac{1}{\left[1 + \left(\dfrac{\sigma_1 \sigma_2 \omega}{n}\right)^2\right]^{\frac{n}{2}}} \tag{3.43}$$

and using Eq. 3.41 we can write the PDF for this average of Gaussian products as:

$$p_w(w) = \frac{n}{\sqrt{\pi}\,\Gamma\left(\dfrac{n}{2}\right)\sigma_1\sigma_2} \left[\frac{n\,|w|}{2\sigma_1\sigma_2}\right]^{\frac{n-1}{2}} K_{\frac{n-1}{2}}\left(\frac{n\,|w|}{\sigma_1\sigma_2}\right) \tag{3.44}$$

where

$$w = \frac{1}{n}\sum_{i=1}^{n} u_i \tag{3.45}$$

and K_ν is the νth order modified Bessel function of the second kind. The variance of this PDF is $\sigma_1^2\sigma_2^2/n$.

It is not at all obvious, but *both* Eqs. 3.43 and 3.44 begin to take on Gaussian shapes as n approaches infinity. We mentioned the Central Limit Theorem previously, which states that the PDF of the sum (or average) of n *independent* random variables approaches a Gaussian shape as n approaches infinity, irrespective of the original PDF shapes. Thus, all we really need are the mean value and the variance of this sum or average, and we can write a Gaussian approximation to the final PDF.

The PDFs for several sets of n averages are shown below in Figure 3–6 (as solid curves), along with the limiting Gaussian shape for infinite n (dotted curve). These PDFs

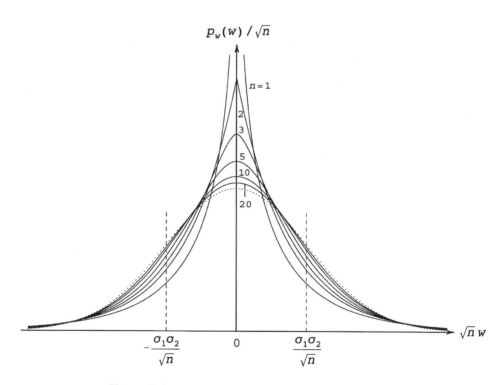

Figure 3–6 PDF of Average of n Products of Gaussian Pairs

are all normalized to have the same *standard deviation* as indicated by the dashed vertical lines. Notice how quickly these curves approach a Gaussian shape as the number of averages increases.

If we calculate the expected value of both sides of Eq. 3.37 we find the mean value of $\hat{W}$ is:

$$E[\hat{W}] = \frac{A_2 W}{A_1 G_o} \tag{3.46}$$

because the mean values of each ensemble average of products is zero. The variance can be written by inspection of Eq. 3.37, since the noise and signal random variables are assumed to be independent (hence uncorrelated). The variance on the loop gain estimate is:

$$\sigma_{\hat{W}}^2 = \frac{|A_2|^2 \, |1 + W|^2}{n \, |A_1|^2 \, |G_o|^2 \sigma^2} \left[\sigma_x^2 + \sigma_2^2 + \frac{|W|^2}{|G_o|^2} \sigma_1^2 \right] \tag{3.47}$$

Since $\hat{W}$ is a complex number at each frequency, we assign *half* of the noise power (variance) to the real part and *half* to the imaginary part. Thus, the Gaussian approximation to the PDF for the real part (or identically for the imaginary part) of $\hat{W}$ is:

$$p_{\hat{W}}(\Re \hat{W}) \approx \frac{1}{\sqrt{\pi} \, \sigma_{\hat{W}}} e^{-\frac{(\Re \hat{W})^2}{\sigma_{\hat{W}}^2}} \tag{3.48}$$

For many applications, a more useful measure of the effects of noise on the loop gain is the *coefficient of variation* (or "noise-to-signal" ratio), obtained by dividing the standard deviation by the mean value. This becomes:

$$\eta = \frac{|1 + W|}{\sqrt{n} \, |W| \, \sigma} \sqrt{\sigma_x^2 + \sigma_2^2 + \frac{|W|^2}{|G_o|^2} \sigma_1^2} \tag{3.49}$$

This quantity is infinite when $W = 0$, and is zero at the point of loop instability when $W = -1$. Otherwise, it tends to be relatively constant as $|W|$ grows, until $|W| \approx |G_o| \sqrt{\sigma_x^2 + \sigma_2^2}/\sigma_1$, and then it tends to grow linearly with $|W|$. Figure 3–7 shows a stereoscopic plot of this function η, over a typical portion of the complex W-plane.

The dashed curve (called a *Nyquist curve*) in the W-plane shows a typical trajectory of loop gain versus frequency, starting with zero frequency along the real W axis to the right and progressing to *higher* frequencies as the curve nears the origin. This is a simple case, where there is only *one* pole within the loop, so the phase change over the positive frequency interval is $-90°$. In many cases, there will be two or more poles in W, and the Nyquist curve will wrap around the origin $-90°$ for each pole. In contrast, any zeros in the loop will contribute a total of $+90°$ of phase change over the positive frequency interval.

Notice the *projection* of this Nyquist curve *onto* the η surface (the heavy space curve). The quality of the measurement tends to be very poor near the origin because the magnitude of the loop gain becomes very small, while the standard deviation of the measurement remains relatively constant. The measurement quality also tends to degrade as the loop gain

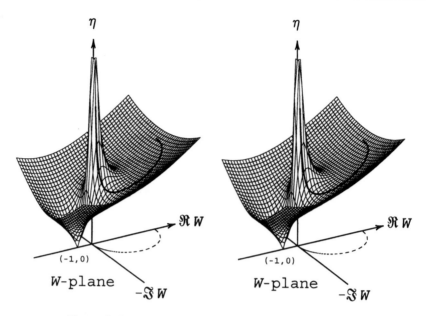

Figure 3–7   Coefficient of Variation η versus Loop Gain W

magnitude gets large, because the noise contribution from the first measurement channel N_1 is multiplied by $|W/G_o|$. Fortunately, the best measurements are obtained for intermediate values of $|W|$, which includes the very important region around the *gain crossover frequency* where $|W| = 1$. The coefficient of variation goes to zero at the point of *instability* (where $W = -1$) because the signals X_1 and X_2 in both measurement channels become "infinite," thereby swamping the instrumentation noise sources N_1 and N_2. The system noise source N_x is greatly reduced by using the *sum* of X_1 and X_2 in the loop gain estimate, instead of *only* X_1. Note that the noise source N_o is part of the composite excitation signal S'.

3.5   EXAMPLE: A NOISY MEASUREMENT WITH BIAS

In the example of the previous section, the loop gain was biased only by a *scaling* factor, which can (in principle) be removed by the proper calibration of the measuring instrument. In most control system loop gain measurements, there are also *additive* bias contributions from various noise terms caused by self-multiplication (or self-rectification). We were able to reduce those bias mechanisms to negligible levels in the previous section by using the *sum* $X_1 + X_2$ instead of just X_1 as the common conjugate multiplier on the numerator and denominator in the estimate of W. It is not always possible to eliminate this sort of bias so easily. To illustrate a more typical situation, in this section we will show the degradation in the loop gain estimate that results from using X_1 *alone*.

First, we will show the bias terms that were deemed to be insignificant in the previous section. A more exact expression for the expected value of $\hat{W}$ from Section 3.4 is:

$$E[\hat{W}] = \frac{A_2 W}{A_1 G_o}\left[1 - \frac{1 + W}{|G_o|^2}\frac{\sigma_1^2}{\sigma^2} + \frac{1 + W}{W}\frac{\sigma_2^2}{\sigma^2} - \left(1 - \frac{A_2}{A_1 G_o}\right)^*\frac{1 + W}{W + |W|^2}\frac{\sigma_x^2}{\sigma^2}\right] \quad (3.50)$$

For a good quality measuring instrument, the input noise on each channel will be at *least* 80 dB below the full scale signal level of that channel. Thus, the ratios σ_1^2/σ^2 and σ_2^2/σ^2 should each be of the order of 10^{-8} or less. The magnitude of W would need to be greater than 10^7 or less than 10^{-7} before the bias from noise sources N_1 and N_2 would be significant.

The control loop noise N_x is harder to predict and can be relatively large in some cases. The bias from this source is negligible for large W values, but it is amplified by small values. However, when the measuring instrument is properly calibrated, $|1 - A_2/(A_1 G_o)|$ is small (say 10^{-3}), so as long as $|W| > .01 \ \sigma_x^2/\sigma^2$ the bias due to N_x should *also* be negligible.

Next, we will formulate an estimate of W using X_1 instead of $X_1 + X_2$, resulting in:

$$\hat{W} = \frac{\overline{X_2 X_1^*}}{\overline{|X_1|^2}} \quad (3.51)$$

As before, we will ignore all cross-terms among the noise sources N_1, N_2, and N_x, giving the approximation:

$$\hat{W} \approx \frac{A_2 W}{A_1 G_o}\left[1 - \frac{1 + W}{\sigma^2 W}\left(\frac{W}{G_o}\overline{N_1 S'^*} - \overline{N_2 S'^*} + \overline{N_x S'^*} + \overline{|N_x|^2}\right) - \frac{|1 + W|^2}{\sigma^2 |G_o|^2}\overline{|N_1|^2}\right] \quad (3.52)$$

The expected value of $\hat{W}$ now becomes:

$$E[\hat{W}] \approx \frac{A_2 W}{A_1 G_o}\left[1 - \frac{1 + W}{W}\frac{\sigma_x^2}{\sigma^2} - \frac{|1 + W|^2}{|G_o|^2}\frac{\sigma_1^2}{\sigma^2}\right] \quad (3.53)$$

In comparing this to Eq. 3.50 we see several differences, including the fact that the bias term due to N_2 is *missing* here. If we continue with the assumption that $\sigma_1^2/\sigma^2 \approx 10^{-8}$, then $|W|$ cannot exceed about 3000 without causing a significant bias in *this* estimate of W. Since $|W|$ can sometimes be as large as 10^7, this bias can cause a considerable error in such cases. In addition, the N_x contribution can be significant for any value of W, but is greatly amplified when $|W|$ is *small*, and the variance is *large*. The quality of a measurement using this technique is decidedly inferior to the one in the previous section.

The definition of *relative bias* in the measurement of W is:

$$\frac{E[\hat{W}] - W}{W} \approx \left(\frac{A_2}{A_1 G_o} - 1\right) - \frac{1 + W}{W}\frac{\sigma_x^2}{\sigma^2} - \frac{|1 + W|^2}{|G_o|^2}\frac{\sigma_1^2}{\sigma^2} \quad (3.54)$$

where we assume the measuring instrument is properly calibrated so $A_2 \approx A_1 G_o$. The *absolute* bias is $E[\hat{W}] - W$.

In this example, the bias on $\hat{W}$ is rather moderate and only affects the measurements of relatively large or small magnitudes of loop gain. However, this is *not* always the case. There are other commonly used test configurations that can produce very large bias errors for nearly every value of *W*.

There are *two* common mechanisms that can cause a bias in a measurement. *First*, whenever random noise is subjected to an *even* order nonlinearity, such as in conjugate multiplication by itself, the average or mean value of the noise will *no* longer be zero, resulting in a bias contribution. *Second*, whenever an erroneous *scale factor* is used on one or more of the measuring channels, a bias is created. This can be especially serious if the measurement algorithm involves the subtraction of two large signals. A small error in the scaling between two similar signals is effectively *amplified* when the actual signal of interest is a small difference between these two large quantities.

We can see from this example that the details of the signal processing algorithm itself can also influence the bias in the final result. For example, we try to select a common complex conjugate multiplier (to remove phase angles from the numerator and denominator) comprising the *least* amount of noise that is *correlated* with either the numerator or the denominator.

We are stressing the dangers of *bias* in a measurement even more than the *random* errors represented by the variance or standard deviation, because these random errors are generally rather obvious and visible. In contrast, bias errors are generally *invisible*, and a user of this biased measurement might easily make bad design decisions based on this erroneous result.

3.6   DISCRETE OR QUANTIZED RANDOM VARIABLES

It is common to find *digital processors* in systems being measured, in which the quantities of interest are represented by *numbers*, each having some finite number of *bits of resolution*. In such cases, the random variables are quantized into *discrete* levels, in contrast to the *continuous* variables that we have discussed in previous sections. Generally, the quantization levels are separated by roughly uniform numeric intervals, although this may not be true when the numbers are represented in a floating point format. For simplicity, we will assume uniform quantization intervals for this discussion.

The probability density functions for discrete random variables comprise a set of "delta functions" that are spaced uniformly along the abscissa of the PDF. A *unit delta function* is defined at a point x_o by the following three rules: (1) The area under the delta function over any interval *including* x_o, no matter how small the interval, is unity; (2) the area under the delta function over any interval *excluding* x_o, no matter how small the interval, is zero, and (3) the shape of the delta function is meaningless and is not defined. The only useful properties of this function are directly related to the two *area* specifications. For example, the integral of the product of any function $f(x)$ times a delta function centered at x_o is $f(x_o)$, expressed as follows:

$$f(x_o) = \int_{-\infty}^{\infty} f(x)\, \delta\,(x - x_o)\, dx \qquad (3.55)$$

where the delta function centered at x_o is denoted by $\delta(x - x_o)$. The integrand is zero except at $x = x_o$, where the unit area under the delta function is multiplied by $f(x_o)$.

It is also possible to define the *nth derivative* of a delta function, which is useful because of the following property:

$$f^{(n)}(x_o) = \int_{-\infty}^{\infty} f(x)\, \delta^{(n)}(x - x_o)\, dx \tag{3.56}$$

where $f^{(n)}(x_o)$ denotes the *n*th derivative of $f(x)$ (relative to x), evaluated at $x = x_o$. The *n*th derivative of the delta function centered at x_o is written as $\delta^{(n)}(x - x_o)$.

The *indefinite* integral of the delta function is the "unit step" function, which is constant to the left of x_o, jumps by $+1$ *at* x_o, and then stays at this new constant level for all x values to the right of x_o. Subsequent integration operations produce ramps and higher order polynomials.

To maintain the unit area property, delta functions *scale* as follows:

$$\delta(x) = |b|\, \delta(bx) \quad , \quad \text{for } |b| > 0 \tag{3.57}$$

We can express the PDF of a discrete random variable, using these delta functions, in the following general form:

$$p_x(x) = \sum_{k=-\infty}^{\infty} a_k \delta(x - k\Delta x) \tag{3.58}$$

where Δx is the space between successive delta functions along the abscissa, and the a_k coefficients define the "amplitude" (meaning area) of each delta function. Since the total area under the PDF must be unity, we require:

$$\sum_{k=-\infty}^{\infty} a_k = 1 \tag{3.59}$$

The *m*th moment of this PDF is:

$$E[x^m] = \sum_{k=-\infty}^{\infty} a_k (k\Delta x)^m = (\Delta x)^m \sum_{k=-\infty}^{\infty} a_k k^m \tag{3.60}$$

The expected value of any function $f(x)$ where x is a quantized random variable is given by:

$$E[f(x)] = \sum_{k=-\infty}^{\infty} a_k f(k\Delta x) \tag{3.61}$$

As before, when $f(x) = e^{i\omega x}$ we get the *characteristic function* for the PDF, so this can be written as:

$$\Phi_x(\omega) = \sum_{k=-\infty}^{\infty} a_k e^{i\omega k\Delta x} = \sum_{k=-\infty}^{\infty} a_k z^k \quad , \quad \text{where } z = e^{i\omega \Delta x} \tag{3.62}$$

Notice this characteristic function is *periodic* in ω, with a period of $2\pi/\Delta x$. It can also be represented as a *power series* in z (defined above), or as a *polynomial* in z *if* there are a finite number of terms in the summation. The a_k are the coefficients of an inverse *Fourier series* representation of the characteristic function (as shown in the first part of Eq. 3.62), and they are also the coefficients of the *inverse z-transform* of the discrete PDF given by Eq. 3.58 (as shown in the second half of Eq. 3.62).

One of the simplest examples of the PDF of a discrete random variable is a *pair* of delta functions representing a *two-state* numerical quantity, say having values 0 and 1. The probability of a "zero" occurring is a_0, and the probability of a "one" occurring is a_1, where $a_0 + a_1 = 1$. If we *sum* n of these binary random variables together, the resulting PDF is the *convolution* of the original PDF with itself $n-1$ times. Delta functions convolve together just like any other functions, so the PDF of this sum (represented by y) becomes:

$$p_y(y) = \sum_{k=0}^{n} \binom{n}{k} a_0^{n-k} a_1^k \, \delta \, (y - k\Delta x) \tag{3.63}$$

where the binomial coefficients are defined by:

$$\binom{n}{k} = \frac{n!}{k! \, (n-k)\,!} \tag{3.64}$$

Recall that $0! = 1$. This is called the *binomial probability density* function, because the coefficients for each delta function can be found from the two original coefficients by the binomial expansion:

$$(a_0 + a_1)^n = \sum_{k=0}^{n} \binom{n}{k} a_0^{n-k} \, a_1^k \tag{3.65}$$

Since $a_0 + a_1 = 1$, we see the above summation must be unity, so the area under $p_y(y)$ is likewise unity.

The mean of the original two-state PDF is $a_1 \Delta x = (1 - a_0)\Delta x$, and the variance is $a_0 a_1 \, (\Delta x)^2$, so these two quantities must be multiplied by n to get the mean and variance of the *sum* of n of these random variables.

As we found with PDFs of the sums and averages of *continuous* random variables, the *envelope* of the PDF for the *sum or average* of n *discrete* random variables also approaches the Gaussian form as n goes to infinity. This envelope is formed by setting its *amplitude* at each discrete abscissa value equal to the *area* under the corresponding delta function centered at that abscissa value. The associated (periodic) *characteristic function* (for $n \to \infty$) will comprise the *sum* of identical Gaussian shapes centered at intervals of $2\pi/\Delta x$ along the ω axis.

Figure 3–8 is an example of the binomial PDF of the sum of 20 two-state discrete random variables, along with the Gaussian envelope approximation to this distribution as $n \to \infty$ (dotted curve). Each vertical line represents a delta function centered at that abscissa value, with the height of the line representing the area under the delta function. The

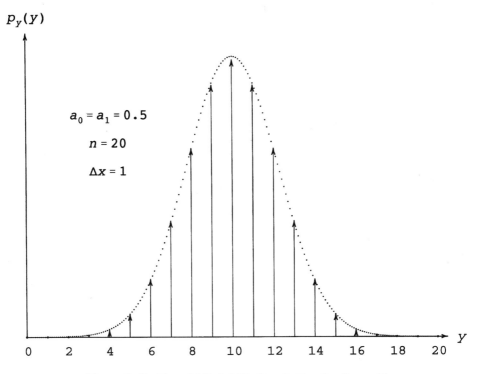

Figure 3–8   Binomial Probability Density Function for $n = 20$

arrows at the top indicate the delta function is indefinite in *actual* height. We have chosen $\Delta x = \Delta y = 1$ for this plot, and also the case where the probability of occurrence of each of the two original states is equal (meaning $a_0 = a_1 = 0.5$).

The characteristic function for this PDF is the polynomial $\Phi_y(\omega) = (a_0 + a_1 z)^n$, where z is given in Eq. 3.62.

3.7   PDFs FOR MIXED RANDOM VARIABLES

In many practical cases of interest, we find mixtures of both *continuous* and *discrete* representations of signals in the systems we want to measure. Discrete PDFs arise within the digital parts of systems, primarily to characterize rounding errors incurred by the various arithmetic operations involved. However, there are often analog-to-digital and digital-to-analog conversion operations that surround the digital components, and errors are produced by *each* of these processes. As an example, consider the PDF of the error in *digitizing* a continuous signal at some *point in time*. If we assume the quantized amplitude is accurate to within plus or minus half of a *quantization interval*, then the PDF of this quantization error will be *rectangular*, centered at zero, and with a width equal to the quantization interval, because we expect all possible errors within this interval will occur with equal probability.

Various methods have been devised to reduce this quantization error, besides the obvious one of using a *higher* resolution analog-to-digital converter. If the signal to be digitized is *repetitive*, then one method is to add random noise (with zero mean value) to the original continuous signal, and then to average several of the resulting digitized samples together in a synchronous manner, so the repetitive components are always aligned in time. If the additive noise is sufficiently large, then several of the adjacent levels of quantization will *also* be excited to some extent. This noise will *then* act as an interpolation mechanism among adjacent quantization levels, giving results at *intermediate values between* these levels after averaging.

We know the mean value of the *average* of n independent random variables is the average of the mean values of *each* individual variable, and likewise the variance of the *average* of n independent random variables is $1/n$ times the average of the individual variances. Thus, the error PDF after n averages will be centered at about the same place along the abscissa, but will be narrower by the square root of n, compared to the PDF before averaging. If we average enough times, this resulting PDF will *also* be narrower than the *original* rectangular PDF, and *that* will improve the quality of all subsequent parameter estimates using this data. Our immediate goal is to determine the amount of noise we should add and the corresponding number of subsequent averages needed to produce a net *reduction* in the variance of our signal after quantization and averaging.

This is a good example to follow in some detail. It is typical of the kinds of calculations you may need to perform when working with mixed (continuous and discrete) random variables, and it will serve to illustrate some of the techniques that often facilitate such calculations. In particular, we will show how to determine the errors in both the *mean value* and the *variance*, introduced by the quantization process. One helpful trick is to use the characteristic functions of the PDFs in this calculation.

For a quantization interval of Δx, the variance of a rectangular PDF of width Δx (centered at the origin) is $(\Delta x)^2/12$. If we assume Gaussian noise, having a zero mean value and a standard deviation of σ_x, is added to a repetitive (nonrandom) signal having a value of μ_x at some particular *time point* within each cycle, then we can calculate the area under *each* delta function of the subsequent PDF *after* digitizing, by integrating this Gaussian PDF over an interval of $\pm \Delta x/2$ centered around each quantization level (denoted by $k\Delta x$). With a bit of thought, you can see this is the same as *convolving* the Gaussian PDF with a *rectangle* having width Δx and height $1/\Delta x$, and then multiplying this result by a *sampling function* comprising an infinite train of delta functions along the abscissa, spaced Δx apart, and *each* having an *area* of $1/\Delta x$. We can then calculate the mean value and the variance of this *new* PDF by evaluating the first and second derivatives (slope and curvature) of the composite characteristic function at the origin. We denote the *average* of n of these discrete random variables by y.

The Gaussian PDF Eq. 3.1 has a characteristic function given by Eq. 3.22, and the unit area rectangle has an inverse Fourier transform of $\sin(\omega\Delta x/2) / (\omega\Delta x/2)$. The process of multiplying the PDF by a sampling function is represented in the transform domain by the *convolution* of the characteristic function with the *inverse Fourier transform* of the sampling function (which is, itself, a similar sampling function in the *transform domain*, comprising an infinite train of unit area delta functions spaced $2\pi/\Delta x$ apart along the ω axis). This is equivalent to simply *replicating* the characteristic function along the ω axis at intervals of $2\pi/\Delta x$. The resulting composite characteristic function is:

$$\Phi_y(\omega) = \sum_{k=-\infty}^{\infty} \frac{sin(\omega\Delta x/2 - \pi k)}{\omega\Delta x/2 - \pi k} e^{i\mu_x\left(\omega - \frac{2\pi k}{\Delta x}\right) - \frac{1}{2}\sigma_x^2\left(\omega - \frac{2\pi k}{\Delta x}\right)^2} \tag{3.66}$$

The first and second moments of the PDF can be obtained from this function by two differentiation operations, relative to ω, as indicated in Eq. 3.21. This is a rather complicated function to differentiate, but the operation can be facilitated by *factoring* each term into three or four simpler expressions. Then, we use the rules for differentiating products and/or quotients to construct the final result from these simpler forms. The expression for the mean value becomes:

$$E[y] = \mu_x + \frac{\Delta x}{\pi} \sum_{k=1}^{\infty} \frac{(-1)^k}{k} e^{-2\left(\frac{k\pi\sigma_x}{\Delta x}\right)^2} sin\left(\frac{2\pi k\mu_x}{\Delta x}\right) \tag{3.67}$$

This is a Fourier *sine series* representation of the mean value. When $\sigma_x = 0$, we have a negative going repetitive "sawtooth" shape centered about the point $(0, \mu_x)$, with a peak amplitude of $\pm \Delta x/2$ and a period of Δx. This represents the special case when *no* noise is added before digitizing. In all cases, the *entire* bias error is caused by the final *quantization* step, since both the Gaussian noise PDF and the convolution rectangle are symmetrical functions about the origin.

Figure 3–9 illustrates this bias error $E[y] - \mu_x$, as a function of the mean value μ_x, for a few values of the normalized standard deviation $\sigma_x/\Delta x$ of the additive noise.

In practice, only the three terms for $k = -1, 0, 1$ are generally significant (at least for $\sigma_x \geq \Delta x/4$), so we can simplify this expression considerably, giving:

$$E[y] \approx \mu_x - \frac{\Delta x}{\pi} e^{-2\left(\frac{\pi\sigma_x}{\Delta x}\right)^2} sin\left(\frac{2\pi\mu_x}{\Delta x}\right) \tag{3.68}$$

We see for this approximation, the bias error is *sinusoidal*, with a *peak* value of:

$$(E[y] - \mu_x)_{peak} = \pm\frac{\Delta x}{\pi} e^{-2\left(\frac{\pi\sigma_x}{\Delta x}\right)^2} \tag{3.69}$$

For example, if $\sigma_x = \Delta x/2$, this peak error is $\pm 0.002289\,\Delta x$.

The variance calculation is somewhat more difficult, but a good *approximation* is:

$$\sigma_y^2 \approx \frac{1}{n}\left[\sigma_x^2 + \frac{(\Delta x)^2}{12}\right] - \frac{1}{n}\left[4\sigma_x^2 + \left(\frac{\Delta x}{\pi}\right)^2\right] e^{-2\left(\frac{\pi\sigma_x}{\Delta x}\right)^2} cos\left(\frac{2\pi\mu_x}{\Delta x}\right) \tag{3.70}$$

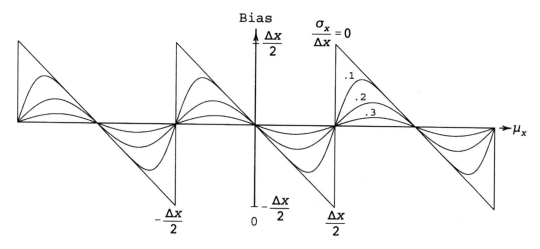

Figure 3–9 Periodic Bias Error Due to Digitizing

The cosine term is normally very small due to the exponential factor and can be ignored in most cases. This gives the variance on the *average* of n of these quantized random variables as:

$$\sigma_y^2 \approx \frac{1}{n}\left[\sigma_x^2 + \frac{(\Delta x)^2}{12}\right] \tag{3.71}$$

This result is not too *surprising*, since we found in section 3.3 that the variances *add* when two functions are convolved together. In this expression, the first term is the variance of the additive Gaussian noise before digitizing, and the second term is the variance of the applied convolution rectangle. The actual digitizing procedure introduces only the cosine term in Eq. 3.70, which is generally negligible. For example, if we choose $\sigma_x = \Delta x/2$, we find the maximum error in Eq. 3.71 is about ± 2.4%, which amounts to about ± 1.2% error in the standard deviation σ_y.

We can now show the conditions under which this method of adding noise before digitizing and then averaging over several records will yield an improvement in variance, compared to the standard quantization method. We simply require:

$$\frac{1}{n}\left[\sigma_x^2 + \frac{(\Delta x)^2}{12}\right] < \frac{(\Delta x)^2}{12} \quad , \quad \text{or} \quad n > 1 + 12\left(\frac{\sigma_x}{\Delta x}\right)^2 \tag{3.72}$$

Another related method that is sometimes used to reduce the effects of digitizing a signal is to subtract a digital replica of the additive Gaussian noise (after quantizing), which was added to the signal *before* quantizing. This has the effect of replacing the variance of the additive noise σ_x^2 with the variance of the error in the digital *formulation* of this correction, due to the finite number of *digits* used in its representation (we assume these digital correction rounding errors are independent of the original quantization errors). Suppose the quantization interval for the digital correction is $\Delta x/M$, where M is considerably larger than unity. Then, the *new* expression for the variance will become:

$$\sigma_y^2 \approx \frac{1}{n}\left(1 + \frac{1}{M^2}\right)\frac{(\Delta x)^2}{12} \tag{3.73}$$

This technique has little appreciable effect on the bias shown above in Eq. 3.67, amounting only to the mean value of the quantized correction PDF, but for large M it almost reduces the variance to its minimum value (for any given number of averages), dictated by the *original* quantization interval Δx. Of course, you can now *increase* the additive noise enough to *reduce* the bias to a negligible level, without any concern about adding more *variance*.

3.8   SOME MATRICES IN PROBABILITY THEORY

Correlation and covariance matrices are used to show relationships (if any) between the elements of a random vector, or a pair of random vectors. The covariance matrix is the expected value of the *outer* vector product of two random vectors with their means removed, as follows:

$$\text{cov}(X,Y) = E[(X - E[X])(Y - E[Y])^T] \tag{3.74}$$

$$= E[XY^T] - E[X]E[Y^T] \tag{3.75}$$

$$\text{cov}(X,X) = \text{cov}(X) = E[XX^T] - |E[X]|^2 \tag{3.76}$$

where the superscript ^{T} denotes the complex conjugate transpose of the vector or matrix. The diagonal elements of a covariance matrix between X and itself are the variances on each element of the vector.

   If we divide all elements in each row and each column by the positive square root of the corresponding diagonal element of the covariance matrix of X with itself, we obtain the correlation matrix. Thus, the diagonal components of a correlation matrix are unity, and the various off-diagonal components are the correlation coefficients between the corresponding elements of X, which can range from -1 to $+1$. Thus we can write:

$$\text{corr}(X,X) = \text{corr}(X) = \sqrt{W}\,\text{cov}(X)\sqrt{W} \tag{3.77}$$

where W is a diagonal matrix of the reciprocals of the variances on the elements of the random vector X.

   Even though the elements of a random vector may be correlated with one another, there is generally a set of combinations of these elements that *are* mutually uncorrelated. We can determine these uncorrelated random vectors by calculating the *eigenvalues* and *eigenvectors* of the covariance matrix. The definition is:

$$AU = \lambda U \tag{3.78}$$

where A is a real nonsingular square matrix, U is called an eigenvector, and λ is called an eigenvalue of the matrix A. If A is an $n \times n$ matrix, there will be n distinct eigenvectors and n eigenvalues. It is possible to show that the eigenvectors are mutually orthogonal, and it is also possible to scale the eigenvalues so that the eigenvectors are of unit length (which makes them orthonormal). We define a matrix Φ whose columns are the orthonormal eigenvectors, and a diagonal matrix D, whose components are the eigenvalues. Then, we can write:

$$A\Phi = \Phi D \tag{3.79}$$

However, since the columns of Φ are orthonormal, we have:

$$\Phi^t\Phi = I = \Phi\Phi^t \tag{3.80}$$

The result is:

$$A = \Phi D \Phi^t \quad , \quad \text{or} \tag{3.81}$$

$$D = \Phi^t A \Phi \tag{3.82}$$

If we replace A by the covariance matrix cov(X), the columns of Φ become newly formed *orthonormal* vectors, and the elements of the diagonal matrix D are the respective variances in each new vector direction.

If two random vectors X and Y are linearly related by a real matrix A, in the manner $Y = AX$, then the covariances are related by:

$$\text{cov}(Y) = A\text{cov}(X)A^T \tag{3.83}$$

$$\text{cov}(Y,X) = A\text{cov}(X) \tag{3.84}$$

These examples illustrate a few applications of matrices involving random vectors.

3.9   SUMMARY

There are many similar problems of the sort we discuss in this chapter, involving the calculation of PDFs and their statistical parameters, although we can only mention a few cases. However, the methods of attack tend to be similar to those described here. Generally, the most difficult aspects are avoiding mistakes in the often complicated algebraic manipulations, and then evaluating the integrals that result.

It is neither within the *scope* nor the *intent* of this book to derive all of the equations we have encountered in this chapter in any detail. The goal is only to *outline* some of the techniques and mathematical methods that are used in this field of probability theory. There are many *other* books that specialize in these topics and that derive these results much more elegantly. You should either work through these relationships yourself, or you should consult *other* books for more assistance. The fact that we skim the surface without delving into the details does not mean that the details are unimportant or can be ignored, but only that we have chosen to keep this book as short and concise as possible, and feel that *repeating* subjects that are already covered well elsewhere is somewhat *counterproductive*.

Since each measurement of the parameters of a given physical system are generally somewhat different, we must consider these measurements to be *random variables*. In order to use such measurements, we must have some knowledge about the expected *accuracy* of each measured parameter, along with the *conditions* under which the measurements are *valid*. We accomplish this task by constructing a *model* of the system under consideration, including the parameters we need to measure, and also including all of the noise sources that might perturb our measurements. In addition, this model must include the *measuring instrument* and *its* noise contributions and the parameter *estimation* algorithms we plan to use. Next, we either calculate or measure (or both) the resulting probability density function (PDF) that is associated with each parameter to be measured, and then we extract mean values, biases in those mean values, variances (or standard deviations), and confidence intervals for some given set of confidence levels for each parameter.

Either the calculation or the measurement of the PDF of each parameter can be somewhat difficult and/or time consuming, and the results will never be perfect. However, without this information, we cannot really *use* our measurements effectively because we cannot place any confidence in their accuracy. Even *with* this information, we can still only guarantee a given accuracy specification over some percentage of the time (say 95% or 99%).

It is certainly important to select the best available signals in the measurement model from which we can extract information about all of the parameters of interest, but it is equally important to design the best possible *signal processing algorithm* with which we ultimately obtain our parameter estimates from this raw data. A poorly chosen processing or estimation algorithm can seriously degrade the accuracy of a measurement, even when using very high quality original data.

To complicate matters further, the processing algorithm may need to be different for different ranges of the parameter values. Some algorithms work best for large values, while other algorithms may be needed for intermediate or small parameter values. Some algorithms may give lower variance values for some of the parameters, compared with other algorithms. The optimum algorithm for measuring *one* parameter may be different from the one needed for *another* parameter. Very often there is a trade-off between a low bias level and a low standard deviation (or variance) on a parameter. An algorithm designed to remove a bias caused by some noise source will depend on the level of that noise, which must therefore be estimated in some way. Designing good estimation algorithms is a *skill*, but it is also an *art* in many ways.

We discuss a measurement as a *random variable*, and review some of the important aspects of *probability theory* to help describe and quantify the accuracy of this "random" measurement. Then we employ a relatively simple control system example to illustrate the application of this random variable theory to a typical physical measurement task. The theory is well developed and documented in many texts and references, but the results obtained when this theory is applied to an actual system can be quite complicated, and it is often necessary to make a number of approximations. A considerable degree of *judgment* may be needed to select these approximations, to insure the final result is sufficiently accurate to satisfy the *end user* of the measurement.

We also introduce *quantized* or *discrete* random variables that are associated with *digital processors* in our systems, and we discuss *mixed* (both continuous and discrete) random variables, to characterize analog-to-digital and digital-to-analog converters.

BIBLIOGRAPHY ON PROBABILITY THEORY

[3:1] Abramowitz, Milton, and Stegan, Irene A., *Handbook of Mathematical Functions with Formulas, Graphs, and Mathematical Tables,* National Bureau of Standards, 1964. This is a good reference on higher mathematical functions, including the modified Bessel functions of the second kind.

[3:2] Bracewell, Ronald N., *The Fourier Transform and Its Applications,* McGraw-Hill, 1986. This is a very good general reference on the Fourier transform.

[3:3] Campbell, George A., and Foster, Ronald M., *Fourier Integrals for Practical Applications,* D. Van Nostrand, 1967. This is an excellent book of Fourier transform pairs, especially for higher functions.

[3:4] Clenshaw, C. W., *Mathematical Tables, Vol. 5,* Chebyshev Series for Mathematical Functions, National Physical Laboratory, Her Majesty's Stationery Office, 1963. This is an excellent compilation of coefficients for the expansion of many higher functions in Chebyshev series form. It was used here to construct the modified Bessel functions of the second kind in Figure 3–6.

[3:5] Goodman, N.R., *Measurement of Matrix Frequency Response Functions and Multiple Coherence Functions,* AFFDL TR 65-56, Research and Technology Division, AFSC, Wright-Patterson AFB, Ohio, Feb. 1965. This is a more thorough treatise on the statistics of frequency response functions (and also on coherence functions), and does not depend upon the many approximations we have used in this chapter.

[3:6] Gradshteyn, I. S., and Ryzhik, I. M., *Tables of Integrals Series and Products,* Translated from Russian by Alan Jeffrey, Academic Press, 1965. This is yet another good reference on all kinds of integrals of higher functions.

[3:7] Gröbner, Wolfgang, and Hofreiter, Nikolaus, *Integraltafel II,* Springer-Verlag, Austria, 1961. This is volume II of a two-volume set of integral tables. The first volume covers indefinite integrals, and the second volume covers definite integrals. This is an excellent reference (in German) for definite integrals, especially for higher mathematical functions.

[3:8] Oliver, Bernard M., and Cage, John M., *Electronic Measurements and Instrumentation,* Chapter 5, Signal Analysis by Digital Techniques, Ronald W. Potter, McGraw-Hill, 1971. A general but abbreviated review of signal processing methods similar to those described in this chapter.

[3:9] Papoulis, Athanasios, *Probability, Random Variables, and Stochastic Processes,* McGraw-Hill, 1965. This is an old standby text on probability theory and covers all of the concepts discussed in this chapter. There are more recent books on the subject, but this one is still excellent.

4

Estimating Parameter Values

4.1 TO MEASURE IS TO ESTIMATE

We could easily paraphrase this section to read, "To Measure Is to Guess," but that sounds a little crude. Perhaps if *guess* is replaced by *educated guess*, we could justify substituting the word *estimate*, and then we might be able to write a few equations describing the estimation *procedure*. Once we have some equations, we have some basis for further discussion. If this idea is not appealing, then another possibility is simply to call measuring an *artform* and to ignore such unpleasant things as possible *errors* in the results.

This is meant to sound somewhat flippant, but it really isn't too far from the truth. In previous chapters we discussed the concept that a measurement model is a mental *abstraction* that should always be kept separate from the physical "thing" being measured and that only the *parameters* of this abstract mental model can ever be determined. We also went to some length to emphasize that measurements are inherently *incorrect*, in the sense that you get somewhat different answers *each* time you try. Your best option is to calculate a set of *confidence intervals* around each parameter in your model, based on a set of *confidence levels* of your choosing. If this approach isn't educated guesswork, what else would you call it?

Actually, there is one more level of *art* that we must explore, because we have not *yet* discussed ways to *decide* when we have adjusted the parameters in our measurement model to fit the raw observation data in the "best" possible manner. We would like to make the *best* measurement we can, given the data we have collected. How do we decide what "best" really means, in this context? There has been a large amount of work on this subject over the years, by many people, under the general heading of *estimation theory*. In this chapter, we will introduce some elements of this theory and will give some examples of its use in this field of measuring. You should feel somewhat more comfortable about the *artform* or *guesswork* aspects of measuring after reading this chapter.

4.2   THE CONCEPT OF ABSTRACT METRIC SPACES

We are all accustomed to thinking and dealing with *three*-dimensional space, but now the goal is to generalize our perspective to *n-dimensional* space (we will restrict our attention to Riemannian spaces that have a well-defined metric tensor, so we can discuss *distances* between points). We will use *analogies* with our familiar three-space whenever we can, but we must *depend* on our mathematical notation to carry most of the burden as we move into these higher dimensionalities.

The reason for introducing higher order abstract spaces is to provide a mechanism for us to better understand some of the concepts and mathematical constructions that occur in estimation theory. True, we cannot actually *visualize* more than three dimensions, but we *can* imagine many of the familiar *concepts* of three-space to carry over into *n*-space. We can also actually *use* three-space for some of our examples to help clarify the ideas and techniques we use in higher dimensionalities.

The basic approach is to assign *one* coordinate in an abstract (existing only in our imagination) *n*-dimensional space to *each* real number that we *observe* in our raw data set. Then, if we observe *n* such numbers, we can represent this set of *n* observations as a *single point* in our *n*-dimensional abstract space.

The next crucial concept is to use our *mathematical model* of the system being measured (having *m* parameters), with all noise sources set to *zero*, to *calculate* the analogous data that we *observe* in the physical world, while *varying* all *m* model parameters over their full respective ranges. When we plot these model output points in our *n*-dimensional abstract space, we get an *m*-dimensional *subspace* (where $m \leq n$, because there can be no more parameters than observations). Remember, measuring is essentially a data *reduction* procedure, where a small number of parameter values are ultimately obtained from a large amount of raw data.

Furthermore, every point in this *m*-dimensional subspace is indexed by the complete set of model parameters (except possibly for a few pathological or degenerate cases). Imagine a *set* of *m coordinates* within this subspace, each of which defines contours for one parameter. In this way, the entire *m*-space is *spanned* by *m* sets of coordinate contours. We will refer to the original abstract *n*-dimensional space of observation points as the *observation space* and the *m*-dimensional subspace of parameter contours as the *parameter subspace*.

As an example, if our observations comprise exactly *three* numbers, then the observation space will be three-dimensional. In this case, we generally expect either one or two parameters in our model, corresponding to either a space *curve* or a space *surface* for the parameter subspace (although it *is* possible to have three parameters). In any case, the entire range of these parameters can be represented as coordinates totally *within* the parameter subspace.

The two-dimensional surface in Figure 4–1 is a parameter subspace embedded in a three-dimensional observation space, where the three observation coordinates are labeled x_1, x_2, and x_3. In this graph, the two sets of contours are actually the *projections* of the two observation coordinates x_1 and x_2 onto the parameter surface. In Figure 4–3 below, we show the same surface but the contours are those for *constant parameter values,* which are usually of more interest.

Now, let's imagine making a few million different sets of *n* observations on the *same* physical system, under *identical conditions,* except that our various noise sources will perturb each set of observations in a slightly different way *each* time. When these points are plotted in our observation space, we get a "cloud" of points, presumably clustered in some way around the "correct" set of parameter values. However, since our parameter space is only a *subspace,* few if any observation points will actually fall *within* this subspace. Most of the observation points will be *outside,* although hopefully nearby. For these outside points, there is *no* possible combination of parameter values in our model that can yield such points. This *could* mean our model is wrong, but it is more likely due to the various random noise perturbations in the system, giving different observation points from what we would otherwise have *expected.*

Figure 4–2 shows the same parameter surface as Figure 4–1, (except for fewer contours), but 300 observation points have been included to show this "cloud" effect. The additive noise is spherically symmetric, having a three-dimensional joint Gaussian PDF,

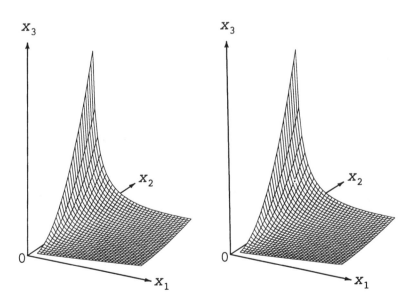

Figure 4–1   A 2-D Parameter Surface Embedded in a 3-D Observation Space

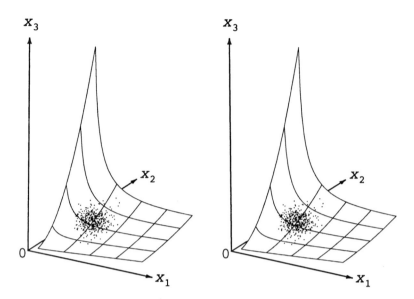

Figure 4–2   A Noise "Cloud" of Observations

centered at the point $x_1 = 1$ and $x_2 = 2$ (which lies *within* the parameter subspace). The contour limits for both of these coordinates range from 0.2 to 3.4, so each interval is 0.8 units in size.

The contours in the parameter surface above are still projections of the *observation* coordinates. In contrast, we show a few of the *parameter contours* within our parameter surface in Figure 4–3 for the same cloud of observation points.

In this form, we can see how *sensitive* each parameter is to noise and how each parameter is related to the others. If two contours for different parameters are nearly *collinear* (or *parallel*), it will be difficult to decide on the two parameter values needed to *represent* a particular point, and consequently *both* estimated values may be considerably in *error*.

We have chosen to represent the coordinates of the n-dimensional observation space by a set of variables x_k, where k ranges from 1 to n. We can represent this set using the notation $\{x_k\}$, or we can define an n-dimensional *vector X*, whose components are the x_k values. In a similar manner, we choose u_j to represent the m parameter variables, where j ranges from 1 to m. This set can be written as $\{u_j\}$ or as the m-dimensional *vector U*. The parameter subspace is defined by the set of n equations:

$$\{x_k = g_k(\{u_j\})\} \tag{4.1}$$

where g is the *mathematical model* of the system being measured, and g_k is simply this model *evaluated* at the n points indexed by k, that comprise *one set* of observations. That is, g represents the output from our model (with all noise sources set to zero) that corre-

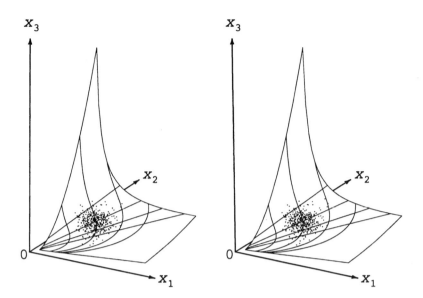

Figure 4–3   Contours of Constant Parameter Values

sponds to the output from the *ideal* physical system (having *no* noise) from which we obtain our set of *n* observations. The *things* we are trying to measure are the parameter values $\{u_j\}$ that define *g*. Since the set of *n* equations in Eq. 4.1 are functions of the *m* parameters u_j, these *define* the *m*-dimensional parameter *subspace* embedded within the *n*-dimensional observation space (where $m \le n$). The vector form is given in Eq. 4.2, where *G* is an *n*-dimensional vector of *functions* whose elements are g_k.

$$X = G(U) \tag{4.2}$$

These are fittingly called *parametric equations*, since each observation coordinate is a function of the parameters of the model. In principle, we can solve for all of the u_j parameters using any *m* of the Equations in 4.1 or 4.2, and then substitute these expressions into the remaining $n - m$ equations, thereby eliminating all references to the parameters in this set of equations. These $n - m$ expressions then *define* the parameter subspace, in terms of a subset of *m* (out of *n*) observation coordinates, without reference to any parameter values or parameter coordinate system at all. However, it can sometimes be difficult to solve *explicitly* for all of the parameters, so this formulation is not always practical or useful.

In a typical real-life measurement session, we make a single set of observations, corresponding to exactly *one point* in the observation space (which will nearly always lie *outside* of the parameter subspace). We must invent some satisfactory way to deduce the point *within* the parameter subspace that "best" corresponds to this single observation point. Even if the observation point *does* miraculously fall within the parameter subspace, there is no reason to think it is at the *best location*, or corresponds to the *best* combination of parameter values. How is it possible to estimate the most accurate set of parameter values from this *one*, seemingly *errant*, observation point?

Of course, you cannot expect to predict something about which you have *no* information. You can either make a wild *guess*, or you can search for *additional* information that may exist, such as from the results of previous estimation attempts. The measurement or the simulation of the *joint PDF* of the observation coordinates is *one* way of describing the results of previous estimates. Most of the various estimation algorithms either make use of this joint PDF, or else use some of its statistical parameters, like mean values, variances, or correlation coefficients.

We will discuss a simple *example* to illustrate the concepts we have been describing, before we proceed to explore the various estimation techniques in more *detail*.

4.3   EXAMPLE: SINGLE-POLE TRANSFER FUNCTION

The stereoscopic figures above were obtained from a model for the measurement of the pole value and the residue value of a *single-pole transfer function* in the Laplace domain. For example, this model could either represent a parallel spring and damper combination in a vehicle suspension system, or a simple electrical lowpass filter. The noise-free model is:

$$H(s) = \frac{a}{s - s_o} \quad , \quad \text{where } a > 0, \text{ and } s_o < 0 \tag{4.3}$$

where s_o is the *pole value*, and a is called the *residue* of the pole. This is analogous to a single term in Eq. 2.17 in Chapter 2, for the transfer function of a vibrating mechanical structure, although in *that* formulation both parameters are generally complex numbers. For simplicity, we have chosen a function having only *real* parameter values for this example.

We can *only* measure the characteristics of this transfer function *on the frequency axis*, where $s = i\omega$ (ω is the angular frequency in radians per second). This is called the *frequency response function*, expressed as:

$$H(i\omega) = \frac{a}{i\omega - s_o} = -\frac{as_o}{s_o^2 + \omega^2} - i\frac{a\omega}{s_o^2 + \omega^2} \tag{4.4}$$

The *principle of analytic continuation* in the theory of complex variables states that if two analytic functions *match* along any finite line segment or if their derivatives all match at a point, then the functions will match *everywhere* in the complex plane. Thus, a representation along the frequency axis is sufficient to deduce the function at *all* other points in the complex plane. If we can measure the parameters in Eq. 4.4, then we know these same parameter values also belong to Eq. 4.3.

If we sample $H(i\omega)$ at three different values of ω, we can *use* these three samples as the *coordinates* in our observation space, and we can then calculate the shape and *para-*

meter coordinate system in our parameter subspace for this model. To keep things simple, let's use the three values: $\omega = \pm 1$ and 0. The three corresponding values of $H(i\omega)$ are:

$$H(\pm i) = -\frac{as_o}{s_o^2 + 1} \mp i \frac{a}{s_o^2 + 1} = x_1 \mp ix_2 \tag{4.5}$$

$$H(0) = -\frac{a}{s_o} = x_3 \tag{4.6}$$

We have assigned *observation coordinates* x_1, x_2, and x_3 to these three samples in a manner such that each coordinate is a *real* number, even though two of the samples are *complex* (conjugate) numbers. The assignment of these coordinates is rather arbitrary, so we have made choices to keep things simple. Thus:

$$x_1 = -\frac{as_o}{s_o^2 + 1} \tag{4.7}$$

$$x_2 = \frac{a}{s_o^2 + 1} \tag{4.8}$$

$$x_3 = -\frac{a}{s_o} \tag{4.9}$$

We can solve for both a and s_o using Eqs. 4.7 and 4.8 to get:

$$s_o = -\frac{x_1}{x_2} \tag{4.10}$$

$$a = \frac{x_1^2 + x_2^2}{x_2} \tag{4.11}$$

Inserting these two parameter expressions into Eq. 4.9 yields the equation for the parameter surface, *independent* of any parameter values and expressed only in the observation space coordinates:

$$x_3 = \frac{x_1^2 + x_2^2}{x_1} \tag{4.12}$$

This is the parameter surface illustrated in Figure 4–1 above. The two sets of constant parameter contour curves can be obtained by pairing either Eq. 4.10 or Eq. 4.11 with Eq. 4.12. Thus, for contours of constant pole value, we hold s_o constant in Eq. 4.10, giving:

$$x_1 = -s_o x_2 \tag{4.13}$$

$$x_3 = -\frac{s_o^2 + 1}{s_o} x_2 \tag{4.14}$$

These two equations define the space curves for constant s_o in terms of the observation coordinates. Likewise, for contours of constant a, we have:

$$x_1 = \sqrt{ax_2 - x_2^2} \tag{4.15}$$

$$x_3 = \frac{ax_2}{\sqrt{ax_2 - x_2^2}} \tag{4.16}$$

A few of these contours are shown in Figure 4–3. The four constant s_o contours are straight lines passing through the origin and comprising the set s_o = −0.25, −0.5, −0.75, and −1, beginning on the left. The four constant a contours are the second set of curves that rise up and to the left, with a = 1.5, 2.5, 3.5, and 4.5, also beginning on the left.

Figure 4–4 shows the frequency response function Eq. 4.4 as a complex space curve versus frequency. We have added some zero mean Gaussian random noise to this curve at each frequency. The three *sample points* are shown by the dashed lines running from the frequency axis to the three noisy points near the curve. This function has *Hermitian symmetry*, meaning the *real part* is an *even* function of frequency, and the *imaginary part* is an *odd* function of frequency. Thus, the two samples at $\omega = \pm 1$ are *complex conjugates* of one another and can both be expressed by the two numbers x_1 and x_2. The third sample at $\omega = 0$ is the *real* number x_3.

We assume the *noise* in this frequency response function originated in the time waveforms that comprised the original data set for this measurement. We also assume the *power spectral density* of this noise is flat over the frequency range of interest, and the noise power is equally divided between the real and imaginary parts of the frequency spectrum. Since a real time waveform transforms into a Hermitian symmetric frequency spectrum, the additive noise must *also* have this symmetry. So, we have added Hermitian symmetric noise to the frequency response function in Figure 4–4. Be careful in practice, because such simplifying assumptions may not always be *valid* in real-world situations.

In the absence of noise, all observation points at *each* frequency would superimpose and would also fall exactly *in* our parameter subspace (the *solid* space curve in Figure 4–4), assuming our model of the measurement is indeed correct. In this case, the coordi-

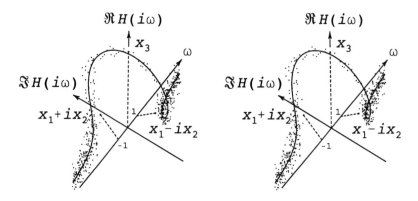

Figure 4–4   Single Pole Frequency Response Function

nates of these three points would produce all the parameter values in our model without any error.

Since this fortuitous event is *very* unlikely to occur, we must invent a strategy to *estimate* a set of parameter values that will "best" justify the *actual* values of the three observed data points. You, as the *end user* of the measurement, will have to decide what *you* think is best. However, there are some commonly accepted techniques which have been developed over the years for you to consider, and we will study some of these in the next few sections. Feel free to invent your own estimation methods, if you like.

4.4   THE LEAST-SQUARES ESTIMATE

One common definition of the *best* parameter values is the set obtained when a *single point* in the parameter subspace is found that has the minimum possible *distance* from the observation point. This is called a *least-squares estimate* because the square of the distance in question is the *sum* of the squares of the differences in each observation coordinate, between the observation point and this *optimum point* in the parameter subspace. This minimum distance is also the result you get by projecting a straight line *perpendicular* to the parameter subspace and passing *through* the observation point. Thus, the least-squares estimate is also the *orthogonal projection* of the observation point into the parameter surface. If we represent the points in the parameter subspace by a set of *m* *nondependent* vectors residing within this subspace, then the *minimum distance* vector will lie *outside* of this subspace and will be *orthogonal* to all *m* vectors in this set. This is the *only* estimation method in this review that does *not* use any information about the *noise sources* in the model.

In order to be precise and unambiguous, we give the mathematical description of this approach next. Denote the *n* observation point coordinates by x_{ok}, so the corresponding observation vector is X_o. The sum of the squares of the component distance differences between the observation point and a point in the parameter subspace (indexed by U), denoted by ϵ, is:

$$\epsilon = \sum_{k=1}^{n} [x_{ok} - g_k(u_j)]^2 = |X_o - G(U)|^2 \tag{4.17}$$

We next *minimize* ϵ with respect to *all* of the model parameters u_j in U by setting the *m* partial derivatives to zero, as follows:

$$\frac{\partial \epsilon}{\partial u_j} = -2 \sum_{k=1}^{n} \frac{\partial g_k(u_j)}{\partial u_j}[x_{ok} - g_k(u_j)] = -2 \left[\frac{\partial G(U)}{\partial U}\right]^t [X_o - G(U)] = 0 \tag{4.18}$$

where the superscript ^{t} denotes the *transpose* of a matrix (in which the rows and columns are interchanged). Note, both X_o and $G(U)$ are *n*-vectors in the observation space.

The partial derivatives in this expression need to be explained in more detail. For *each* value of *j*, we calculate the *n* partial derivatives of $g_k(u_j)$ with respect to u_j, which are the components (expressed in the coordinates of the *observation* space) of a vector *in the* parameter subspace that is. *tangent* to the u_j coordinate at that point. Unless some of the parameter coordinates are exactly *collinear*, we get *m unique* tangent vectors (each tangent to *one* of the *m* parameter coordinates), which form a *complete* set of *basis vectors* for this parameter subspace at any particular point. This means any other vector in the parameter subspace can be uniquely represented by a *linear combination* of these basis vectors.

In the matrix-vector form of Eq. 4.18, the factor comprising the transpose of the matrix of partial derivatives of *G* with respect to *U* is an *m* × *n* *rectangular* matrix (*m* rows and *n* columns) in which each *row* is the transpose of the parameter subspace vector (or basis vector) that is *tangent* to the associated u_j coordinate line. There are *m* such rows, one for each of the *m* parameters in the model.

The second factor in Eq. 4.18 is the *n*-vector of the vector difference between the *observation point* (denoted by X_o) and the *desired* (but *unknown*) parameter subspace point, denoted by *G(U)* (where *U* comprises the parameter coordinates u_j). Since *all m* components of this matrix-vector product are *zero*, we recognize that the difference vector $X_o - G(U)$ must be *orthogonal* to all of the basis vectors in the parameter subspace. This means the difference vector is *perpendicular* to the parameter subspace, in a multidimensional sense. This justifies our earlier assertion that the least-squares estimate is the *orthogonal projection* of the observation point into the parameter subspace.

We can rewrite the matrix form of Eq. 4.18 as follows:

$$\left[\frac{\partial G(U)}{\partial U}\right]^t X_o = \left[\frac{\partial G(U)}{\partial U}\right]^t G(U) \qquad (4.19)$$

The *left* side is an *m*-vector representing the *projection* of the observation *n*-vector X_o into the parameter subspace, and the *right* side represents a similar projection of the *model n*-vector *G(U)* into the parameter subspace. *Both* projections are represented in terms of the *basis vectors* comprising the rows of the transposed partial derivative matrix. We have *m* equations in the *m* unknown parameter values u_j.

The actual solution of Eq. 4.19 for the *optimum* set of parameter values (components of *U*) may be difficult in many cases. These are often sets of *nonlinear* equations that can only be solved by *iterative techniques* after a suitable starting *approximation* for the parameter vector has been selected.

It is very possible for *multiple* solutions of Eq. 4.19 to exist, and it is also possible for there to be *no unique* solution. For example, suppose the parameter subspace includes a "spherical" region, and suppose the observation point is at the center of curvature of this spherical region. Then there will be an *infinite* number of solution vectors that are *all* perpendicular to the parameter subspace and that *all* pass through this observation point. Any solution to Eq. 4.19 will be a *local* solution, in which all vectors in the immediate *vicinity* will be longer than the solution vector. However, there is no assurance that shorter solution vectors might not exist somewhere *else* in the parameter subspace. Thus, the solution you find may *not* be the *best* one in a *global* sense.

There are times when *G(U)* is a *linear* function of *U*, which corresponds to a multidimensional "plane" for the parameter subspace. For this to occur, either the measurement model is *inherently* linear, or else a *linear approximation* to a nonlinear model has been chosen. This linearizing approach is often used *locally* when iterating towards a solution of nonlinear equations. For these special cases, the least-squares estimate can be written in *closed form* as a matrix-vector expression. Let's define:

$$G(U) = TU \qquad (4.20)$$

where T is an $n \times m$ *constant* transformation matrix. We can avoid a constant offset vector in Eq. 4.20 by locating the origins for X and U at the same point. Recall, U is an m-vector and $G(U)$ is an n-vector. The elements of this matrix T are simply the *partial derivatives* of G with respect to the elements of U. The linearized version of Eq. 4.19 is:

$$T^t X_o = T^t T U \qquad (4.21)$$

Solving for the linear least-squares estimate of U gives:

$$\hat{U} = (T^t T)^{-1} T^t X_o \qquad (4.22)$$

We can substitute this estimate back into the *original* error equation 4.17 to get the *least-squared* error:

$$\epsilon_{\min} = |[I - T(T^t T)^{-1} T^t] X_o|^2 \qquad (4.23)$$

where I is the $n \times n$ identity matrix. Notice, we need to *invert* the $m \times m$ matrix $T^t T$ to obtain this optimum solution. The quantity $(T^t T)^{-1} T^t$ is called a *left-handed pseudoinverse* of T, since we get the $m \times m$ identity matrix I if we premultiply T by this quantity. However, this inverse is *not* unique, as it would be if T were a square matrix. Since T has more *rows* than *columns*, it is only *possible* to define a *left*-handed inverse in this case.

We can use our single-pole transfer function measurement discussed above as an example of this nonlinear least-squares estimation procedure in action. We write the observation vector X_o and the model vector $G(U)$ as:

$$X_o = \begin{bmatrix} x_{o1} & x_{o2} & x_{o3} \end{bmatrix}^t \qquad (4.24)$$

$$G(U) = \begin{bmatrix} \dfrac{-as_o}{s_o^2 + 1} & \dfrac{a}{s_o^2 + 1} & \dfrac{-a}{s_o} \end{bmatrix}^t \qquad (4.25)$$

where the parameter vector is $U = \begin{bmatrix} a & s_o \end{bmatrix}^t$. The two transposed basis vectors in the parameter subspace are the *rows* of the transposed partial derivative matrix, given by:

$$\left[\frac{\partial G(U)}{\partial U} \right]^t = \begin{bmatrix} \dfrac{-s_o}{s_o^2 + 1} & \dfrac{1}{s_o^2 + 1} & \dfrac{-1}{s_o} \\[2mm] \dfrac{a(s_o^2 - 1)}{(s_o^2 + 1)^2} & \dfrac{-2as_o}{(s_o^2 + 1)^2} & \dfrac{a}{s_o^2} \end{bmatrix} \qquad (4.26)$$

From Eq. 4.19, we can write the two equations (in the two parameters a and s_o) that must be solved:

$$-\frac{x_{o1}s_o}{s_o^2 + 1} + \frac{x_{o2}}{s_o^2 + 1} - \frac{x_{o3}}{s_o} = a\left[\frac{1}{s_o^2 + 1} + \frac{1}{s_o^2}\right] \tag{4.27}$$

$$\frac{x_{o1}(s_o^2 - 1)}{(s_o^2 + 1)^2} - \frac{2x_{o2}s_o}{(s_o^2 + 1)^2} + \frac{x_{o3}}{s_o^2} = -a\left[\frac{s_o}{(s_o^2 + 1)^2} + \frac{1}{s_o^3}\right] \tag{4.28}$$

We can readily eliminate the a parameter by forming the quotient of these two equations, leaving a nonlinear equation (in this case, a quartic polynomial) in s_o. After a bit of algebra we get:

$$2x_{o2}s_o^4 + (3x_{o1} - x_{o3})s_o^3 + (2x_{o1} - x_{o3})s_o - x_{o2} = 0 \tag{4.29}$$

$$a = -s_o\frac{(x_{o1} + x_{o3})s_o^2 - x_{o2}s_o + x_{o3}}{2s_o^2 + 1} \tag{4.30}$$

In the example illustrated in Figure 4–4, the sample values are:

$$x_{01} = 0.949063$$

$$x_{o2} = 1.323042$$

$$x_{o3} = 5.142195$$

Their noise-free original values were 1, 2, and 5, respectively. Notice, x_{o2} is *considerably* in error. There are four roots to this fourth order polynomial in Eq. 4.29, so we expect four values for s_o. Three of these are *extraneous roots* that were introduced by the mathematical manipulations we used to obtain Eq. 4.29 from the original pair Eqs. 4.27 and 4.28. The correct root can be determined by substituting all four values of s_o (and the corresponding values for a) into the original pair of equations. The extraneous roots will not satisfy these equations. In this example, the four roots are:

$$s_o = 1.530332, -0.1511106 \pm i0.939550, -0.360789$$

The *nominal* (noise-free) value should be -0.5, and the *correct* root choice is $s_o = -0.360789$. There is a positive root and a complex conjugate pair of roots that are extraneous. When we substitute this estimated value of s_o into Eq. 4.27 or Eq. 4.30, we get the estimate for a, which is $a = 1.835647$ (the *nominal* value is 2.5). Since the error in x_{o2} is so large, we get correspondingly large errors in our estimates of *both* a and s_o.

We have included Figure 4–5 to show the frequency response function *corresponding* to these estimated parameters (dashed curve) along with the original (solid) curve. Since this function is described by only *two* parameters, it is not feasible to construct a solution that passes exactly through the *three* noisy samples, but the estimated shape passes as closely as *possible* (in a least-squares sense) to these samples.

This least-squares estimation technique is rather intuitive, since you would logically expect that the true set of parameter values would be those for which the parameter subspace is *closest* to the observation point. However, there may be other factors to consider.

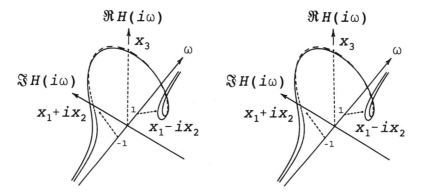

Figure 4–5 Single-Pole Estimated Frequency Response Function

One of the rules of estimation theory is to make use of *all* of the available information, whenever possible. Suppose the "cloud" of simulated observation points is *not* spherically symmetric, but instead looks somewhat ellipsoidal. The *asymmetry* of the cloud indicates that the uncertainty in the observations is greater in some directions than in others.

You would intuitively tend to *weight* the contributions from *noisy* data *less* than the contributions from "clean" data. This technique is called a *weighted least-squares* estimation procedure. The weighting function is generally proportional to the *reciprocal* of the *variance* of each component of the observation and is applied to that *corresponding* component of the squared distance difference. This technique *effectively* converts or reshapes the ellipsoidal cloud of observation points into a *spherical* cloud, thereby reducing the large errors that would otherwise accumulate from the noisiest data.

There may be other reasons for *weighting* some of the data differently. For example, certain regions may have more influence over the parameter values than other regions. Generally, the part of the frequency response function that is *closest* to a pole (and therefore having the largest *magnitude*) has the most influence over the pole location, so observations that are *near* that part of the function should probably be weighted more heavily than others.

In this method, some minimum knowledge of the *statistics* (like the variance in each direction) in the observation space must generally be available. We obtain these either by actual measurement (by repeating the observations a large number of times), or else we *calculate* the required statistics from our *model* of the measurement, which hopefully includes all of the significant noise sources. Of course, the model must also be *accurate* or else our calculations will be incorrect. This case, where the observation space PDF is *nonspherical,* is illustrated in Figure 4–6.

In this figure, we have kept the *total* noise variance the same, but have made the standard deviation of the x_1 coordinate four times that of the other two coordinates. When each squared component is weighted by dividing by the *relative* variance in that compo-

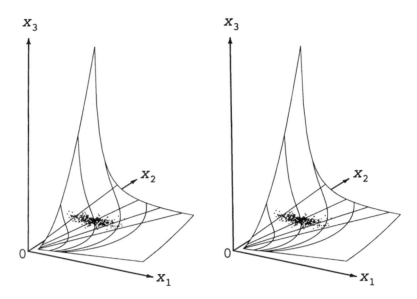

Figure 4–6   Asymmetrical Observation Noise

nent (the component variance normalized by the *sum* of all component variances), we get the spherical distribution shown in Figure 4–3.

4.5   MAXIMUM LIKELIHOOD ESTIMATION

Another possible approach is to use our model to *simulate* the measurement procedure (often called *Monte Carlo simulation*). Imagine that we assign independent random values to each *noise source* in our model and then calculate the resulting observation point. This observation point is *not likely* to lie within the parameter subspace, since *that* space was constructed with all model noise sources set to *zero*. If we repeat this task a few million times, we will obtain a *cloud* of points (approximating a *joint probability density function*) in the observation space, around this single (*known*) point in the parameter subspace. Of course, we might prefer to *calculate* this joint PDF using our measurement model, instead of using Monte Carlo simulation. Let's *repeat* this PDF determination procedure at *every point* (or for every possible combination of parameters) *throughout* the parameter subspace.

Now, we make *one set of observations*, giving exactly *one* observation point. We try all possible parameter combinations until we find the set where the associated *joint PDF is a maximum* at this *observation point*. Although the observation point is *exterior* to the parameter subspace, the joint PDFs for each combination of parameters *also* extend *outside* of this space (so the single observation point will fall *somewhere* on *each* of these joint PDFs). The resulting set of parameter values are the most *likely* combination, because they give the *highest probability* for the occurrence of the set of *observed* values. Fittingly, this technique is called *maximum likelihood estimation*. This approach is only as good as the joint PDFs of the observations, but it seems like a good intuitive method, and it is very popular. For *spherically symmetric* joint PDFs, this method will give the same result as the least-squares method (namely the *closest* point within the parameter subspace to the observation point), but for asymmetric PDFs, the results will be different.

Now, we introduce a few equations so we can precisely describe this maximum likelihood estimation method. We want an expression for the *joint PDF* in observation space coordinates, centered at *each* point *in* the parameter subspace. All parameter subspace points are described by the measurement model n-vector $G(U)$, whose elements are $g_k(u_j)$. Here, k indexes the n observation space coordinates ($1 \le k \le n$) and j indexes the m parameter coordinates in the parameter subspace ($1 \le j \le m$). If we assume Gaussian noise statistics, the joint PDF around any point in the parameter subspace can be written as:

$$p_X(X;U) = \frac{1}{(2\pi)^{\frac{n}{2}} \prod\limits_{k=1}^{n} \sigma_k} e^{-\frac{1}{2} \sum\limits_{k=1}^{n} \frac{[x_k - g_k(u_j)]^2}{\sigma_k^2}} \qquad (4.31)$$

This is an n-dimensional Gaussian PDF in the n independent random variables x_k, each having a standard deviation σ_k and a mean value $g_k(u_j)$, where u_j are the m parameters of the model that are to be *measured* or *estimated*. Of course, some *other* joint PDF might be more appropriate in your application instead of a Gaussian shape, in which case you would use the expression for *that* PDF.

Now, we want to *position* this joint PDF so the single observation point (an n-vector with elements x_{ok}) occurs at the point of *maximum* probability on the joint PDF. We accomplish this task by setting $x_k = x_{ok}$ for all k, and then varying the u_j parameters until $p_X(X;U)$ is maximized. Form the partial derivative of p_X with respect to each parameter u_j and set the result to zero, giving m equations in the m unknown parameters:

$$\frac{\partial p_X}{\partial u_j} = \frac{1}{(2\pi)^{\frac{n}{2}} \prod\limits_{k=1}^{n} \sigma_k} e^{-\frac{1}{2} \sum\limits_{k=1}^{n} \frac{[x_{ok} - g_k(u_j)]^2}{\sigma_k^2}} \sum\limits_{k=1}^{n} \frac{\partial g_k(u_j)}{\partial u_j} \frac{x_{ok} - g_k(u_j)}{\sigma_k^2} = 0 \qquad (4.32)$$

Only the *last summation* in this equation can produce this zero value, so we can write:

$$\sum\limits_{k=1}^{n} \frac{\partial g_k(u_j)}{\partial u_j} \frac{x_{ok} - g_k(u_j)}{\sigma_k^2} = 0 \qquad (4.33)$$

Compare this *maximum likelihood* condition with the *least-squares* condition given by Eq. 4.18. If the variance of each component is constant, then these two estimates are identical (at least when using a Gaussian joint PDF). This is also the same form as the *weighted* least-squares technique, with the weighting function for each component being equal to the reciprocal of the variance for *that* component. However, if the joint PDF is not a Gaussian shape, these equivalences will generally *not* hold.

We can write Eq. 4.33 in a matrix-vector form by defining a *diagonal* weighting matrix W, whose elements are the weighting factors on each component of the difference (or error) vector. The result is:

$$\left[\frac{\partial G(U)}{\partial U}\right]^t W[X_o - G(U)] = 0 \tag{4.34}$$

The diagonal elements of W are $1/\sigma_k^2$ for this Gaussian case. As before, X_o is the n-vector describing the observation point, and $G(U)$ is an n-vector (a function of the parameter m-vector U), representing the measurement model. The transposed *rows* of the transposed partial derivative matrix form a complete set of *basis* vectors at each point *within* the parameter subspace.

As we found for the least-squares estimate, if we *linearize* the parameter space so $G(U) = TU$ (with coincident origins for X and U), we can write this maximum likelihood estimate in *closed form* as a matrix-vector product, given by:

$$\hat{U} = (T^t W T)^{-1} T^t W X_o \tag{4.35}$$

For a Gaussian PDF, this is the same result we obtained for the *weighted* least-squares estimate, where the weighting matrix W is diagonal with elements $1/\sigma_k^2$. As before, we recognize the matrix $(T^t W T)^{-1} T^t W$ as a *left-handed pseudoinverse* of T, but *now* defined for *any* weighting matrix W. This shows the *ambiguity* inherent in the pseudoinverse of a *nonsquare* matrix. For a *square* matrix, the W matrix is *cancelled* by the W^{-1} factor inside the parentheses (in which case, $\hat{U} = T^{-1}X_o$).

4.6   ESTIMATION USING BAYES THEOREM

The most satisfying way to estimate our parameter values would be to somehow determine the *joint PDF* for these parameters (*within* the parameter space itself) *after* an observation has been made, and then to choose something like either the mean, mode, or median of this PDF as our *best guess* of the parameter values. From this joint PDF we could also obtain confidence intervals for each parameter for some given confidence level. At the same time, we would like to account for any *prior* information that we might have about the allowed parameter ranges, or about the likelihood of some values occurring with different probabilities, either based on previous observations or on some other source of prior information.

We discussed Bayes theorem at the end of section 3.3 in Chapter 3, and this relation provides a means for accomplishing these goals. We know the vector of parameter values U to be measured is actually a *random* vector, since all measurements are random quantities. The observation vector X is also a random vector, so we will define a *new* joint PDF $P_{XU}(X,U)$ to include *both* of these random vectors. Using Bayes theorem obtained from Eq. 3.27 we can write:

$$p_{XU}(X,U) = p_{X|U}(X|U)p_U(U) = p_{U|X}(U|X)p_X(X) \qquad (4.36)$$

This expression illustrates *two* different ways to *factor* the joint PDF of X and U in terms of conditional PDFs. Furthermore, it relates the probability of U given X to the probability of X given U, which allows us to determine the PDF of our parameters *after* an observation, once we have obtained the PDF of the observations for any given parameter vector from our measurement model.

The left side of Eq. 4.36 is simply an $(n + m)$-dimensional joint PDF, treating the n observation components and the m parameter components in an equal manner. If we integrate this PDF over all of the components of X and U, we get unity. If we integrate the two parts of Eq. 4.36 separately with respect to X and U, we get the following four expressions:

$$\int_{-\infty}^{\infty} p_{X|U}(X|U)\, dX = 1 \qquad (4.37)$$

$$\int_{-\infty}^{\infty} p_{U|X}(U|X)\, dU = 1 \qquad (4.38)$$

$$\int_{-\infty}^{\infty} p_{X|U}(X|U)\, p_U(U)\, dU = p_X(X) \qquad (4.39)$$

$$\int_{-\infty}^{\infty} p_{U|X}(U|X)\, p_X(X)\, dX = p_U(U) \qquad (4.40)$$

where these integrals are actually multiple integrals over all elements of the integration vector.

The first pair of integrals Eqs. 4.37 and 4.38 show that the two conditional PDFs indeed have *unit* total "volume" independent of the *fixed* component values, as we require of any PDF. The last pair of integrals Eqs. 4.39 and 4.40 show that the *expected values* of these conditional PDFs, relative to the components that are held fixed, are actually the joint PDFs of the *variable* components.

We can write Bayes theorem is several ways, depending on what is *known* and what is *unknown*. In our application, we *choose* the a priori PDF of our parameters $p_U(U)$ *before* we make any measurements. This choice is based on all prior knowledge we have about the values of these parameters. Then, from our measurement model we calculate the PDF of our *observations* for *each* possible set of parameter values. In the maximum likelihood estimation technique discussed in section 4.5 we called this $p_X(X;U)$, but we *should* call it $p_{X|U}(X|U)$ because the PDF in the X coordinates is defined for *each* set of fixed parameter values, U. That is, this is a PDF of the random vector X, *given* a particular vector U. There will always be a different PDF in X for *each* U, because U at *least* determines the location of the *mean value* of the PDF of X, and it may *also* determine the *variance* and/or the *shape* of the PDF of X.

If we multiply the conditional PDF $p_{X|U}(X|U)$ times the a priori PDF of the parameters $p_U(U)$, we get the "shape" of the conditional PDF in U for a given observation X_o. In order to turn this into a *true* PDF, we must force its multidimensional volume to be *unity*. We can normalize this shape by dividing by the constant $p_X(X_o)$, which is given by Eq. 4.39 above, for $X = X_o$. Notice that this divisor is determined *solely* by the observation point. The resulting conditional PDF $p_{U|X}(U|X_o)$ is called the *a posteriori* PDF of the *parameters*, because this is the PDF *after* the observation has been made, in contrast to the *a priori* PDF $p_U(U)$. We also need to emphasize that this PDF lies solely *within* the parameter subspace as a function of U and does *not* extend into the general observation space. The result is:

$$p_{U|X}(U|X_o) = \frac{p_{X|U}(X_o|U)p_U(U)}{p_X(X_o)} = \frac{p_{X|U}(X_o|U)p_U(U)}{\int_{-\infty}^{\infty} p_{X|U}(X_o|U)p_U(U)\,dU} \qquad (4.41)$$

Writing Eq. 4.41 in a slightly different way gives:

$$p_{U|X}(U|X_o) = \left[\frac{p_{X|U}(X_o|U)}{p_X(X_o)} \right] p_U(U) \qquad (4.42)$$

The quantity in brackets modifies the *a priori* parameter PDF $p_U(U)$ *before* the observation X_o, to produce the *a posteriori* parameter PDF $p_{U|X}(U|X_o)$, which we get *after* the observation. The numerator within the bracket is the PDF of X given U (evaluated at X_o), which is a function of U. The denominator is this same quantity averaged over *all possible values* of U and is therefore a *constant* after the observation. If $p_U(U)$ is relatively constant over all parameter values, then the shape of the conditional PDF of U given X_o will be about the same as the conditional PDF of X given U, evaluated at the observation point X_o. However, if $p_U(U)$ changes rapidly with respect to U then *that* function begins to dictate the shape of the result.

In Figure 4–7, we show the conditional PDF of X (given U) for nine particular values of the parameter vector U. Of course, there are an *infinite* number of these PDFs, one for each possible value of U, but you can understand the procedure with only a few examples of such distributions. We have *also* applied the *a priori* PDF for the parameters $p_U(U)$ to these distributions, which is indicated by the *relative sizes* of each cloud of points, resulting in the joint PDF $p_{XU}(X,U)$, as shown in Eq. 4.36. It appears in the figure that each PDF is rather localized and isolated from its neighbors, but in fact the PDF for *each* set of parameter values generally covers the *entire* observation space, at least to some extent. Thus, after we make *one* set of observations, denoted in this figure by the *point* (or vector) X_o, this joint PDF will have *some non-zero* value at this observation point, no matter *what* parameter vector values are involved. In this manner, we can construct the *entire* conditional PDF for the parameter vector, $p_{U|X}(U|X_o)$, given a *single* observation point, by dividing by $p_X(X_o)$.

So far, this approach is very similar to the one we described for maximum likelihood estimation, with the *generalization* that the *shape* of the PDF (including its various moments) in the observation coordinates can *vary* over the parameter subspace as a function of the parameter vector U. In the maximum likelihood formulation, we only allow the *mean value* (or position within the parameter subspace) to vary with U. Bayes relation al-

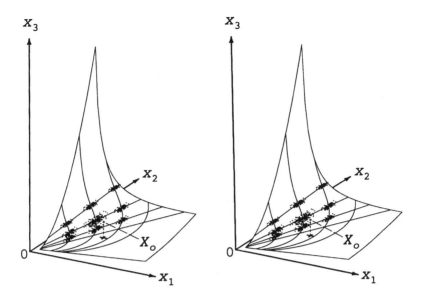

Figure 4–7   PDFs of Observation Noise versus Parameter Values (X_o Is Observation Point Vector)

lows us to incorporate *any* prior known *parameter* distribution into the final parameter estimate.

Having obtained the *a posteriori* PDF for the parameter set, we are now in a good position to study the *statistics* of the parameters and to decide which parameter values we will select as our *best* estimates. For example, we can establish confidence intervals for each parameter corresponding to any prescribed confidence level, and we can find the mean, mode, or median of the conditional parameter distribution. Just remember, we are working strictly *inside* of the parameter *subspace* from here on, thanks to Bayes theorem.

There are *two* common estimation methods we will describe at this point. The first method, *Bayesian mean-squared-error* (BMSE) estimation, selects a parameter value such that the *squared error* measured from this value is minimized when integrated over the *entire* parameter subspace. As before, we indicate estimated values by a caret over the symbol. So, we want to minimize ϵ with respect to $\hat{U}$, where:

$$\epsilon = \int_{-\infty}^{\infty} (U - \hat{U})^2 p_{U|X}(U|X_o)dU \tag{4.43}$$

If we set the partial derivatives of ϵ with respect to the components of $\hat{U}$ equal to zero, we find the BMSE estimate is:

$$\hat{U} = \int_{-\infty}^{\infty} U\, p_{U|X}(U|X_o)dU = E[U|X_o] \tag{4.44}$$

which is the *expected value* (or mean) of the *a posteriori* PDF of the parameters U, given a single set of observations X_o. This solution is valid for *any* conditional PDF in U, whether of Gaussian form or not.

Notice when we substitute this BMSE estimate back into Eq. 4.43, we find ϵ becomes the *variance* of the conditional PDF $p_{U|X}(U|X_o)$, and hence of the parameter vector U. Unfortunately, the evaluation of the integrals Eq. 4.43 and/or Eq. 4.44 are often difficult, so a closed form representation of this BMSE estimate may not exist.

The second Bayes method, *maximum a posteriori (MAP) estimation,* selects the *mode* or point of *maximum* probability on this *a posteriori* conditional PDF $p_{U|X}(U|X_o)$ as the "best" estimate of the parameter values. Thus, we must form the m partial derivatives of this PDF Eq. 4.41 with respect to each of the m parameters in U, and equate each derivative to zero, which is:

$$\frac{\partial}{\partial U}\left[p_{X|U}(X|U)p_U(U)\right] = 0 \tag{4.45}$$

The MAP estimate $\hat{U}$ will be the solution vector U of these m equations. To show an example of this estimate, we will assume both of the PDFs in Eq. 4.45 have Gaussian distributions (which we must *know* before we can perform the differentiation). We use Eq. 4.31 for the conditional PDF $p_{X|U}(X|U)$, and we define the Gaussian PDF of U as:

$$p_U(U) = \frac{1}{(2\pi)^{\frac{m}{2}} \prod_{j=1}^{m} \tau_j} e^{-\frac{1}{2}\sum_{j=1}^{m}\frac{(u_j - u_{oj})^2}{\tau_j^2}} \tag{4.46}$$

where the mean values are u_{oj}, and the variances are τ_j^2. If we substitute these two Gaussian PDFs into Eq. 4.45 and do the indicated differentiation with respect to each component of U, we get the following result:

$$\left[\frac{\partial G(U)}{\partial U}\right]^t W[X_o - G(U)] = Q(U - U_o) \tag{4.47}$$

where, as before, W is a real diagonal weighting matrix with elements $1/\sigma_k^2$. We now have a *second* diagonal weighting matrix Q, with elements $1/\tau_j^2$.

Compare Eq. 4.47 to the maximum likelihood solution given by Eq. 4.34. These two methods give identical solutions *if* the elements of Q are very *small* (meaning large variance values on all parameters), which corresponds to a nearly constant PDF for U (meaning little *a priori* knowledge of any *preferred* values for U). When $p_U(U)$ becomes an infinitesimal constant, the conditional PDF for U, given in Eq. 4.41 becomes:

$$p_{U|X}(U|X_o) = \frac{p_{X|U}(X_o|U)}{\displaystyle\int_{-\infty}^{\infty} p_{X|U}(X_o|U)dU} \tag{4.48}$$

In contrast, if the elements of Q become very large, meaning the PDF for U is very concentrated around the selected mean U_o, then the solution for Eq. 4.47 approaches $U = \hat{U} \approx U_o$. Here is a self-fulfilling prophecy because if we *assume* the solution is U_o by virtue of the choice of the *a priori* PDF for U, then indeed the solution *turns out* to be U_o.

As we found for the least-squares and the maximum likelihood estimates, when the parameter space is *linear* in all of the parameter values, we can write $G(U) = TU$ (with co-incident origins for X and U), and then we can solve Eq. 4.47 in closed form. The linearized version of Eq. 4.47 becomes:

$$(T'WT + Q)\, U = T'WX_o + Q\, U_o \tag{4.49}$$

The solution for this linearized MAP estimate is:

$$\hat{U} = (T'WT + Q)^{-1}\, (T'WX_o + Q\, U_o) \tag{4.50}$$

If we set $Q = 0$, we get the linearized estimate for *either* the maximum likelihood method *or* the weighted least-squares method, at least for Gaussian PDFs. If we *also* set $W = I$, we get the linearized least-squares solution.

The expected value of this parameter estimate is:

$$E[\hat{U}] = (T'WT + Q)^{-1}\, (T'WE[X_o] + Q\, U_o) \tag{4.51}$$

For $Q = 0$ and $E[X_o] = E[G(U)] = TE[U]$, we find $E[\hat{U}] = E[U]$, so the estimate is *unbiased* if the original observation noise is unbiased. For large Q, we find the expected value of the estimate approaches U_o, as we would anticipate.

By subtracting Eq. 4.51 from Eq. 4.50, we get a *zero mean random vector* in the parameter estimates, from which we can calculate the *covariance matrix* for the *parameters*. The *diagonals* of the covariance matrix are the *variances* on each parameter estimate, and the off-diagonal elements are related to the *cross*-correlation between different parameters. We can write:

$$\hat{U} - E[\hat{U}] = (T'WT + Q)^{-1}T'W(X_o - E[X_o]) \tag{4.52}$$

The *covariance matrix* is defined as the *expected value* of the *outer* vector product of a *zero mean* random vector times its conjugate transpose. The covariance matrices for $\hat{U}$ and X_o are therefore defined as follows (where ^{T} denotes the conjugate transpose):

$$\text{cov}(\hat{U}) = E[(\hat{U} - E[\hat{U}])\, (\hat{U}^T - E[\hat{U}^T])] \tag{4.53}$$

$$\text{cov}(X_o) = E[(X_o - E[X_o])\, (X_o^T - E[X_o^T])] \tag{4.54}$$

Using these definitions in conjunction with Eq. 4.52 gives:

$$\text{cov}(\hat{U}) = (T'WT + Q)^{-1}\, T'W\, \text{cov}\,(X_o)WT * (T^TWT* + Q)^{-1} \tag{4.55}$$

Given the covariance between the components of our observation vector X_o, along with our linear measurement model described by T and the two weighting matrices W and Q, we can calculate the covariance between the components of our estimated (or measured) parameters using equation 4.55. If the set of *observations* are uncorrelated, then the corresponding covariance matrix cov(X_o) will be diagonal, with the variances of each observation *on* the diagonal. A similar statement applies to the *parameter* estimates and their associated covariance matrix cov($\hat{U}$). We get the matrix of *correlation coefficients* for either case by dividing each row *and* column by the square root of the diagonal element (standard deviation) for *that* row and column.

Of course, these expressions only apply to *linear* parameter spaces. The corresponding results for *nonlinear* parameter spaces are generally more complicated.

Figure 4–8 shows the *a posteriori* PDF for the parameters as a *cloud of points confined* to the *parameter surface*. Compare this PDF to the one shown in Figure 4–3. Bayes theorem essentially *maps* the observation *n*-space PDF of Figure 4–3 into the parameter *m*-space PDF of Figure 4–8 below. All estimation methods based upon Bayes theorem use only the *parameter* subspace PDF.

There is one *caveat* we should emphasize about the use of Bayes theorem in estimating parameter values. The choice you make for the PDF of the parameters $p_U(U)$ will *influence* the estimate for these parameter values. If you are *sure* of your choice, fine, but if you simply *guess* at the proper PDF for *U*, the estimates may become a *self-fulfilling prophecy*. The answers you get may be what you *want* or *expect*, but they may *not* be correct. It is easy to misuse these methods in cases for which they were not designed.

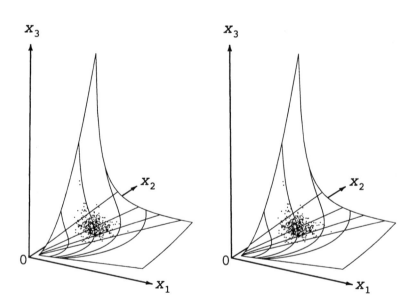

Figure 4–8 *A Posteriori* PDF of Parameters (Within Parameter Space)

4.7   SEQUENTIAL ESTIMATION

There are times when you would like to *begin* with a crude parameter estimate and then *refine* that estimate as more data is collected. Our goal is to update these estimates without *completely* recalculating all of the relevant matrix and vector quantities for *each new* set of data. We will only show this procedure for cases where the measurement model is *linear* in the parameters, because the general case is often rather complicated. Four of the estimation methods we have discussed lend themselves to this linearized sequential approach (least-squares, weighted least-squares, maximum likelihood, and MAP). If we derive this procedure for the MAP estimate given in Eq. 4.50 then we can readily obtain corresponding results for the other methods.

First, we need a few definitions. The *new* incremental observation vector will be called ΔX_o, and the corresponding incremental corrections to the parameter vector estimate will be called $\Delta \hat{U}$. We also need additional terms in T, called ΔT, which describe the additional elements of T and extra terms ΔW in the weighting matrix W to apply to the new observations. These extra terms in T can be calculated ahead of time and do *not* depend upon the new observations. The extra terms in W typically depend upon the variances we expect on the new observations, but would also be precalculated in most cases. The dimensionality of the observation space *increases* by the number of elements in ΔX_o, but the dimensionality of the parameter subspace remains *unchanged*.

We can write *two* versions of Eq. 4.49, one for the current estimate and one for the updated estimate, as follows:

$$(T'WT + Q)\,\hat{U} = T'WX_o + QU_o \tag{4.56}$$

$$(T'WT + \Delta T'\Delta W \Delta T + Q)\,(\hat{U} + \Delta \hat{U}) = T'WX_o + \Delta T'\Delta W \Delta X_o + QU_o \tag{4.57}$$

Now, we subtract the first expression from the second and solve for $\Delta \hat{U}$, giving:

$$\Delta \hat{U} = (T'WT + \Delta T'\Delta W \Delta T + Q)^{-1}\Delta T'\Delta W\,(\Delta X_o - \Delta T\hat{U}) \tag{4.58}$$

This parameter vector update depends on *both* the incremental *new data* ΔX_o and the *old* parameter estimate $\hat{U}$. If the new observations *exactly* fit the predictions of the old parameter set, then the parameter corrections will be *zero* because $\Delta X_o = \Delta T\hat{U}$. (recall that for *no noise*, $X_o = G(\hat{U}) = T\hat{U}$). Otherwise, the parameter vector will be updated to reflect the new data.

It appears that a new matrix *inverse* is required in Eq. 4.58 for *each* new data increment. However, there is a way to limit the size of this matrix to the *number* of new observations, by means of the *Sherman-Morrison-Woodbury* matrix identity:

$$(A + BD^{-1}C)^{-1} = A^{-1} - A^{-1}B\,(D + CA^{-1}B)^{-1}CA^{-1} \tag{4.59}$$

Once A is inverted, the inverse of $(A + BD^{-1}C)$ can be obtained from the inverse of $(D + CA^{-1}B)$. In Eq. 4.58, the matrix to be inverted is $m \times m$ in size, but if only r new data points are appended to the estimate (where $r < m$), we can use Eq. 4.59 to reduce the size of this matrix inverse to $r \times r$. If $r = 1$, this matrix inverse becomes the *reciprocal* of a *scalar* quantity. We make the substitutions:

$$A = T'WT + Q \quad (m \times m)$$

$$B = \Delta T' \quad (m \times r)$$

$$C = \Delta T \quad (r \times m)$$

$$D = \Delta W^{-1} \quad (r \times r)$$

After a little algebra, can write:

$$\Delta \hat{U} = \Delta S (\Delta X_o - \Delta T \hat{U}) \quad \text{and} \tag{4.60}$$

$$\hat{U} + \Delta \hat{U} = \hat{U} + \Delta S(\Delta X_o - \Delta T \hat{U}) \tag{4.61}$$

$$= (I - \Delta S \Delta T)\hat{U} + \Delta S \Delta X_o \tag{4.62}$$

where

$$\Delta S = \Delta V(I + \Delta T \Delta V)^{-1} \quad (m \times r) \tag{4.63}$$

$$\Delta V = (T'WT + Q)^{-1} \Delta T' \Delta W \quad (m \times r) \tag{4.64}$$

We can also write the *updated* version of $(T'WT + Q)^{-1}$ as:

$$(T'WT + \Delta T' \Delta W \Delta T + Q)^{-1} = (I - \Delta S \Delta T)(T'WT + Q)^{-1} \tag{4.65}$$

The only required *new* matrix inverse is the one in Eq. 4.63, which is $r \times r$ in size, and hence relatively small, especially when $r = 1$. Since most of these quantities are independent of both the new observation data and the old parameter estimate, they can be precalculated, if desired.

The parameter m-vector upgrade $\Delta \hat{U}$ involves two matrix-vector products (both with the r *new* observations and with the *old* parameter m-vector), comprising only $2mr$ (complex) multiplications and r subtractions, while the upgrade in Eq. 4.65 requires only the *product* of a pair of $m \times m$ matrices (which can also be precalculated because they are independent of the observation data).

Equation Eq. 4.60 is the *sequential linearized MAP estimate update,* and the resulting $\hat{U} + \Delta \hat{U}$ is *equivalent* to the *non*sequential or batch estimate given by Eq. 4.50. To get the maximum likelihood sequential estimate or the weighted least-squares sequential estimate, we set $Q = 0$, and to get the least-squares sequential estimate, we also set $W = I$ and $\Delta W = I$.

The covariance matrix for $\hat{U}$ is given by Eq. 4.55. For sequential estimation, we would *also* like to update this covariance matrix in a *sequential* manner. The calculation is similar to that used above to obtain the updated parameter vector, giving:

$$\text{cov}(\hat{U} + \Delta \hat{U}) = (I - \Delta S \Delta T) \text{cov}(\hat{U})(I - \Delta S \Delta T)^T + \Delta S \text{cov}(\Delta X_o) \Delta S^T \tag{4.66}$$

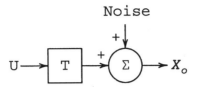

Figure 4–9   Linear System Model

We diagram the linear system model and this sequential estimation technique in Figures 4–9 above and 4–10 below.

In Figure 4–10, we have added a delay element denoted by a/z. This sequential estimator processes data sampled in the time domain at intervals of Δt seconds, so it is appropriate to use the z-transform to represent a unit of delay (given by z^{-1}). Recall that the Laplace domain representation is $z = \exp(s\Delta t)$.

When $a = 1$, we have an ideal integrator that produces exactly the same estimate of the elements of $\hat{U}$ as the original nonsequential form. However, by allowing a to be less than unity (but positive), we introduce a *lowpass filter,* which weights the most recent time samples heavier than earlier samples. The estimator tends to "forget" the effects of earlier observations and therefore allows the algorithm to "track" slowly varying parameters. The impulse response of this filter in the time domain is such that successive time samples are multiplied by successively higher powers of a. In particular, we have:

$$\hat{U} + \Delta\hat{U} = \frac{\Delta\hat{U}}{1 - az^{-1}} \quad , \quad \text{so} \tag{4.67}$$

$$\hat{U} + \Delta\hat{U} = \Delta\hat{U}\sum_{k=0}^{\infty} a^k z^{-k} \tag{4.68}$$

The lowpass filter pole occurs at $z = a$, or at $s = (\ln a)/\Delta t$. The estimator will tend to track any parameter components with angular frequencies less than this pole value.

We can see from Figure 4–10 that the sequential estimator attempts to predict the next ΔX_o sample from the currently estimated parameter vector $\hat{U}$, by means of the incre-

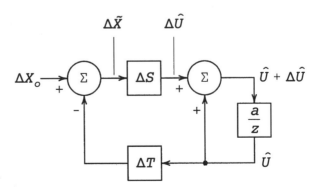

Figure 4–10   Sequential Estimator

mental model matrix ΔT, thus forming a prediction error $\Delta \tilde{X} = \Delta X_o - \Delta T \hat{U}$. This error is then multiplied by a gain matrix ΔS to obtain an incremental correction $\Delta \hat{U}$ to the parameter estimate. The correction is then added to the old parameter estimate $\hat{U}$ to get an updated estimate. If the predicted value of ΔX_o is correct, then the old parameter vector is retained without correction.

4.8   THE KALMAN FILTER

There is a popular class of linear sequential estimators generically called *Kalman filters*, which are subsets of the procedure we have just discussed. These are used primarily to estimate the mean value of a signal or waveform at a point in time, based upon some *previous* set of time domain observations. The model for this estimator is usually some linear filter (often called the "plant"), and the parameter to be adjusted is usually the *gain* of the filter, so that the *mean value* of the observed time waveform is "tracked" by the filter. There are also *extended* Kalman filters that allow *nonlinear* elements in the system model, and/or *non*-Gaussian noise statistics on the internal noise sources. However, as you might expect for nonlinear estimators, the computational load is greatly increased for these extended filters.

Kalman filters are interesting and useful sequential estimators for many applications involving *linear* time domain models, and we can mold the general sequential estimator into the Kalman form in a simple way. First, we set $Q = 0$ to eliminate any preferred parameter values. Then we make the model matrix T (as well as ΔT) into a convolution matrix (which will be of Toeplitz form), forcing the parameter vector to be a time waveform. The gain matrix ΔS (also called K) adjusts the estimate to make the mean value of the error vector (also called the *innovation vector*) as near zero as possible. This, in turn, minimizes the second moment of the error vector, leaving only its variance. There is a vast amount of existing literature devoted to Kalman filters, so we will not pursue this subject any further in this book. See references [4:3] and [4:4] for more details.

4.9   GENERAL COMMENTS ON ESTIMATION METHODS

Among the estimation methods we have discussed, the least-squares method requires the *least* information about the noise perturbations, namely none at *all*. The weighted least-squares method *can* be used without any noise information as well, but it often does a better job if the *variances* on each observation component are known, and used. The maximum likelihood estimation (MLE) procedure requires a knowledge of the *joint PDF* of the observation vector, so the *maximum* point can be found. The Bayes mean-squared-error (BMSE) method requires knowledge of the mean value of the *a posteriori* parameter PDF, which involves the joint PDF of the observations, as well as a knowledge of the *a priori* joint PDF of all of the parameters. The MAP estimate requires *about* the same information as the BMSE technique, except only the maximum point (*mode*) of the *a posteriori* parameter PDF is needed, rather than the mean value.

There is no "best" estimation algorithm for *all* situations. The results are more accurate if you use all of the *prior* information you have about the noise sources *and* the parameter values, but do not try to use methods that require this extra information if you do *not* have it. Otherwise, you will tend to get answers you may *want*, but they might not be the *best* answers.

Sometimes the measurement model is *linear* in the parameters, either because the system in question is inherently linear, or because the system has been defined to be *locally* linear during the process of iterating towards the solution of a *nonlinear* system. In the linear case, many of the estimates can be obtained in closed form by means of matrix-vector operations.

We have, so far, not discussed the questions of *bias* and *minimum variance* to any extent in our parameter estimates. All of the estimation methods we have mentioned can be biased, and the variances on each estimated value may *not* have their minimum possible values. Often, the variance can be *reduced* by allowing the bias to *increase*, and vice versa. It can sometimes be difficult to construct an estimation algorithm that gives *both* zero bias *and* minimum variance simultaneously. Much of the literature on estimation theory is centered around the bias and variance properties of various algorithms, and there is usually a great *emphasis* on finding the "optimum" estimators for each situation (in which the bias is zero and the variance is the minimum possible value).

Unfortunately, these optimum estimators tend to be hard to find, and they may not even *exist*. In many practical cases, the computation required to realize these optimum techniques is unreasonably *heavy*, and some loss of "optimality" may not really be *that* important. The *zero bias* property is often more important than that of minimum variance, because the variance can nearly always be reduced by further averaging using additional data. If there is a significant bias, this additional averaging will *not* remove it, and it may eventually cause unacceptable errors in the measurement. Of course, if the bias is small enough, it can be ignored. There is no substitute for *knowing* the levels of both bias and variance in the measured results, so you can decide if they are important for your application or not. There is very little reason to make measurements that are far *better* than you need, because this tends to be a waste of valuable time.

We can estimate the variance either by making many sets of observations or by calculating this quantity from our measurement model. The biases are best calculated from the model because it may not be practical to collect enough actual data to reduce the noise sufficiently to *show* any bias values with adequate accuracy. Our ultimate goal is to calculate confidence intervals for each parameter, for some specified set of confidence levels. Again, the measurement model is generally the most feasible way to obtain this information.

There is a question that arises fairly often as to whether it is best to estimate parameters in *one* step, using all of the observations that are available, or to collect a few observations with which to calculate some *initial* parameter values, and then to repeat this process until the observations are *all* included. There may be several factors that dictate the best answer. Is the processing time (in your computer) smaller for one method than for the other? Do you want *some* crude results as soon as possible, and then allow these results to improve with time? In the case of nonlinear models, is the nonlinearity easier to handle computationally for one method compared to the other? Is the bias and/or variance in the final parameters better in one case than in the other? You will have to consider these various factors for your particular measurement, because a general answer cannot be given. However, having *said* that, there are a few characteristics that may help in making your decision.

For linear measurement models, the statistics (mean, bias, variance, PDF, confidence intervals, etc.) are *independent* of the number or sizes of any *sub*-estimates. In section 4.7, we discussed sequential estimation techniques, where we simply use *portions* of the T, W, and X_o matrices (or vectors) for each sequential estimate, but ultimately, the final calculation combines these portions to give exactly the *same* parameter estimates we would get if we made the estimate using all of the observations at *once*.

For nonlinear models the answer is not so easy. It is possible to construct sequential estimation algorithms for nonlinear models, but the nonlinearity may affect the *statistics* of the resulting parameter estimates in different ways, depending on where the nonlinearity appears in the procedure. As a rule, it is *best* to reduce the noise on an estimate as much as possible *before* a nonlinearity is introduced. Passing a random variable through a nonlinear element often introduces some bias, and it also changes the shape of the PDF. This means the variance will change, and it may be either larger or smaller.

For example, we found in section 3.4 in chapter 3 that a frequency response function has an *infinite* variance if it is calculated as the quotient of two Gaussian random variables. However, if the numerator *and* denominator are both multiplied by the complex conjugate of the denominator, and *both* numerator and denominator are averaged separately *before* the division, the variance becomes finite. Thus, for this example, it is *always* best to estimate the numerator and denominator separately, using all of the available observations, and then to apply the division nonlinearity as the *last* step.

In contrast, if the PDF on the observations has an exponential form, meaning there are large noise spikes in *one* direction (like the output from a photomultiplier tube at low light levels, for example), it is often best to *clip* this signal to reduce the variance caused by these large spikes, *before* the observations are subsequently used. As a matter of fact, for *non*-Gaussian noise superimposed on some very *small* signal, there exists an *optimum nonlinearity* that will *maximize* the signal-to-noise ratio.

4.10   SUMMARY OF ESTIMATION TECHNIQUES

Our goal in this chapter is to discuss various "best" ways to estimate the values of the parameters in our measurement model, *given* some finite amount of data that we have collected. It is somewhat heretical to refer to our measurement as a *guess*, so we attempt to place the *art* of measuring on a "firm" mathematical foundation by using the concepts of *estimation theory*. We hope to *quantify* the probable errors in our measurements or estimates, so we can subsequently *use* this information in some practical applications.

There are several textbooks on estimation theory, but they tend to be heavy on mathematics and light on concepts and explanations. As we said in the introduction to this book, it is important to be able to "walk" with *one* foot in the mathematical world of our measurement model and the *other* foot in our physical world of practical applications. Many of the equations in this chapter look rather complicated, but most of these have a relatively simple geometrical interpretation, and they *usually* represent a relatively simple concept, so we especially want to perform this kind of balancing act between theory and practice in this chapter.

We introduce the concept of an abstract *multi*dimensional vector space, in which *each* set of n related observations appear as a *single point* in an n-dimensional *observation space*. Embedded *within* this space is an m-dimensional *subspace* defined by our measurement model ($m \leq n$), which comprises the m model parameters we want to measure. In general, our *observation* point will be *exterior* to the parameter subspace, so the estimation problem is to select the point *within* the parameter subspace that "best" corresponds to this *wild* observation point. We find in many cases the definition of best is neither obvious nor well defined.

Among the many standard methods of estimating parameters, we have chosen to discuss five, namely, (1) least-squares estimation (LSE), (2) weighted least-squares estimation (WLSE), (4) maximum likelihood estimation (MLE), (3) Bayesian mean-squared error estimation (BMSE), and (5) maximum *a posteriori* estimation (MAP). The mathematical definitions of these methods are given, but they are also explained in terms of our abstract observation and parameter spaces. We also briefly discuss *sequential estimation* techniques, which are useful if the observations are obtained sequentially over some interval of time. This allows you to begin with rather crude parameter estimates, and then to *upgrade* these estimates as you collect additional data.

As an example to clarify these concepts, we show how to estimate the two parameters (the *pole* location and the *residue* at the pole) of a *single-pole transfer function* (in the Laplace domain) by observing three noisy points on the corresponding frequency response function.

It is important to make the best possible measurements and to characterize the accuracy of this information as *well* as possible, but it is easy to get carried away with the mathematical techniques and the geometrical abstractions that are rampant in this field, and to imagine a degree of precision in your final results that may not be entirely *justified*. Among the five estimation methods we discuss, none of them do a *perfect* job, and yet all of them *usually* give reasonably good results. Keep in mind this is *not* a precise field of activity, but it often tends to *look* that way because of the imposing equations and the special "buzzwords" which abound. The very nature of the phrase "estimation theory" is something of an oxymoron. You should not be overly intimidated by the vast amount of literature, or by the many claims of *optimality* in this field.

BIBLIOGRAPHY ON ESTIMATION THEORY

[4:1]   Deutsch, R., *Estimation Theory,* Prentice-Hall, 1965. A rather old reference on estimation theory, but still good.

[4:2]   Gelb, Arther, Editor, *Applied Optimal Estimation,* The Analytic Sciences Corp., The M.I.T. Press, 1974.

[4:3] Kalman, R. E., A New Approach to Linear Filtering and Prediction Problems, *Transactions of the ASME Journal of Basic Engineering,* March, 1960, pp. 35-45.

[4:4] Kay, Steven M., *Fundamentals of Statistical Signal Processing—Estimation Theory,* Prentice-Hall, 1993. An up-to-date treatise on estimation theory with words of explanation in between the equations. Also discusses several other estimation techniques, including Wiener and Kalman filtering.

[4:5] Miller, James H., and Thomas, John B., "Detectors for Discrete-Time Signals in Non-Gaussian Noise," *IEEE Transactions on Information Theory, IT-18* (2), Mar. 1972, pp. 241–250.

CHAPTER 5

A Few Examples in More Detail

5.1 PREVIEW OF FOUR EXAMPLES

As mentioned in the Preface, we have selected four examples of measurements of varying difficulty to illustrate the concepts we have discussed so far. All four examples involve *nonlinear* estimation equations, although the first three examples are *linear* systems in the sense that their behavior is described by linear differential equations in time. The *first* example involves the measurement of the DC resistance of a battery or power supply. This would seem to be one of the simplest measurements you might encounter, but we will see that looks *can* be deceiving. The *second* example, a control system measurement, is more typical of the measurements you are likely to confront and uses a linear *approximation* to a nonlinear measurement model. The *third* example is a mechanical problem requiring the measurement of the *modal* parameters of a vibrating mechanical structure (the parameters are complex *modal vectors* and *pole* values). This is similar to the control system, but involves a more complicated model, including *double* poles and an *asymmetric* system matrix. The *fourth* example is the measurement of *position* coordinates using the Global Positioning System (GPS) with Earth-orbiting satellites. Even though this comprises a nonlinear measurement model, a *closed form* solution does exist.

These four examples are in different fields of activity, and seem to be different in their basic nature, but they *all* fit into the measurement structure we have established in the earlier chapters. Unfortunately, in a small book such as this, it is not practical to discuss examples from a large number of diverse fields, but we *have* described several *tools* in previous chapters that you can use in attacking your own unique measurement tasks. Just keep in mind the buzzwords may be different in each field, but the underlying *concepts* of measuring are universal.

5.2   MEASURING THE DC RESISTANCE OF A BATTERY

We established a measurement model for this example in section 2.3 of chapter 2, and we wrote the corresponding model equation in Eq. 2.1. For easy reference, we reproduce the two associated Figures 5–1 and 5–2 and Eq. 5.1 below. The model equation describing the measurement is:

$$E_x = A_x \left[(E + I_x R + N_o) \frac{R_x}{R + R_x} + N_x \right] \tag{5.1}$$

The *primary* parameter to be measured is R, but we will include E as a *secondary* parameter because *it* may not be known accurately enough to use in this equation. These *two* parameters must be measured *simultaneously* in order to get accurate values for *either* of them individually. We can use any combination of R_x and/or I_x to excite the system, but we must use at least *two* different sets of (R_x, I_x) excitation values, since there are *two* parameter values to be estimated. Our observations are strictly of the output voltage E_x, which we will simply call x in the following discussion.

With two unknowns, the parameter space will be *two*-dimensional, but we will need *more* than two observations, since we have noise sources N_o and N_x that will perturb our data. This does *not* mean every excitation must be different, but there must be at least *two* different *sets* of excitation values in the measurement. For the *kth* observation, corresponding to excitation values R_{xk} and I_{xk}, we will observe or read E_{xk}, and this will become a *new* coordinate x_k in our k-dimensional *observation* space. Notice E_x is a *nonlinear* function of R (although a linear function of E), so our parameter subspace will *not* be a linear plane surface.

Recall the parameter subspace is obtained from the measurement model equations by setting all *noise* sources to zero. In our three-dimensional observation space, the resulting set of parametric equations describing the parameter surface are:

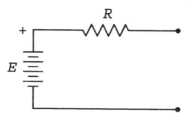

Figure 5–1   Simple Battery Model

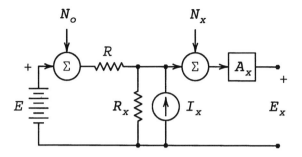

Figure 5–2   DC Measurement Model

$$x_1(R,E) = (E + I_{x1}R)\,\frac{A_x R_{x1}}{R + R_{x1}} \tag{5.2}$$

$$x_2(R,E) = (E + I_{x2}R)\,\frac{A_x R_{x2}}{R + R_{x2}} \tag{5.3}$$

$$x_3(R,E) = (E + I_{x3}R)\,\frac{A_x R_{x3}}{R + R_{x3}} \tag{5.4}$$

We can use the first two equations Eqs. 5.2 and 5.3 to solve for R and E and then substitute these parameters into the third equation Eq. 5.4 to get the third coordinate value. We obtain:

$$R = \frac{x_2 - x_1}{\left(\dfrac{x_1}{R_{x1}} - A_x I_{x1}\right) - \left(\dfrac{x_2}{R_{x2}} - A_x I_{x2}\right)} \tag{5.5}$$

$$E = \frac{1}{A_x}\,\frac{x_2\left(\dfrac{x_1}{R_{x1}} - A_x I_{x1}\right) - x_1\left(\dfrac{x_2}{R_{x2}} - A_x I_{x2}\right)}{\left(\dfrac{x_1}{R_{x1}} - A_x I_{x1}\right) - \left(\dfrac{x_2}{R_{x2}} - A_x I_{x2}\right)} \tag{5.6}$$

$$x_3(x_1,x_2) = \frac{x_2\left(\dfrac{x_1}{R_{x1}} - A_x I_{x1} + A_x I_{x3}\right) - x_1\left(\dfrac{x_2}{R_{x2}} - A_x I_{x2} + A_x I_{x3}\right)}{\left(\dfrac{x_1}{R_{x1}} - \dfrac{x_1}{R_{x3}} - A_x I_{x1}\right) - \left(\dfrac{x_2}{R_{x2}} - \dfrac{x_2}{R_{x3}} - A_x I_{x2}\right)} \tag{5.7}$$

We will *illustrate* this 2-D parameter surface embedded in a 3-D observation space, but for better accuracy we will *derive* the estimation equations for an n-dimensional observation space.

In this example, the shape of the parameter subspace depends on the *input excitation*, as well as on the two parameters of interest. Contrast this to the single-pole frequency response measurement that we discussed in chapter 4 (see Eq. 4.12 and Figure 4–4), where the input excitation was *removed* from consideration by the definition of a frequency response or transfer function. In the present example, we allow combinations of two kinds of inputs, either changes in the load resistance R_x or the injection of a test current I_x (or both). We make three observations of the battery terminal voltage, under the three input conditions listed below (we assume $A_x = 1$ in all cases).

1. For the x_1 observation: $R_{x1} = 0.5, I_{x1} = 10$
2. For the x_2 observation: $R_{x2} = 0.5, I_{x2} = -10$
3. For the x_3 observation: $R_{x3} = 1, I_{x3} = 0$

Figure 5–3 shows the parameter subspace described by Eq. 5.7.

Using Eqs. 5.5 and 5.6, we can replace the observation space coordinates projected into the parameter subspace by coordinates of constant *parameter values*. This view is shown in Figure 5–4, where constant R contours are the lines going upward and to the right, and constant E contours are those going upward and to the left. The line for $R = 0$ is the one that begins at the origin.

The five constant R contours range between 0 and 2 with an increment of 0.5, and the five constant E contours go from 5 to 21 with an increment of 4. The parameter surface ranges between 0 and 15 in both x_1 and x_2 directions. Notice these two sets of contours become *collinear* for sufficiently large values of E and R, meaning they asymptotically approach parallel straight lines.

Let's assume both noise sources N_o and N_x have Gaussian probability density functions with zero mean values, and are independent of one another. We define the variances to be σ_o^2 and σ_1^2, respectively. Since the model Eq. 5.1 is linear in both noise sources, we know the noise on the observations E_x will also have a Gaussian shape with a composite variance of:

$$\sigma_x^2 = \sigma_o^2 \left(\frac{A_x R_x}{R + R_x} \right)^2 + A_x^2 \sigma_1^2 \tag{5.8}$$

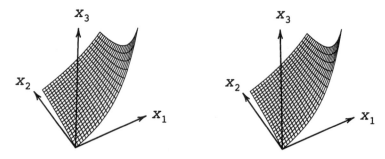

Figure 5–3   Parameter Space for R and E

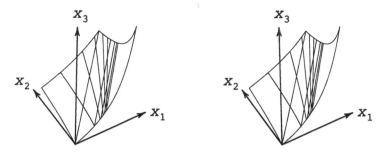

Figure 5–4   Coordinates of Constant R and E

Note that this variance is a function of the parameter R, so we actually will not *know* this final value until we finish the measurement. However, in practice $R \ll R_x$, so we can begin with a good *approximation* of this quantity.

In Figure 5–5, we show a cluster of 300 observation points around the *correct point* ($R = 0.2$ and $E = 13$) on the parameter surface. This is Gaussian noise with a variance of unity.

In a practical measurement, we will read *three* values of E_x (or x), thereby getting only *one* of the points in the cluster, and from that one point we must decide the "closest" pair of parameter values *on* the parameter surface. Since we are assuming Gaussian noise, we know from chapter 4 that both a weighted least-squares estimation method and a maximum likelihood method will yield the same results. We do not really know anything about the ranges or probabilities of the two parameter values, so we should *not* use any methods based on Bayes theorem. We are also assuming the variance is the same on all observations, so we have no need to use a weighting function.

The best solution to our measurement problem is probably the least-squares formulation given by Eq. 4.19 in chapter 4. The parameter vector U has the two components R and E, and the measurement model vector $G(U)$ comprises the three components (x_1, x_2, x_3) given by Eqs. 5.2 through 5.4. The observation vector X_o comprises the three

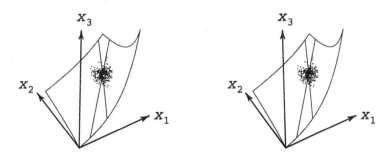

Figure 5–5   300 Noisy Observation Points

components (x_{o1}, x_{o2}, x_{o3}). The components of the partial derivative matrix can be readily obtained by differentiating the elements of G with respect to both parameters. We show these quantities below.

$$G(U) = A_x \begin{bmatrix} \dfrac{R_{x1}\,(E + I_{x1}R)}{R + R_{x1}} \\[2ex] \dfrac{R_{x2}\,(E + I_{x2}R)}{R + R_{x2}} \\[2ex] \dfrac{R_{x3}\,(E + I_{x3}R)}{R + R_{x3}} \end{bmatrix} \tag{5.9}$$

$$\left[\frac{\partial G(U)}{\partial U} \right]^t = A_x \begin{bmatrix} \dfrac{R_{x1}\,(I_{x1}R_{x1} - E)}{(R + R_{x1})^2} & \dfrac{R_{x2}\,(I_{x2}R_{x2} - E)}{(R + R_{x2})^2} & \dfrac{R_{x3}\,(I_{x3}R_{x3} - E)}{(R + R_{x3})^2} \\[3ex] \dfrac{R_{x1}}{R + R_{x1}} & \dfrac{R_{x2}}{R + R_{x2}} & \dfrac{R_{x3}}{R + R_{x3}} \end{bmatrix} \tag{5.10}$$

Recall, each row of Eq. 5.10 is a transposed tangent vector at a point *in* the parameter subspace. Thus, our least-squares solution will be the subspace *point* where a *perpendicular* vector passes through the *observation* point X_o. We will repeat Eq. 4.19 below, for reference.

$$\left[\frac{\partial G(U)}{\partial U} \right]^t X_o = \left[\frac{\partial G(U)}{\partial U} \right]^t G(U) \tag{5.11}$$

Probably the best way to solve a set of nonlinear equations like these is to form a *linearized* version of $G(U)$, as indicated in Eq. 4.20, *but* to leave the partial derivative matrix *as is*, in its nonlinear form. If the partial derivative matrix is obtained from the linearized version of $G(U)$, then the tangent plane to the parameter subspace will sometimes have the wrong slope, which can throw the iterative solution off considerably.

Initial *trial* values for the parameters are inserted, and the resulting equation is then solved in a manner similar to Eq. 4.22. The newly calculated parameter values are substituted back into the *original* matrices to obtain a new set of element values. If this process is continued, the solution will usually converge to the correct values. Basically, the initial parameter values must be sufficiently close to the final solution so successive iterations give *better* solutions each time. If the equations are heavily nonlinear, then the initial starting values must be fairly close to the correct values. For *mildly* nonlinear behavior, the starting values tend not to be very critical.

In our example, the battery resistance R is generally very small relative to any normal value of load resistance R_x, so this iterative method will work fine. Our linearized model can be represented by $G(U) \approx TU$, where T is a matrix of constants given by:

$$T = A_x \begin{bmatrix} \dfrac{I_{x1}R_{x1}}{R + R_{x1}} & \dfrac{R_{x1}}{R + R_{x1}} \\[2ex] \dfrac{I_{x2}R_{x2}}{R + R_{x2}} & \dfrac{R_{x2}}{R + R_{x2}} \\[2ex] \dfrac{I_{x3}R_{x3}}{R + R_{x3}} & \dfrac{R_{x3}}{R + R_{x3}} \end{bmatrix} \tag{5.12}$$

Analogous to Eq. 4.22, we can write the approximate solution to Eq. 5.11 as:

$$\hat{U} \approx \left[\left(\frac{\partial G(U)}{\partial U} \right)^t T \right]^{-1} \left(\frac{\partial G(U)}{\partial U} \right)^t X_o \tag{5.13}$$

where $U^t = [R\ E]$, and $X_o^t = [x_{o1}\ x_{o2}\ x_{o3}]$. We hold R constant in the denominator of each element of Eq. 5.9 and Eq. 5.10 to get an initial representation for T, and we also hold E constant in each element of Eq. 5.10. We then substitute the elements of $\hat{U}$ from Eq. 5.13 back into Eq. 5.9 and 5.10 and repeat the procedure as many times as necessary to obtain a convergent solution.

If we *happened* to observe $X_o^t = [75/7\ 55/7\ 65/6]$, then we would get $\hat{U}^t = U^t = [0.2\ 13]$, which would be the *correct* result. However, due to noise, we expect to observe a somewhat different X_o. Let's say we actually observe:

$$X_o^t = \begin{bmatrix} 11 & 9 & 10 \end{bmatrix} \tag{5.14}$$

After seven iterations, we calculate $R = 0.08435$ and $E = 11.3771$. These are certainly *poor* approximations to the true values of $R = 0.2$ and $E = 13$, but this is *also* a very poor set of observations.

The way to extend this method of solution to *more* than three observations is readily apparent from Eq. 5.13 above. We simply append the additional observations to X_o and add corresponding rows to both $G(U)$ and T.

We now have a method for solving the least-squares equations for estimates of the parameter values, but since the observations are *random variables*, the parameter estimates will likewise be random variables. We would really like to know the PDF (probability density function) for *each* parameter estimate, *given* the PDF for the observations. In most nonlinear cases this is very difficult to calculate. Sometimes the best approach is to use *Monte Carlo* simulation, where random noise is added to the observations in a computer *simulation* of the measurement, and the corresponding noise in the parameter estimates are used to form approximations to the parameter PDFs and to the various parameter moments.

In practice, it is often adequate if we only determine the *bias* in the mean value and the *variance* of each parameter estimate. If there is no observation noise and the model is correct, then the observation point lies *within* the parameter subspace, and the estimates are *exact* solutions to the measurement model equations. This is true whether or *not* the model equations are linear in the parameters. In the presence of symmetrical noise (like zero mean Gaussian noise) on the observations, the least-squares solution is *still* unbiased, provided the measurement model is *linear* in the parameters, because the least-squares *projection* of the observation PDF onto each parameter contour is always a Gaussian PDF, with *no* intrinsic bias *due* to the projection.

However, this lack of bias is *not* valid if the model equation is nonlinear in one or more parameters, even when the additive observation noise *is* Gaussian with zero mean value. Furthermore, even if the model is linear in *most* of its parameters, it only takes *one* nonlinear parameter to sometimes influence the least-squares estimates of the remaining *linear* parameters. We can see this effect in the example that we discussed above. This *mixing* of the linear and nonlinear parameters occurs via the matrix inverse shown in Eq. 5.13, because the nonlinear *determinant* of the original matrix appears in the denominator of *all* elements of the inverse.

One of the most practical ways to determine the bias in these parameters is to use the Monte Carlo approach in a computer simulation, including the range of expected parameter values and observation noise. This is not very elegant from a mathematical perspective, but it is a *practical* method.

We would also like some measure of the *variance* on our parameter estimates, once we have settled on a best solution for their values. We can write an expression for the *covariance* of $\hat{U}$ from Eq. 5.13 by multiplying the expected value of the outer vector product of $\hat{U}$ minus its mean value times its conjugate transpose.

We get:

$$\text{cov}(\hat{U}) = \left[\left(\frac{\partial G(U)}{\partial U} \right)^t T \right]^{-1} \left(\frac{\partial G(U)}{\partial U} \right)^t \text{cov}(X_o) \left(\frac{\partial G(U)}{\partial U} \right)^* \left[T^T \left(\frac{\partial G(U)}{\partial U} \right)^* \right]^{-1} \quad (5.15)$$

For the above example where $\hat{U}^t = U^t = [0.2 \ 13]$ and the variance on each observation is given by Eq. 5.8, we get a parameter vector covariance of:

$$\text{cov}(\hat{U}) = \sigma_x^2 \begin{bmatrix} 0.014458 & 0 \\ 0 & 0.58314 \end{bmatrix} \quad (5.16)$$

The upper left element is the variance on R and the lower right element is the variance on E. Since the resistance value is smaller than the voltage value by a factor of 65, you might expect the ratio of variances to be related by the *square* of that factor. However, the terminal voltage observations are generally more sensitive to changes in *some* parameters than in others, so any additive noise in the system will affect the parameter estimates that *least* affect the voltage, *more* than the others. In this case, the battery resistance is determined by the difference between two relatively large terminal voltages, and it is also in parallel with the load resistance R_x, so we would expect its *coefficient of variation* (standard deviation divided by mean value) to be larger than *that* for E (it is larger by a factor of 10.235).

Since the *off-diagonal terms* in the covariance matrix are zero, there is no *cross-correlation* between the noise on the two parameter estimates. This seems rather surprising since it is apparent from Figure 5–5 that the two constant parameter contours are *not* orthogonal to one another at the solution point. The reason for this result is due to a fortuitous choice of the input excitation values for the three observations. In this case, the columns of T are orthogonal, and $\text{cov}(X_o) = \sigma_x^2 I$, so $\text{cov}(\hat{U})$ is diagonal. Generally, the noise on the various parameter estimates *will* be mutually correlated, at least to some extent.

We would like to see how the covariance matrix for the parameter estimates in Eq. 5.15 is *reduced* by including additional observations in the procedure. We intuitively feel the parameter variance values should be reduced by a factor of n as we include n times more observations in the estimate. Each matrix product involving the summation of n similar elements will introduce a factor of n into the resulting variance. So, each product of the partial derivative matrix with T introduces a factor of n into the denominator, and the factor to the left of $\text{cov}(X_o)$ times its conjugate introduces a single factor of n into the numerator. Thus, the covariance of the parameter estimates is *inversely* proportional to the number of observation points n.

This is easier to see in Eq. 5.13, where we get a factor of n in the denominator from the inverse matrix in brackets and a factor of $\sqrt{n}$ in the numerator from the multiplication with X_o, where the noise *sums* in a root-mean-square fashion (we assume the observation noise is uncorrelated between samples). The net result is that the noise on each parameter estimate is *reduced* by $\sqrt{n}$ if we make n observations.

There is another way to estimate these battery parameters, suggested by Eqs. 5.5 and 5.6, in which we solved the nonlinear equations for R and E using only *two* observations. We could solve for a *new pair* of (R,E) values each time we make a new observation and simply *average* these calculated parameter values together to get our final estimates. We still expect to get variance reductions by a factor of n for each parameter, since we are averaging that number of estimates together. This is equivalent in Figure 5–5 to projecting each observation point (x_{o1}, x_{o2}) into a horizontal parameter space (since we do not have a third observation coordinate x_{o3}).

However, this is *seldom* a good method because the observation noise enters via the denominators of both equations in the form of terms involving x_1 and x_2, and this noise becomes *distorted* by the division operation. This distortion mechanism introduces a *bias* in the parameter estimates that cannot be removed by averaging, and it also causes the noise PDF to change its shape. Even if the original observation noise was of Gaussian form, the parameter PDFs would *still* comprise additional distortion components. This might either increase or decrease the variance, but it would somewhat complicate the determination of *confidence intervals* for each parameter.

In contrast, the least-squares method that we discussed previously *reduces* the noise amplitude by $\sqrt{n}$ *before* any nonlinearities are encountered. Any bias that might result from such nonlinearities is likewise *reduced*, although there may still be *some* residual distortion in the PDFs.

Having *discounted* the value of this second measurement method, we will backtrack somewhat and point out that this method works fine if the nonlinearities and noise are sufficiently *small*, or if the system equations are actually *linear*. The question as to which method to use then becomes primarily a matter of relative computation times. One potential advantage of this method is that it is *sequential*, giving early estimates of both R and E, which then become more accurate as new observations are processed.

5.3   CLOSED-LOOP CONTROL SYSTEM MEASUREMENTS

We discussed *one* of many possible closed-loop control system measurement models in chapter 2, with a block diagram shown in Figure 2–3 and with the corresponding set of Eqs. 2.2 through 2.5. These are reproduced below as Figure 5–6 and Eqs. 5.17 through 5.20, for the reader's convenience.

The equations describing this model are:

$$X_1 = (S' + N_x)\frac{A_1 G_0}{1 + W} + A_1 N_1 \tag{5.17}$$

$$X_2 = S'\frac{A_2 W}{1 + W} - N_x\frac{A_2}{1 + W} + A_2 N_2 \tag{5.18}$$

$$S' = R - S - N_0 \tag{5.19}$$

$$W = GH \tag{5.20}$$

We also studied this measurement in chapter 3, section 3.4, where we derived an algorithm for processing many observations from this control system to get a *frequency response function*, from which we can proceed to estimate the parameters that describe the system. We reproduce Eqs. 3.36 through 3.38 from chapter 3 for the estimated frequency response function as Eqs. 5.21 through 5.23, for your convenience.

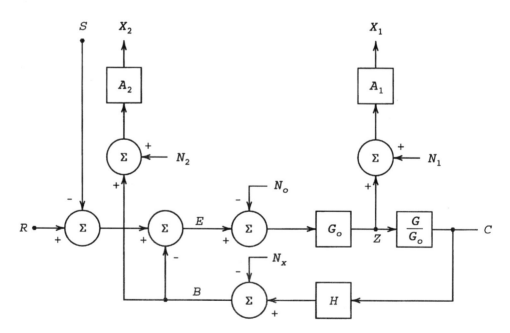

Figure 5–6   Typical Control System

$$\hat{W} = \frac{\overline{X_2 X_1^*} + \overline{|X_2|^2}}{\overline{|X_1|^2} + \overline{X_1 X_2^*}}$$ (5.21)

$$\hat{W} = \frac{A_2 W}{A_1 G_o} \left[1 - \frac{1 + W}{W} \frac{\overline{N_x S'^*}}{\sigma^2} + \frac{1 + W}{W} \frac{\overline{N_2 S'^*}}{\sigma^2} - \frac{1 + W}{G_o} \frac{\overline{N_1 S'^*}}{\sigma^2} \right]$$ (5.22)

where

$$\sigma^2 = \sigma_S^2 + \sigma_R^2 + \sigma_o^2$$ (5.23)

and σ_S^2, σ_R^2, and σ_o^2 are the respective variances of the three signals S, R, and N_o. We see σ^2 represents the variance (or power) in the *composite* input signal S'.

In this section, we will *simulate* the data obtained from a typical control system and will describe a weighted least-squares estimation algorithm that we can use to measure the control system parameter values. As in section 4.3 in chapter 4, our observation space will comprise samples of *frequency response functions*, and our measurement model will comprise the sum of several terms generally involving complex *poles*, and their corresponding complex *residues* in the *s*-plane.

Before getting into the details of the measurement procedure, we will *digress* somewhat and discuss the way a control system works and the way a designer *thinks* about the system parameters. We want to select a good control system *design* so our subsequent measurements will be typical of those actually encountered in practice.

In Figure 5–6, under ideal conditions the error E at the output of the primary summing junction is very small, so signal B is nearly identical to the input reference signal R, and the system output C is very nearly R/H. In practice, the error E may *not* always be so small, especially at high frequencies or during fast transient events. Due to phase lags or time delays in the loop, the tracking signal B tends to respond relatively *slowly* to changes in the input R, resulting in a sizable E waveform during these *catch-up* intervals. This effect can be counteracted to some extent by increasing the *loop gain* (at least at low and moderate frequencies), but if this is carried *too* far, the system will generally become *unstable* and will break into a sustained oscillation at some relatively high frequency. Once this happens, there can be a lot of damage to some components of the system. The *primary goal* of the control system designer is to make the system *track* the input as accurately (and as fast) as possible while maintaining sufficient margin in the parameters to prevent instabilities or system oscillation.

You could argue that all we *need* to measure is the behavior of the closed-loop system between the *input* terminal R and the *output* terminal C, without any concern for the values of the parameters *inside* of the loop. This may be suitable in some cases, but generally the designer (and the user) wants the ability to change the loop gain and to insert various *compensation networks* inside the loop to optimize the performance of the system, as well as to control the *margin of stability* of the system. This requires a detailed and accurate knowledge of the poles and residues of the loop, represented by $W = GH$. This information is usually *not* available from *just* the C/R transfer characteristic (due to the H block in the model), although this C/R characteristic may *still* be needed in addition to W.

Once we have measured the parameters of the loop transfer function W, we can optimize the control system behavior by simulating it in our computer. We can add various compensation networks and vary the loop gain factor until we get acceptable results by way of response time (or bandwidth) and stability margin. We can also evaluate the noise performance of the system (especially to sources of noise *internal* to the loop), and we can even study nonlinear *distortion* components generated within the loop.

For this discussion, we will assume $H = 1$, with all of the poles of the loop residing in G. In most control systems, there will be a *dominant pole* at some low frequency, plus one or more poles at much higher frequencies, although sometimes there are other poles nearby at intermediate frequencies. For simplicity in this example, we will assume *two* high-frequency poles, in addition to the dominant *low*-frequency pole, making a total of three poles in the loop. We can adjust the loop gain either for *critical damping*, or for some amount of *overshoot* on the step response, and we can also study the conditions for loop instability. We can write the loop equation as:

$$W = G = \frac{K}{(s - s_1)\,(s - s_2)\,(s - s_3)} \tag{5.24}$$

where s_1, s_2, and s_3 are the three poles and K defines the gain factor. When we close the loop, we can write the actual control system transfer function as:

$$T = \frac{C}{R} = \frac{W}{1 + W} = \frac{K}{(s - s_1)\,(s - s_2)\,(s - s_3) + K} \tag{5.25}$$

By adjusting the gain factor K, we can alter the locations of the three *new* poles (roots of the denominator polynomial) to get the *optimum* response for the control system. Note the new poles start at their *original* values when $K = 0$ and move to *new* locations as K increases (K must be a positive number). One of the common ways to illustrate this behavior is by means of a *root locus plot,* as shown in Figure 5–7. For the initial pole values, we choose $s_1 = -.001$, $s_2 = -1$, and $s_3 = -1.25$.

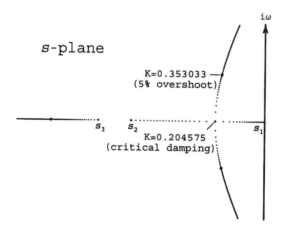

Figure 5–7   Root Loci of Poles

As we increase the value of K, the two poles s_1 and s_2 begin to move *towards* one another, while s_3 moves further to the left. Critical damping occurs when s_1 and s_2 merge together at -0.368780 (and where $K = 0.204575$), as illustrated in Figure 5–7. This configuration gives a step response that rises as quickly as possible *without* having any ringing or overshoot, as shown by the dashed line in Figure 5–8. For some control system applications, this may represent the optimum design. However, if *some* overshoot can be tolerated (say 5%) then the step response risetime can be *reduced* by a factor of *two* by selecting a somewhat higher value for K (namely 0.353033). For this case, the two poles s_1 and s_2 move *away* from the negative real s axis and become a *complex conjugate pair* at $-0.320585 \pm i0.342491$. If K is further increased to 2.81757, the pole trajectories intersect the $i\omega$ axis, at which point the control system becomes *unstable* and breaks into a steady-state oscillation at an angular frequency of ω radians per second.

The frequency response functions obtained by evaluating both Eqs. 5.24 and 5.25 along the $i\omega$ axis are shown superimposed together in Figure 5–9. We have chosen K to give 5% overshoot on the step response, as shown in Figure 5–8.

The open-loop -3 dB bandwidth is 0.001, due to the dominant pole at s_1, while the closed-loop -3 dB bandwidth is 0.480. At the same time, the low-frequency gain drops from 49.018 dB to -0.0307 dB as we close the loop.

Having settled upon a typical control system design, we will return to the task of measuring the system parameter values from observations of the *frequency response* function using the algorithm shown in Eq. 5.21. For brevity, we will assume the scaling error in the estimate of W (the factor $A_2/(A_1 G_o)$ in Eq. 5.22) has been removed via a calibration procedure, so the estimate of W differs from the true W *only* by the additive observation

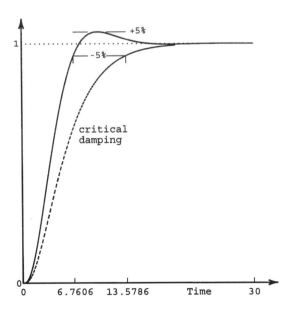

Figure 5–8 Normalized Step Response

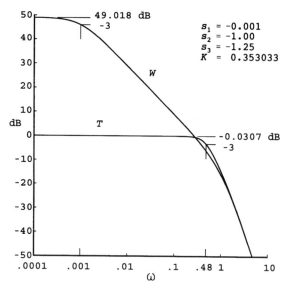

Figure 5–9   Frequency Response Functions

noise. We will assume all of the noise terms in Eq. 5.22 are independent Gaussian random variables having zero mean values.

Our measurement job simply amounts to adjusting the four parameters in our control system model expressed by Eq. 5.24 so the squared error magnitude $|W - \hat{W}|^2$ is *minimized*, where W is shown in Eq. 5.24 and the estimate is obtained by way of Eq. 5.21. We will use the least-squares (or weighted least-squares) technique discussed in section 4.4 of chapter 4, where the observation vector components are the values of $\hat{W}$ at each frequency, and the measurement model $G(U)$ is the same as W in Eq. 5.24. The elements of the parameter vector U comprise the three open-loop pole values s_1, s_2, and s_3 along with the gain factor K. The solution is contained in Eq. 4.19 (or 4.34 if a weighting function is used. *Note*: Do not confuse the *weighting* matrix W in Eq. 4.34 with the *loop gain* variable W in the current control system model). We require:

$$\left[\frac{\partial W(U)}{\partial U}\right]^T (W(U) - \hat{W}) = 0 \tag{5.26}$$

where $U = [s_1 \; s_2 \; s_3 \; K]^t$, and $W(U)$ is given by Eq. 5.24 above. Notice, the samples of both $\hat{W}$ and W are *complex numbers* (having real and imaginary parts). We define the superscript ^{T} to denote the *complex conjugate transpose* of a matrix.

In this example, the observation data (elements of frequency response vector $\hat{W}$) have been obtained from Eq. 5.21, which comprises quotient of sums of auto- and cross-spectra involving the two quantities X_1 and X_2. These, in turn, are obtained by taking the Fourier transforms of the corresponding pair of *time* waveforms acquired by the measuring analyzer from the control system. Thus, our set of frequency response function observations are not really "raw" data in the sense that no processing has been done, but rather represent some intermediate state where the original observation noise has been reduced by averaging, and certain potential sources of bias have already been removed. However, there is still the need to reduce the data further by estimating the best set of four parameter values from an entire vector of frequency response data.

This is certainly not the *only* way to handle the data to make this measurement. For example, it is possible to estimate our control system parameters directly from the sampled *time waveforms*, without using the Fourier transform, or without even introducing the frequency domain, or the Laplace transform, at *all*. Each method will generally have advantages and disadvantages, depending upon the application at hand.

Unfortunately, Eq. 5.26 is nonlinear in the parameters, so it is best solved by linearizing it to some extent and then proceeding with an *iterative* approach. This can be time consuming, and there is always the question of stable *convergence* after a reasonable number of iterations. Another alternative is to *reformulate* the problem in some other way. For example, it might be acceptable to minimize something *other* than the errors between the frequency response functions. The nonlinearity in this problem comes from the poles in the denominator of W. Suppose we multiply both W and $\hat{W}$ by the denominator of W, and then minimize *this* resulting difference. This is *still* not a completely linear problem, but we can use linear algebra to obtain a set of polynomial coefficients (for the Laplace variable $s = i\omega$) that minimize this modified error function, and then use a standard polynomial root solving algorithm to get the final pole and zero values. This last step is nonlinear, but is well understood and can be controlled to insure a complete set of roots in a timely manner, and it is the *last* step in the process so nonlinearities have a minimum effect on biases due to noise. Thus, we might choose to minimize:

$$|K - (i\omega - s_1)(i\omega - s_2)(i\omega - s_3)\hat{W}|^2 \qquad (5.27)$$

This will produce a *cubic polynomial* in the angular frequency variable ω. The *coefficients* of this polynomial are linear functions of the observations, so we can minimize this expression using linear matrix algebra. The four unknown parameters now become the polynomial coefficients instead of the three pole values and gain factor. The idea is for the three *pole* factors to remove *all* frequency dependence from the observed response function $\hat{W}$, leaving a *constant* value (plus observation noise), which is then removed by adjusting K. Notice if we choose the squared magnitude of the (original) denominator as a diagonal *weighting matrix* in the formulation given in Eq. 5.27, we obtain the original least-squares form of Eq. 5.26. The only problem is that we do not *know* this weighting function ahead of time, so we can only use some approximation.

It is useful to consider *other* polynomial functions (such as Chebyshev polynomials) in place of the powers of $i\omega$ in the above representation. The choice is primarily dictated by numerical considerations in the computations, but as a rule Chebyshev polynomials work much better than powers of s. These auxiliary polynomial functions can be easily converted back to powers of s after the optimum coefficients have been found, so a standard polynomial root solver can still be used.

We will illustrate this *linearized* solution for the polynomial coefficients in somewhat more detail and will generalize the equations to handle arbitrary polynomial orders for both numerator and denominator. We will also allow any complete set of polynomial functions to be used as *basis* functions for the solution. For any given set of polynomial basis functions, we will use the notation $R_k(\omega_j)$, where k is the *order* of the function (beginning with zero), and j is the sampling *index* along the frequency axis. We can express *any* function in the observation space as a linear combination of these basis functions, so the numerator and denominator polynomial shapes can be written respectively as:

$$P(\omega_j) = \sum_{k=0}^{p} c_k R_k(\omega_j) \tag{5.28}$$

$$Q(\omega_j) = \sum_{k=0}^{q} d_k R_k(\omega_j) \tag{5.29}$$

where c_k and d_k are the numerator basis function coefficients and the denominator basis function coefficients, respectively. Note the numerator polynomial order is p, and the denominator polynomial order is q. In matrix-vector form, we can write:

$$P = \phi C \tag{5.30}$$

$$Q = \theta D \tag{5.31}$$

where the elements of the vectors C and D are the c_k and d_k coefficients, respectively, and the columns of both ϕ and θ are the basis vectors $R_k(\omega_j)$. The matrix ϕ has $p + 1$ columns, and θ has $q + 1$ columns, both of which begin with the *constant* vector $R_0(\omega_j)$. If we have n observation points along the ω axis, then the size of ϕ will be $n \times (p + 1)$, and the size of θ will be $n \times (q + 1)$.

As indicated in our example in Eq. 5.27, we want to minimize the quantity:

$$|\phi C - \hat{W}\theta D|^2 \tag{5.32}$$

where we now write $\hat{W}$ as a *diagonal matrix* of the observations of the frequency response function, rather than as a vector. We can see by setting the partial derivatives of Eq. 5.32 with respect to both C and D to zero, that this scalar quantity will be minimized when the difference vector is orthogonal to *each* of the individual vectors that form the difference. Thus, Eq. 5.32 will be minimized when the following pair of equations are solved for C and D:

$$\phi^T(\phi C - \hat{W}\theta D) = 0 \tag{5.33}$$

$$\theta^T \hat{W}^T(\phi C - \hat{W}\theta D) = 0 \tag{5.34}$$

Remember, the superscript ^{T} denotes the *complex conjugate* transpose of a matrix or vector. We have two equations in the two unknowns C and D, so it is straightforward to solve for these coefficient vectors. One method is to express C in terms of D, giving a *single* equation in D, which we can then solve. Next, we can get C by back substitution. For example, from Eq. 5.33 we can write:

$$C = (\phi^T\phi)^{-1}\phi^T\hat{W}\theta D \tag{5.35}$$

Substituting this back into Eq. 5.34 gives an expression involving *only* the vector D as:

$$[\theta^T \hat{W}^T \phi \, (\phi^T \phi)^{-1} \phi^T \hat{W} \, \theta - \theta^T \hat{W}^T \hat{W} \, \theta] \, D = 0 \qquad (5.36)$$

The vector D is the solution to this *homogeneous* equation involving both the frequency response observations $\hat{W}$ and the basis vectors (columns of θ and ϕ). One of the best ways to solve equations of this sort is by means of the *Gram-Schmidt orthogonalization technique*, where D is chosen as the vector that is *most* orthogonal to all of the rows of the matrix in brackets. Once D is found from Eq. 5.36, it can be substituted back into Eq. 5.35 to obtain C.

There is one rather serious problem with this solution technique. *All* of the measured elements of *both* C and D are *biased* by the noise on the spectral data (diagonal elements of $\hat{W}$). This bias occurs when the noise is multiplied by its *self-conjugate*, as occurs in the $\theta^T \hat{W}^T \hat{W} \theta$ term in Eq. 5.36. Once this bias is introduced into D, it propagates into C as well. This bias can be removed if the *variance* on each spectral element of $\hat{W}$ is subtracted from the $\hat{W}^T \hat{W}$ product before further use. An example of this bias error is given in Table 5–1.

We have employed this technique to estimate the four parameters of our control system model, and the results are shown in Figure 5–10. The noisy spectrum represents the original set of observations in the frequency domain, and the solid curve is the best least-squares fit that we found. The dashed line represents the *true* shape of the response function, but it is only visible along the lower right-hand tail of the function. The measured pole and gain values are listed in the table within Figure 5–10. The measured DC gain is 0.086 dB greater than the true value.

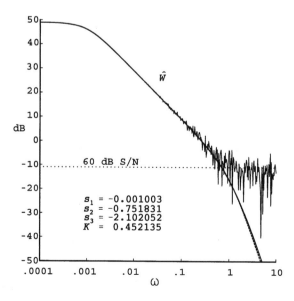

Figure 5–10 Curve Fitting Results

The dominant pole at −0.001 is measured very accurately, as is the magnitude of the function at zero frequency. However, the other two poles are very much in error, even though the estimated frequency response function fits very closely to the true shape (dashed line). Notice that the influence of these two large poles occurs very near the noise level, which was chosen to be 60 dB below the DC value. Thus, we should not expect much in the way of accuracy for *either* of these large pole estimates.

Actually, it is rather surprising that the fitting algorithm was able to find these two poles at all. In this particular case, the numerator and denominator orders were prespecified. When the algorithm was allowed to select the orders automatically, it selected only two poles, but added a pair of zeros. This choice actually produced a somewhat better fit to the given data than did the correct configuration. However, this sort of behavior depends on the details of the noise for any particular data record and would be different for another record.

In general, poles and zeros that are *far* from the frequency axis are more difficult to measure than those *nearby*. By analogy, it is something like walking along the $i\omega$ axis, looking into the left half of the *s*-plane through a *fog bank*. The farther away a feature is, the more difficult it is to see and to measure. However, by the same reasoning, the farther a feature is located from the frequency axis, the less *effect* it has on the response function, and the less important it is, at least in practical terms. There may be little difference in how many poles and/or zeros are assumed, or in precisely where they are located, as long as the net effect is the same *within the given noise level* along the *frequency axis*. This noise level is critical, because if it were reduced, then errors in feature locations would become more noticeable. Hence, to carry the fog analogy a little further, the *density* of the fog bank in the left half plane is proportional to the *noise level* along the *frequency axis*.

Our measurement of the control system parameters would not be complete without some idea of the expected variance on each estimated parameter value. These variance values can be *calculated* mathematically from Eqs. 5.35 and 5.36, or they can be estimated by means of a Monte Carlo random *simulation* of the observation noise in your computer. We have used this later method, and give the results in Table 5–1.

We used 10,000 averages to obtain each table entry, and we used 1024 points in the frequency response of the control system, giving a spacing of 1/512 between adjacent fre-

Table 5–1   Statistics for Control System Parameters

Estimated Parameter	Without Bias Correction		With Bias Correction	
	Mean Value	**Std. Dev.**	**Mean Value**	**Std. Dev.**
s_1	−0.000909	9.38E−6	−0.000992	1.69E−5
s_2	−0.1418	0.02726	−0.9971	0.1219
s_3	−0.7565	0.01692	−1.2461	0.4333
K	0.1505	0.00760	0.3606	0.0516
$K/|s_1 s_2 s_3|$	288.95	1.874	285.08	1.812

quency samples. The noise power was held constant throughout the frequency range, fixed at 60 dB below the DC value of the frequency response.

Note the *serious* errors in the estimated mean values of the pole locations when the noise bias corrections are *not* used. In general, the measured pole locations are biased towards the *right* (more positive values) when the observation noise is significant. Also note the large standard deviations on the two poles located *farthest* from the frequency axis, compared to the closest pole. This occurs because the effects of these far poles on the frequency response are very near the −60 dB *noise level*. It is also interesting to note the standard deviation on the DC gain is much smaller than you might predict from the standard deviations of the four constituent parameters. This is because the noise on these four parameters are *mutually correlated* to a considerable extent. In fact, the DC gain is the most accurately estimated parameter in the group, with the lowest frequency pole value coming in second. The farthest pole is the *least* accurate.

There are many fine points and techniques that we cannot cover in this short discussion of control system measurements, but we have at least illustrated some basic methods and have highlighted several ways to avoid some of the pitfalls, so you can make more accurate measurements of the loop parameters. You should carefully evaluate each possible method (via the measurement model) *before* making any measurements, and before using the resulting data, because some methods are much better (or worse) than others. You should also determine the expected *variance* and *bias* for each measured parameter, so you will be aware of the general quality of the final results.

5.4   VIBRATION MODES OF MECHANICAL STRUCTURES

In section 2.5 of chapter 2, we discussed a mathematical model of the modes of vibration of a mechanical structure, using the Laplace transform and the frequency domain. The resulting model Eqs. 2.17 and 2.18 are rewritten below as Eqs. 5.37 and 5.38.

$$H(s) = \sum_{j=1}^{n} \sum_{k=1}^{p_j} \frac{a_{jk}}{(s - s_j)^k} \tag{5.37}$$

where the *residue* matrix is:

$$a_{jk} = \sum_{\ell=0}^{p_j - k} u_{k+\ell} v_{p_j - \ell}^t \tag{5.38}$$

This is the *transfer function matrix* in the Laplace domain of a mechanical structure having n poles s_j indexed by j, each having a multiplicity p_j. In general, there is at least one *modal* and one *bimodal* vector associated with *each* multiplicity of *each pole value* (modal and bimodal vectors are identical for symmetric system matrices). The details of this modal *model* are explained more completely in section 2.5 of chapter 2. Notice that this transfer function matrix resembles a partial fraction form of Eq. 5.24, which we used to describe the previous control system example. This should not be surprising, since we are using the Laplace transform representation to describe a set of time domain *linear dif-*

ferential equations in both cases. It does not matter whether these systems are electrical or mechanical in nature.

We can use the same technique we introduced in section 5.3 to construct a least-squares fit to each *frequency response function* we obtain from the mechanical structure, thereby measuring the *pole* values and the amplitudes (or *residues*) of each term in the above summation Eq. 5.37. We form *each* modal vector from the residues of the terms corresponding to *that* particular pole value. Each component of a modal vector gives the amplitude of that mode of vibration at a *physical* point on the structure. Since the poles are *global parameters* of the structure, the "best" pole values can be obtained either by *averaging* the measured values for each structural point together, or by using a *simultaneous* fitting procedure in which all transfer matrix terms are fitted at the *same* time, thereby producing only *one* set of estimated pole values.

There *are* a few differences between the modal fitting procedure and the control system fitting procedure. As a rule, modal poles tend to be *lightly damped,* giving frequency response functions that are rather localized along the frequency axis. Consequently, the frequency response may only be significant in a narrow *band* near the poles of interest, which can be some distance away from the frequency origin. The use of basis polynomials having Hermitian symmetry around the origin is *still* the correct form in a theoretical sense, but often does not work well in practice because the various polynomials in the set may appear to be very similar to one another within a narrow frequency interval (each one looks like a *straight line* segment). A better approach is to define a set of basis polynomials that are *orthogonal* over the frequency interval of *interest* and to forego any symmetry restrictions.

In a modal system, there are likely to be many modes with poles that are either *above* or *below* the frequency band of interest, but that have "tails" that spread *into* this band. These must be represented by introducing "extra" modes into the fitting procedure, to allow the *desired* modes to be measured accurately. However, it is important to recognize that these extra terms are *not* a part of the final set of measured parameters, but are *catalyst modes* that must be discarded at some point.

Depending on the method of excitation, it is very possible that a mode of vibration is not given sufficient amplitude to be visible above the noise level. If it *is* visible, it may be weak and difficult to measure accurately. Sometimes, a mode is excited strongly, but simply has a small amplitude at certain points on the structure (called nodal points). During the fitting procedure, these components will either *not* be found or will be rather inaccurate, so allowances must be made for these cases. You should always excite the structure at *more* than one point, to be sure *all* modes are excited. For example, if the structure is a rectangular plate, you might inadvertently excite all of the modes in the *long* direction without exciting *any* short-direction modes at all, unless you properly move the point of excitation and make a *second* set of measurements.

Since we use the same least-squares fitting technique we discussed for the control system (in the previous section), we have the same potential bias problem caused by the noise power in each frequency response estimate. You should always remove this bias by subtracting the noise variance from the conjugate product of the frequency response times itself, in any least-squares formulation. For *lightly* damped modes, this bias correction is particularly critical, since the poles are already very close to the frequency axis, and this bias generally moves all poles to the *right* (*less* damping). Without the bias correction a pole may easily be offset enough to *erroneously* indicate a right-plane pole, and hence an unstable system.

As with any measurement, it is very important to obtain some sort of estimate of the *variance* in each measured quantity. It is typical in a complicated system for all parameter estimates to interact with each other, so their individual noise perturbations are often highly correlated. It is very difficult to predict the resulting error statistics for each parameter in isolation. It is possible to calculate these interrelations by means of the *covariance* matrix, but often the best way is via Monte Carlo simulation of the measurement a large number of times, using typical noise contamination in the frequency response waveforms (derived from a measurement model), and then to construct a set of histograms of parameter errors. At the same time, you can approximate the various covariance matrix elements and find the cross-correlation coefficients between parameters. This is not a very elegant procedure from a theoretical perspective, but it is a practical method and can give good usable results.

Generally, the parameters of any *lightly* damped modes will be measured most accurately, and will also exhibit a high degree of correlation between errors in the *pole* value and errors in the modal vector *strength* (or residue). Modes with poles farther away from the frequency axis will have progressively noisier parameter estimates. Of course, the errors will be larger if the frequency response magnitude is small (and hence noisy) near the pole. If several poles are clustered together, the *individual* parameter values will tend to be very noisy, but they will *correlate* in a manner such that the *overall* effects of the cluster will be accurately represented along the frequency axis. Keep in mind, the only *visible* part of the *s*-plane in this Laplace formulation is the *frequency axis*. Hence, the quality of any parameter measurement is determined by its effect along the frequency axis, and not by its effect anywhere else in the plane.

As a guideline, *if* it is difficult to make accurate parameter estimates in certain cases, then conversely those parameters will generally have *little effect* along the frequency axis. At the risk of sounding somewhat facetious, if you can't measure it, then it probably doesn't *matter*!

One major difference between structural vibration and control system measurements is the need to make *many* frequency response estimates in order to obtain the modal vector components. Each frequency response measurement (between different points on the structure) results in *one* of the components of each modal vector. In general, the poles are complex and occur as complex conjugate pairs, and the *same* is true of the corresponding modal vectors.

In the absence of damping in the system, all modal vectors would be purely *imaginary*. However, some damping is always present, and this results in an additional *real* part for each vector. The actual physical motion of the structure (corresponding to a particular mode of vibration) comprises contributions from each of the two conjugate pairs of poles and modal vectors and is always a *real* quantity. However, the damping in each mode introduces different phase angles into the motion at each point on the structure. These combined modal vector pairs result in "standing waves" on a structure, although these waves actually appear to *roll* across the structure rather than to stand in place, because the motion at some points will *lag behind* the motion at other points.

It is beyond the scope of this section to give the complete details of an actual example of modal measurements on a structure, but we can illustrate some of the procedures and potential problems associated with measurements of this sort, using a simple mechanical model comprising a device called a *gyroscope*. We discussed some of the assumptions implied in using a linear lumped model of a mechanical structure in section 2.5 of chapter 2, including Eqs. 2.6 through 2.11. We will pick up our story with Eqs. 2.12 and 2.13, which we repeat below as Eqs. 5.39 and 5.40:

$$BX = F \tag{5.39}$$

$$X = B^{-1}F = HF \text{ , where } H = B^{-1} \tag{5.40}$$

The elements of the system matrix B are of the form $ms^2 + cs + k$. The transfer function matrix H, shown above in Eq. 5.37, is the *inverse* of B. When we measure the characteristics of a vibrating mechanical structure, we estimate *some* of the elements of H, evaluated along the *frequency axis (frequency response functions)*. Our measurement task is to use these *parts* of the transfer function matrix to obtain our best estimates of *all* the parameters of H in the partial fraction form shown in Eq. 5.37, namely the set of pole values and the set of modal vector components.

One interesting example that illustrates many of the important characteristics of a vibrating mechanical structure is a pair of masses coupled to orthogonal points on a set of gimbals supporting a rotating disc (a gyroscope) by means of springs and dampers. This is an *asymmetric* system having six poles and six *pairs* of modal vectors (excluding rigid body modes). It is possible for two pairs of poles to coalesce into a pair of *double poles* (each having a multiplicity of two). The geometry of this example is shown in Figure 5–11.

In Figure 5–11, we have a disc rotating around the z-axis with an *angular momentum M*, connected to a pair of mass-spring-damper resonators attached at *orthogonal* points on the x and y axes at distances (from the z axis of rotation) a and b, respectively. Applied forces f_1 and f_2 on the masses m_1 and m_2 cause displacements z_1, z_2, z_3, and z_4, which depend upon the spring coefficients k_1 and k_2, the damping coefficients c_1 and c_2, and the angular momentum M of the disc (the angular momentum of the disc is the product of its moment of inertia about the z-axis and the angular velocity of rotation of the disc). This is a right-handed coordinate system with the axis labels denoting the positive direction of each coordinate. We will restrict our attention to small displacements so the system equations will be linear. In this example, all forces and displacements are confined to the z direction.

We first characterize the *gyroscopic* effects of the rotating disc, and then we obtain the system equations by writing *force balance* expressions at *each* of the four nodes in the model.

If we apply a force f_3 at point 3, we are applying a torque around the y-axis of $\tau_y = -af_3$, where the sign is determined by wrapping the fingers of the right hand around the y-axis in the direction of the torque and taking the positive sign in the direction of the

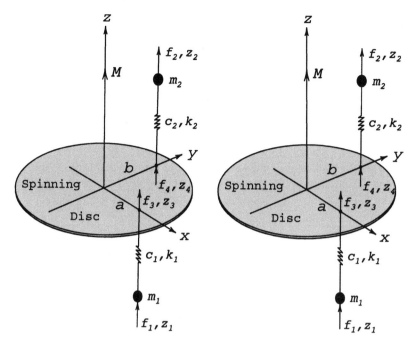

Figure 5–11   Example of a Mechanical System: The Gyroscope

thumb. This torque is equal to the *time derivative* of the *total* angular momentum in the y direction (the angular momentum vector for the spinning disc is perpendicular to the plane of rotation).

Thus, in an infinitesimal time dt we get an infinitesimal change in the y component of the angular momentum of the disc $dM_y = \tau_y\,dt = -af_3 dt$. If we *vectorially* add this increment to the original z component of angular momentum (M) we get a *composite* angular momentum vector that is infinitesimally tilted towards the negative y direction. This implies that the rotating disc is likewise tilted by this angle $-dM_y/M$ radians (in dt seconds), in a positive direction around the x-axis, and this corresponds to an *angular velocity* around the x-axis of $\omega_x = -\tau_y/M$. If the applied force f_3 is held constant, then the gyroscope will continue to rotate or *precess* around the x-axis at an average angular velocity of ω_x radians per second.

In addition, a portion of the applied torque τ_y produces the time derivative of a *new* angular momentum component in the y direction, which is $I_y\dot{\omega}_y$, where I_y is the moment of inertia of the disc around the y-axis and $\dot{\omega}_y$ is the angular acceleration around the y-axis.

By the same argument, a torque τ_x around the x-axis will introduce an angular velocity $\omega_y = \tau_x/M$ around the y-axis, along with the product of the moment of inertia and the angular acceleration around the x-axis. These two simple equations are sufficient to describe the behavior of a gyroscope when arbitrary torques are applied (at least for a *uniform* disc rotating around an axis *perpendicular* to the disc). We can write these equations as follows:

$$\tau_x = I_x \dot{\omega}_x + M\omega_y \tag{5.41}$$

$$\tau_y = I_y \dot{\omega}_y - M\omega_x \tag{5.42}$$

We will combine these into a single matrix equation and simultaneously take the Laplace transform, giving:

$$\begin{bmatrix} T_x \\ T_y \end{bmatrix} = \begin{bmatrix} sI_x & M \\ -M & sI_y \end{bmatrix} \begin{bmatrix} \Omega_x \\ \Omega_y \end{bmatrix} \tag{5.43}$$

where T is the Laplace transform of the torque τ, and Ω is the Laplace transform of the angular velocity ω. As usual, the Laplace variable s represents time domain differentiation. The *inverse* of this matrix gives the vector of angular velocities:

$$\begin{bmatrix} \Omega_x \\ \Omega_y \end{bmatrix} = \frac{1}{s^2 I_x I_y + M^2} \begin{bmatrix} sI_y & -M \\ M & sI_x \end{bmatrix} \begin{bmatrix} T_x \\ T_y \end{bmatrix} \tag{5.44}$$

To illustrate the use of these relations, imagine a *unit impulse of torque* applied around the y-axis (represented by $T_y = 1$), with no external constraints on the x-axis torque ($T_x = 0$). We recognize there are a pair of poles *on* the imaginary s-axis located at $s = \pm iM/\sqrt{I_x I_y}$. The resulting time domain waveforms will be *sinusoidal* having an angular frequency of $M/\sqrt{I_x I_y}$ radians per second. In particular, we get:

$$\phi_x = \frac{1}{M} \left[\cos\left(\frac{Mt}{\sqrt{I_x I_y}} \right) - 1 \right] \tag{5.45}$$

$$\phi_y = \frac{1}{M} \sqrt{\frac{I_x}{I_y}} \sin\left(\frac{Mt}{\sqrt{I_x I_y}} \right) \tag{5.46}$$

where the ϕ's are the angles of rotation (in radians) around their respective axes. Notice that this represents a *nutation* of the spin axis at a rate of $M/\sqrt{I_x I_y}$ radians per second, with the indicated amplitudes in each direction, and with the axis returning to its original position after each cycle. This *oscillatory* motion is a characteristic trait of a "free" gyroscope, in which all external torques are *zero* after the initial impulse.

The units do not appear to be correct in the above pair of equations, but note that there is an implied convolution with the unit torque impulse that caused this motion, which has the units of angular momentum M, so the units cancel, as expected for an angular quantity.

Beginning with a pair of conjugate complex poles *on* the frequency axis, it is relatively easy to push these poles into the *right half* of the s-plane, thereby introducing an instability or *growing* oscillation into the system. Imagine a motorcycle traveling around a curve on a rough highway. The front wheel (a gyroscope) is leaning into the curve, and the vertical highway perturbations are exciting the wheel with some force components that are *perpendicular* to the plane of rotation of the wheel. The resulting *nutation* of the front axle will tend to periodically *lean* the bike in a left-right direction, while *simultane-*

ously turning the wheel to the left and right (with a 90° phase lag). The *axis* of rotation of the front wheel will *itself* rotate (nutate) in an elliptical manner.

If the rider attempts to counteract this dual set of oscillations, but *lags* somewhat behind, the resulting poles can easily cross into the right half-plane, and the oscillations will quickly grow in amplitude, *especially* if the road irregularities happen to include strong components near the *nutation frequency*. The author can verify these predictions from firsthand experience, having been thrown from a motorcycle under similar conditions! There is no damping built into an ordinary gyroscope to keep the system stable, so some sort of external damping is usually needed.

It is interesting to set $T_x = 0$ in Eq. 5.43 and then to eliminate Ω_x, giving an expression relating the applied torque T_y and the resulting angular velocity Ω_y. We get:

$$T_y = \left(s^2 I_y + \frac{M^2}{I_x} \right) \Phi_y \tag{5.47}$$

where Φ is the Laplace transform of the angular displacement ϕ in radians. We see the first term is an angular mass represented by the moment of inertia I_y around the y-axis, and the second term is a series connected angular stiffness M^2/I_x around the y-axis caused by the spin of the disc. This effective stiffness is proportional to the *square* of the angular momentum of the disc and *inversely* proportional to the moment of inertia around the x-axis.

If we rewrite Eq. 5.43 in terms of the forces and displacements shown in Figure 5–11, we obtain:

$$\begin{bmatrix} F_3 \\ F_4 \end{bmatrix} = \begin{bmatrix} \dfrac{s^2 I_y}{a^2} & \dfrac{sM}{ab} \\ -\dfrac{sM}{ab} & \dfrac{s^2 I_x}{b^2} \end{bmatrix} \begin{bmatrix} Z_3 \\ Z_4 \end{bmatrix} \tag{5.48}$$

where the *F*s represent the Laplace transforms of the forces *f*, and the *Z*s represent the Laplace transforms of the displacements *z*. This matrix-vector equation completely describes the behavior of the gyroscope in Figure 5–11.

In many cases, the spin momentum M is very large compared to terms involving either I_x or I_y, and the frequencies of interest are low compared to the nutation frequency, so we can effectively represent the gyroscope by the simplified equation:

$$\begin{bmatrix} F_3 \\ F_4 \end{bmatrix} \approx \frac{sM}{ab} \begin{bmatrix} 0 & 1 \\ -1 & 0 \end{bmatrix} \begin{bmatrix} Z_3 \\ Z_4 \end{bmatrix} \tag{5.49}$$

Notice the system matrix describing the gyroscope is *asymmetric*. This means the system matrix for *any* system involving active rotating components cannot be *completely* symmetric.

We are now in a position to write the four force balance equations at the four nodes of the system. Writing these equations in the Laplace domain gives:

$$F_1 = s^2 m_1 Z_1 + (sc_1 + k_1)(Z_1 - Z_3) \tag{5.50}$$

$$F_2 = s^2 m_2 Z_2 + (sc_2 + k_2)(Z_2 - Z_4) \tag{5.51}$$

$$F_3 = s\frac{M}{ab} Z_4 + s^2 \frac{I_y}{a^2} Z_3 + (sc_1 + k_1)(Z_3 - Z_1) \tag{5.52}$$

$$F_4 = -s\frac{M}{ab} Z_3 + s^2 \frac{I_x}{b^2} Z_4 + (sc_2 + k_2)(Z_4 - Z_2) \tag{5.53}$$

We are assuming all z displacements are measured relative to their individual *quiescent values* (values taken when all spring forces are zero) to simplify the equations. The effects of the gyroscope spin are represented by the two terms involving M/ab.

We can write these four linear equations as a single matrix expression in the Laplace domain, as follows:

$$F = BZ \tag{5.54}$$

where the four components of the force vector F are F_1 through F_4, the four components of the displacement vector Z are Z_1 through Z_4, and the system matrix B is given by:

$$B = \begin{bmatrix} s^2 m_1 + sc_1 + k_1 & 0 & -(sc_1 + k_1) & 0 \\ 0 & s^2 m_2 + sc_2 + k_2 & 0 & -(sc_2 + k_2) \\ -(sc_1 + k_1) & 0 & s^2 \dfrac{I_y}{a^2} + sc_1 + k_1 & s\dfrac{M}{ab} \\ 0 & -(sc_2 + k_2) & -s\dfrac{M}{ab} & s^2 \dfrac{I_x}{b^2} + sc_2 + k_2 \end{bmatrix} \tag{5.55}$$

The modal vectors are values of Z obtained when $F = 0$ *and* when the determinant of the system matrix B is also zero. The determinant of B can be written as:

$$\det B = s^2 \frac{M^2}{a^2 b^2} (s^2 m_1 + sc_1 + k_1)(s^2 m_2 + sc_2 + k_2) \tag{5.56}$$

$$+ s^4 \left[\frac{I_y}{a^2}(s^2 m_1 + sc_1 + k_1) + m_1(sc_1 + k_1)\right]\left[\frac{I_x}{b^2}(s^2 m_2 + sc_2 + k_2) + m_2(sc_2 + k_2)\right]$$

The "poles" of the system are the values of s for which $\det B = 0$. Notice, s^2 can be factored out of Eq. 5.56, leaving a sixth-order polynomial, indicating six poles for the system. Modal vectors associated with powers of s are called *rigid body modes*, since they correspond to zero vibration frequency. We will mostly ignore these modes and concentrate on the remaining six modes having *non*-zero vibration frequencies.

To make this example more interesting, we will choose the components of our system to produce a pair of *double* poles (multiplicity two), along with a pair of single poles. The parameter values we will use are given by:

$$\frac{m_1}{k_1} = 0.28360258 \qquad \frac{c_1}{k_1} = 0.90084829 \qquad \frac{I_y}{a^2 k_1} = 0.02$$

$$\frac{m_2}{k_2} = 1.85454262 \qquad \frac{c_2}{k_2} = 2.12727235 \qquad \frac{I_x}{b^2 k_2} = 0.05$$

$$\mu = \frac{M}{ab\sqrt{k_1 k_2}} = 1.45002732$$

The resulting pole values are:

$$s_1 = -0.75010560 + i0.65992332, \text{multiplicity} = 2$$

$$s_1^* = -0.75010560 - i0.65992332, \text{multiplicity} = 2$$

$$s_2 = -44.4554729 + i45.1236193, \text{multiplicity} = 1$$

$$s_2^* = -44.4554729 - i45.1236193, \text{multiplicity} = 1$$

There is also a rigid body mode corresponding to a pole at $s = 0$.

As we discussed in section 2.5 of chapter 2, for a *simple* pole (unit multiplicity) at s_1, the associated modal vector u is obtained from the homogeneous system equation $Bu = 0$. In the vicinity of the pole, *both* B and u will be functions of the Laplace variable s, and all of the elements of Bu will comprise *first order* zeros of the form $s - s_1$. At the pole, the modal vector becomes a *constant* (independent of s), and also becomes *orthogonal* to all *rows* of the B matrix evaluated at the pole.

For a *multiple* pole, with a multiplicity of ν at s_1, each element of the vector Bu will comprise a νth order zero of the form $(s - s_1)^\nu$ at the pole, where u is a Taylor's series expansion of a *composite* modal vector (a function of s) around the pole value. This means the first $\nu - 1$ *derivatives* of Bu with respect to s will also go to zero at the pole, in addition to Bu itself. There will be a *new* modal vector coefficient associated with the pole for *each* of these derivatives, giving a total of ν modal vectors. These are *constant* vectors (independent of s) that define a ν-dimensional *subspace* (within the complete modal vector space) that belongs entirely to this multiple pole. Whenever a pole of multiplicity ν occurs, it must be assumed that poles having all *lower* multiplicities will also appear. The modal vector coefficient for $Bu = 0$ belongs to the pole of highest multiplicity. The modal vector obtained by setting the first derivative of Bu to zero belongs to the next lower multiplicity pole, *but* the *previous* modal vector can *also* appear with this pole. In general, for any given multiplicity and pole value, all modal vectors associated with those poles of *higher multiplicity* are *also* a part of the vector space associated with that *given* multiplicity.

When the system matrix B is *not* symmetric, there will be *twice* the number of vectors associated with each pole. These could be called left and right modal vectors, but in this note we will call this second set *bimodal* vectors. These are defined by $v'B = B'v = 0$, where v is the bimodal vector. If B is not symmetric, this vector will be different from that obtained from $Bu = 0$. Thus, for multiple poles, we must actually contend with a total of 2ν modal/bimodal vectors associated with each pole of multiplicity ν.

For our gyroscope example, we have the following modal and bimodal vectors. The two modal vectors for the double pole are:

$$u_1 = \begin{bmatrix} -0.37782325 - i0.57923476 \\ -0.27253415 - i0.80928795 \\ 0.29448293 + i0.28671401 \\ -0.32924409 - i0.03254375 \end{bmatrix} \tag{5.57}$$

$$u_2 = \begin{bmatrix} 1 \\ -0.51956466 - i0.19411382 \\ 0.66150558 - i0.24529551 \\ 0.15132014 - i0.13762966 \end{bmatrix} \tag{5.58}$$

The corresponding two bimodal vectors for the double pole are:

$$v_1 = \begin{bmatrix} -0.37782325 - i0.57923476 \\ 0.27253415 + i0.80928795 \\ 0.29448293 + i0.28671401 \\ 0.32924409 + i0.03254375 \end{bmatrix} \tag{5.59}$$

$$v_2 = \begin{bmatrix} 1 \\ 0.51956466 + i0.19411382 \\ 0.66150558 - i0.24529551 \\ -0.15132014 + i0.13762966 \end{bmatrix} \tag{5.60}$$

The arbitrary amplitude of the second vector is set by making the first element *unity*. The *otherwise arbitrary* coefficient within the first vector is set to make the first and second vectors *orthogonal* to one another ($u_1^T u_2 = 0$ and $v_1^T v_2 = 0$, where the ^{T} symbol denotes the complex conjugate transpose). For the remaining single pole, we have the modal and bimodal vectors given by:

$$u_3 = \begin{bmatrix} 1 \\ -0.01152253 - i0.22646668 \\ -13.3491122 + i14.2012223 \\ 9.34815205 + i8.19051559 \end{bmatrix} \tag{5.61}$$

$$v_3 = \begin{bmatrix} 1 \\ 0.01152253 + i0.22646668 \\ -13.3491122 + i14.2012223 \\ -9.34815205 - i8.19051559 \end{bmatrix} \tag{5.62}$$

Notice the bimodal vectors differ from the modal vectors *only* in the sign reversals on elements two and four.

For those readers who are surprised to see *complex* modal vector elements, this is the result when *damping* is included in the system model. With zero damping, all of the elements of a *displacement* modal vector are purely imaginary. In a real physical system, the complex poles always appear in *conjugate pairs*, so the modal vectors also appear in conjugate pairs. The actual physical motion of a mechanical structure is the *sum* of the contributions from each mode (comprising the product of a modal vector component *and* a complex exponential in the time domain), so the imaginary parts cancel and only the real parts remain. A complex conjugate pair of modal vectors will result in an oscillatory vibration in which the *phase* of the oscillation is different at *each* point on the structure. Instead of getting a "standing wave" over the structure at some frequency, as we would expect if damping were zero, we get a "rolling wave" that appears to move at some velocity.

The transfer matrix for the *double pole* can be written as:

$$H_1(s) = \begin{bmatrix} u_1 & u_2 \end{bmatrix} \begin{bmatrix} 0 & \dfrac{1}{s - s_1} \\ \dfrac{1}{s - s_1} & \dfrac{1}{(s - s_1)^2} \end{bmatrix} \begin{bmatrix} v_1^t \\ v_2^t \end{bmatrix} \tag{5.63}$$

$$= \frac{u_1 v_2^t + u_2 v_1^t}{s - s_1} + \frac{u_2 v_2^t}{(s - s_1)^2} \tag{5.64}$$

In the time domain, the corresponding impulse response matrix is:

$$h_1(t) = (u_1 v_2^t + u_2 v_1^t)e^{s_1 t} + (u_2 v_2^t)te^{s_1 t} \tag{5.65}$$

Note that t is used both for time and the vector transpose. When the complex conjugate term is added from the conjugate pole, we get twice the real part of Eq. 5.65, giving:

$$h(t) = e^{-\sigma_1 t}[R \cos(\omega_1 t) - I \sin(\omega_1 t)] \tag{5.66}$$

where

$$R = 2\Re \left(u_1 v_2^t + u_2 v_1^t + u_2 v_2^t t \right)$$

$$I = 2\Im \left(u_1 v_2^t + u_2 v_1^t + u_2 v_2^t t \right)$$

$$\sigma_1 = -\Re(s_1)$$

$$\omega_1 = \Im(s_1)$$

Here, $\Re()$ denotes the real part, and $\Im()$ denotes the imaginary part of a complex quantity.

The relative phase angles between points on the structure indexed by j and k are given by α_{jk}, where $\tan(\alpha_{jk}) = I_{jk}/R_{jk}$, and I_{jk} and R_{jk} are the elements of the I and R matrices given above. If the modal vectors were purely imaginary, then I would be zero and all phase angles would be the *same* across the entire structure.

The second term in Eq. 5.65 involving $te^{s_1 t}$ is due to the multiplicity of *two* on the pole and represents a linearly growing sinusoid in time, multiplied by the decaying exponential factor from the real part of s_1. This sort of term would be absent if all pole multiplicities were unity. The complete transfer function matrix is represented as:

$$H(s) = \Theta \Lambda^{-1}(s)\, \Psi \tag{5.67}$$

where the columns of Θ are the modal vectors, suitably scaled, and the rows of Ψ are the transposed bimodal vectors, also suitably scaled. The proper scale factors for each mode can be determined by inverting the system matrix B or by actual measurement of the corresponding elements of the transfer matrix $H(i\omega)$ on the structure (along the frequency axis). Thus, we define:

$$\Theta = \begin{bmatrix} u_0 & u_1 & u_2 & u_3 & u_1^* & u_2^* & u_3^* \end{bmatrix} \tag{5.68}$$

$$\Psi^t = \begin{bmatrix} v_0 & v_1 & v_2 & v_3 & v_1^* & v_2^* & v_3^* \end{bmatrix} \tag{5.69}$$

Notice, the complex conjugates (denoted by the * symbol) of the modal and bimodal vectors must *also* be included.

The rigid body mode is represented by u_o and v_o. In this case, $u_o = v_o$ and both vectors comprise two orthogonal parts, one part involving elements 1 and 3, and the other part involving elements 2 and 4. In particular:

$$u_0, v_0 = \begin{bmatrix} 0 \\ 1 \\ 0 \\ 1 \end{bmatrix}, \begin{bmatrix} 1 \\ 0 \\ 1 \\ 0 \end{bmatrix} \tag{5.70}$$

This is an example of a *repeated* mode at $s = 0$, where the pole multiplicity is unity but there are *two orthogonal* modal vectors associated with the pole. In this case, the first vector in Eq. 5.70 occurs in columns 1 and 3 of the transfer matrix, and the second vector occurs in columns 2 and 4. This means a *constant force* at either nodes 1 or 3 in Figure 5–11 will produce a constant *velocity* at nodes 2 and 4 (note the $1/s$ factor), while a constant force at either nodes 2 or 4 will produce a constant velocity at nodes 1 and 3. This is a description of the *precession* of a gyroscope, as indicated previously in Eq. 5.49.

The poles of the system are represented by $\Lambda^{-1}(s)$ as follows:

$$
\Lambda^{-1}(s) = \begin{bmatrix}
\dfrac{1}{s} & 0 & 0 & 0 & 0 & 0 & 0 \\[2ex]
0 & 0 & \dfrac{1}{s-s_1} & 0 & 0 & 0 & 0 \\[2ex]
0 & \dfrac{1}{s-s_1} & \dfrac{1}{(s-s_1)^2} & 0 & 0 & 0 & 0 \\[2ex]
0 & 0 & 0 & \dfrac{1}{s-s_2} & 0 & 0 & 0 \\[2ex]
0 & 0 & 0 & 0 & 0 & \dfrac{1}{s-s_1^*} & 0 \\[2ex]
0 & 0 & 0 & 0 & \dfrac{1}{s-s_1^*} & \dfrac{1}{(s-s_1^*)^2} & 0 \\[2ex]
0 & 0 & 0 & 0 & 0 & 0 & \dfrac{1}{s-s_2^*}
\end{bmatrix} \quad (5.71)
$$

This form of $H(s)$ expressed in Eq. 5.67 is simply a way of representing each element of the transfer matrix as a *partial fraction* in s. Each pole with its associated modal and bimodal vectors represents *one* solution to the system equations (these are *differential equations* in the *time domain*), and the *total solution* is the *sum* of all of these components. All of the *spatial* information about the solution is carried by the modal and bimodal vectors, and all of the *frequency* or *time* domain behavior is carried by the poles. These poles are "global" in nature, meaning they are *common* to *all* points in the structure. Thus, the spatial information is contained in Θ and Ψ, and the temporal information is contained in $\Lambda^{-1}(s)$. In general, *each column* of $H(s)$ comprises *all* of the poles *and* modal vectors in the system, and *each row* comprises all of the poles and bimodal vectors. Thus, it is often only necessary to measure *one* row and/or column of the transfer matrix to obtain *all* of the modal information about the system.

It is easy to become confused as to when the *conjugate transpose* of a matrix or vector is appropriate, and when only the *transpose* is needed. In modal and transfer function theory it is important to preserve the phase angles of complex matrix and vector elements. In these situations the simple transpose is generally used. An apparent exception occurs when both the numerator and denominator of a frequency response function are multiplied by the complex conjugate of the denominator. However, this procedure still preserves the phase angles of the frequency response function itself at each frequency.

Whenever magnitudes or squared magnitudes of complex quantities are involved, we use the conjugate transpose operation to effectively remove phase angles from consideration. This is needed in least-squares estimation algorithms, and when vectors are orthogonalized. We also need to remove phase in the calcualtion of covariance and correlation matrixes of complex vectors. Sometimes these procedures are used together in some manner, so considerable care is needed to write the resulting expressions correctly.

We will construct the elements of the first *column* of the transfer function matrix along the *frequency axis* (where $s = i2\pi f$), and then add some random noise to the resulting frequency response functions, thereby simulating the results we would get if we actually measured these functions on a *real* gyroscope. Then, we will invoke a *curve fitting algorithm* to estimate the pole values and the residues for each pole. By repeating this process many times, using different noise values, we can estimate the bias and the variance of each measured parameter.

The four transfer functions between the applied force F_1 and the resulting displacements Z_1 through Z_4 (in the Laplace domain) are:

$$H_{11}(s) = \frac{s^2 \dfrac{M^2}{a^2 b^2}\left(s^2 m_2 + s c_2 + k_2\right)}{\det B}$$

(5.72)

$$+ \frac{s^2 \left(s^2 \dfrac{I_y}{a^2} + s c_1 + k_1\right)\left[\dfrac{I_x}{b^2}\left(s^2 m_2 + s c_2 + k_2\right) + m_2\left(s c_2 + k_2\right)\right]}{\det B}$$

$$H_{21}(s) = s\,\frac{M}{ab}\,\frac{\left(s c_1 + k_1\right)\left(s c_2 + k_2\right)}{\det B}$$

(5.73)

$$H_{31}(s) = \frac{s^2\left(s c_1 + k_1\right)\left[\dfrac{I_x}{b^2}\left(s^2 m_2 + s c_2 + k_2\right) + m_2\left(s c_2 + k_2\right)\right]}{\det B}$$

(5.74)

$$H_{41}(s) = s\,\frac{M}{ab}\,\frac{\left(s c_1 + k_1\right)\left(s^2 m_2 + s c_2 + k_2\right)}{\det B}$$

(5.75)

where det B is shown in Eq. 5.56. There is an s factor in *all* of the numerators *and* in the common denominator that cancel, so the numerators are actually *lower* in order by one, and the denominator becomes a seventh-order polynomial. Furthermore, the remaining factor of s in the denominator corresponds to a rigid body *displacement* mode proportional to the integral of the applied force. We obtain the *velocity versus force* transfer function if we remove this denominator s factor, so there are only *six velocity* transfer function poles and modal vector pairs, and the resulting denominator becomes a *sixth-order* polynomial in s.

We show the *magnitude* and *phase angle* versus frequency for each of these four transfer functions, evaluated along the positive frequency axis in Figures 5–12 through 5–15. These are called *frequency response functions*. One of the basic properties of analytic functions of a complex variable (of which these transfer functions are examples) is, they are completely defined throughout the entire complex plane, *if* they are known along any finite or infinite line segment, or *if* their derivatives are all known at any point in the plane. Thus, we only need to measure a set of frequency response functions to determine the *entire* transfer function throughout the complex plane.

The *double pole* occurs near the center of each plot, while the remaining single pole occurs near the right edge.

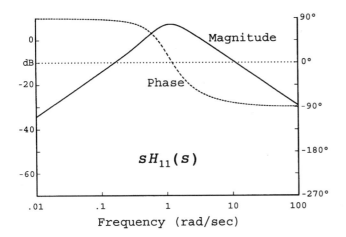

Figure 5–12 Velocity Frequency Response Function sZ_1 vs. F_1

These are *velocity transfer functions,* obtained by multiplying the original displacement transfer matrix elements by s. In Figures 5–12 and 5–14 the velocities are zero at $s = 0$ for a constant applied force F_1, but the *displacements* have the values of:

$$Z_3 = \frac{a^2 b^2}{M^2} \left(m_2 + \frac{I_x}{b^2} \right) F_1 \quad , \quad Z_1 = Z_3 + \frac{F_1}{k_1} \tag{5.76}$$

Thus, the gyroscope tilts in the direction of the applied force, but this tilt is inversely proportional to the *square* of the angular momentum M of the spinning disc and proportional to the effective mass at node 2.

In Figures 5–13 and 5–15, the *precessional velocities* are proportional to the applied force F_1 when $s = 0$, as given by:

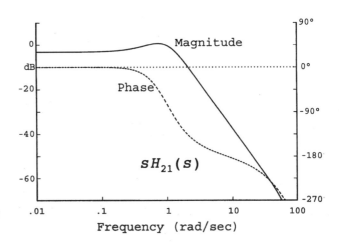

Figure 5–13 Velocity Frequency Response Function sZ_2 vs. F_1

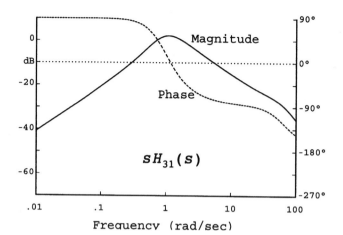

$sH_{31}(s)$

Frequency (rad/sec)

Figure 5-14 Velosity Frequency Response Function sZ_3 vs. F_1

$$sZ_2, sZ_4 = \frac{ab}{M} F_1 \quad , \quad \text{for } s = 0 \tag{5.77}$$

and are inversely proportional to the angular momentum M.

You might notice it is difficult to detect the presence of a pole with multiplicity *two* in these plots. The phase of the transfer function changes by $-180°$ as a single pole is passed along the positive frequency axis, so you would expect a double pole to change the phase by $-360°$. There are two reasons this does not occur in this example. First, the damping is heavy, and none of the poles are close to the frequency axis, so it is difficult to see the effect of any one pole. Second (and most important), there are *zeros* in the s-plane nearby that will *cancel* the phase introduced by the poles to some extent. For example, in Figure 5–12 there are four zeros in the transfer function, in addition to the one at the origin.

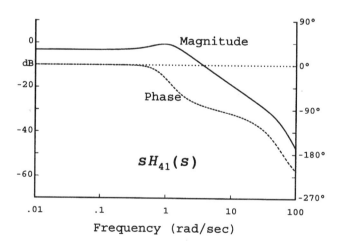

$sH_{41}(s)$

Figure 5-15 Velosity Frequency Response Function sZ_4 vs. F_1

Frequency (rad/sec)

$$\text{Zeros in } H_{11}(s): \quad -0.68064026 \pm i\, 0.27202294$$

$$-43.6868208 \pm i\, 45.9686726$$

$$\text{Zeros in } H_{21}(s): \quad -0.47008555$$

$$-1.11006482$$

$$\text{Zeros in } H_{31}(s): \quad -0.47525503$$

$$-1.11006482$$

$$-43.2172524$$

$$\text{Zeros in } H_{41}(s): \quad -0.57353019 \pm i\, 0.45856257$$

$$-1.11006482$$

The best indicator of a double pole in *this* example is visible in Figure 5–13, where the magnitude *initially* rolls off at a rate of 40 dB per decade of frequency, which is *twice* as fast as for a *single* pole (the roll-off rate increases even more after the remaining single pole is passed). This is the transfer function completely *through* the system, from an applied force at node 1 to a consequent velocity at node 2.

For *lightly* damped poles, the phase change near a multiple pole will usually be more obvious, as will the roll-off rate of the magnitude. However, it is still possible to have some zeros nearby, especially in driving point transfer functions (input impedances), where the *total* phase change is restricted to ±90°.

In Figures 5–16 and 5–17, we show the results of curve fitting to *noisy* frequency response functions for the $sH_{11}(s)$ component of the transfer matrix. We described this least-squares curve fitting technique for the control system example in section 5.3 of this chapter. We added noise to the frequency response function shown in Figure 5–12, with an *rms* noise level 125 dB below the *peak* value of the magnitude of the function. This is a *very* small amount of noise, but for this example the parameter estimates are very *sensitive* to small perturbations in the frequency response function. The small circles denote noise-free parameter values.

Figure 5–16 shows the locus of the two pairs of poles that constitute the "double poles" in the system, along with the locus of the pair of nearby zeros in the transfer function. It is rather obvious these pole estimates are seldom coincident, so they actually look like a pair of *single* poles very *close* together. However, they are *true* double poles in the mechanical system, and since they are so close together, it is best to *model* them as double poles. The *average* value of each pair is very close to the *correct* double pole value, so we use this average value in the decomposition from rational fraction to partial fraction form in *s*, using the double pole partial fraction model, thereby getting double pole *residue* values.

Figure 5–17 shows the corresponding locus of the residue values for both the multiplicity *two* poles and the multiplicity *one* poles. We have used 200 sets of measurements for each plot, so there are 200 points in each trajectory group. These groups of points

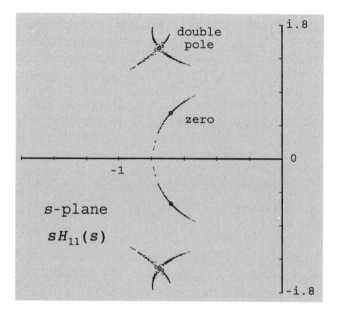

Figure 5–16   Pole-Zero Loci

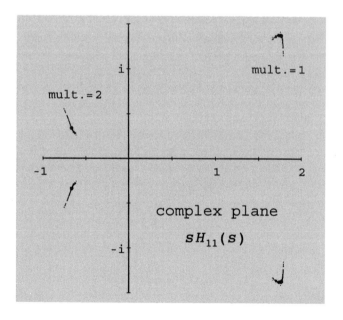

Figure 5–17   Residue Loci

comprise approximations to the probability density functions for each parameter. We have previously discussed the need for measuring both the *bias* and the *variance* (or standard deviation) on each parameter estimate, along with its probability density function, if possible. However, in this case, these various parameter estimates are highly *correlated* with one another, so it may not be very meaningful to determine their individual statistics (although it is certainly possible).

For each of the measurements, the *curve fit* is very close, so the parameters interact in a way that results in an accurate *fit*, even though the *individual* parameter estimates vary considerably. In part, this behavior is due to the poles and zeros being some distance from the frequency axis, and in part it is due to the canceling effects of pole-zero clusters. The same plots for the single pole and zero, which are much farther away from the origin, are not shown, but they are much more variable because of these factors.

The same sort of noise plots are shown for the remaining elements of the first column of the transfer matrix. Figures 5–18 and 5–19 correspond to the transfer function between an applied force at node 1 and the resulting velocity of node 2 in the gyroscope system of Figure 5–11.

The parameters for this element of the matrix are less susceptible to additive noise than those in the previous case because the zeros are farther from the double pole and hence provide a smaller degree of shielding or cancellation.

Figures 5–20 and 5–21 show the noise loci for the poles, zeros, and residues for the transfer function element between an applied force at node 1 and the velocity of node number 3.

The parameters for the transfer matrix element between an applied force at node 1 and the velocity of node 4, as shown in Figures 5–22 and 5–23, are rather poor because of the shielding effects of the pair of zeros near the double pole, in addition to the zero on the negative real axis.

This example was chosen to have heavy damping to illustrate the concept of *complex modes*, but one consequence of this choice is the sensitivity of the resulting parameter estimates to small perturbations and noise on the collected data. In practice, the modal representation of a system works best for lightly damped structures, in which the poles are close to the frequency axis. In these cases, the various modes of vibration are less *coupled* to one another, so there is less correlation between their parameters. In theory, a modal formulation is as valid for a *sandbag* (at least one with *linear* friction forces) as it is for a tuning fork, but in practice it is *most* useful for lightly damped systems.

The four *residue* values for each pole in our gyroscope example form the components of the modal vector (or vectors) for that pole. These are summarized below.

$$w_1 = \begin{bmatrix} 1.7683585 + i1.3718264 \\ -0.0148147 - i0.3887247 \\ 0.8540240 + i0.3217323 \\ 0.5833834 - i0.1029379 \end{bmatrix} \tag{5.78}$$

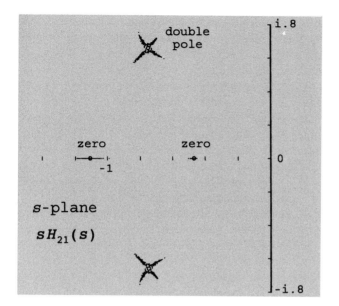

Figure 5–18   Pole-Zero Loci

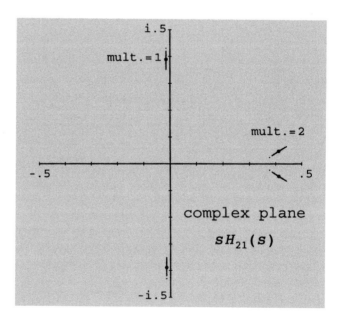

Figure 5–19   Residue Loci

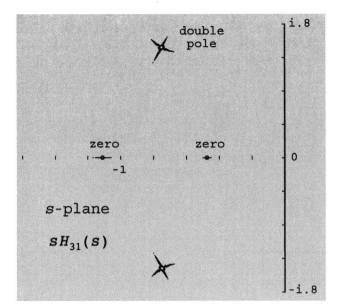

Figure 5–20   Pole-Zero Loci

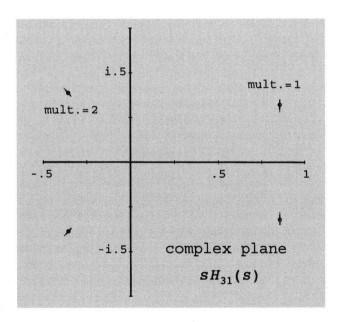

Figure 5–21   Residue Loci

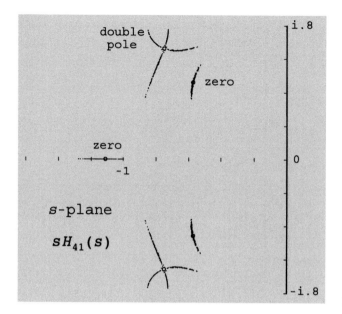

Figure 5–22   Pole-Zero Loci

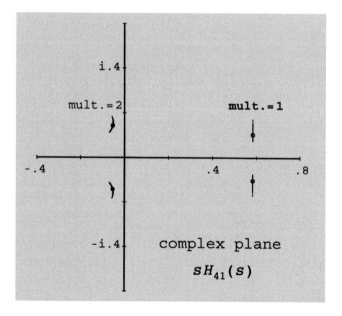

Figure 5–23   Residue Loci

$$
w_2 = \begin{bmatrix} -0.6656659 + i0.3383196 \\ 0.4115290 - i0.0465640 \\ -0.3573534 + i0.3870852 \\ -0.0541658 + i0.1428100 \end{bmatrix}
\tag{5.79}
$$

$$
w_3 = \begin{bmatrix} -0.0053280 + i0.0651457 \\ 0.0148147 + i0.0004560 \\ -0.8540240 - i0.9453007 \\ -0.5833834 + i0.5653525 \end{bmatrix}
\tag{5.80}
$$

The first vector w_1 belongs to the *unit* multiplicity part of the double pole, while the second vector represents the multiplicity *two* part of the pole (at $s_1 = -0.75010560 + i0.65992332$). The third vector w_3 is associated with the large single pole (at $s_2 = -44.4554729 + i45.1236193$). There is also a set of three complex *conjugate* modal vectors associated with the conjugates of these three poles. There is no rigid body mode in this case.

The w_2 vector is *collinear* with the modal vector u_2 (given in Eq. 5.58), and the vector w_3 is collinear with the modal vector u_3 (given in Eq. 5.61). However, w_1 is a linear *combination* of u_1 and u_2, which are orthogonal to one another. When u_2 is removed from w_1 (in a least-squares sense, using w_2), the *resultant* is collinear with u_1 (given in Eq. 5.57). Furthermore, this remanent portion of w_1 is scaled *relative* to w_2 in exactly the same way u_1 is scaled *relative* to u_2 (see Eq. 5.64). This precise interrelationship is needed to insure that the matrix-vector product $B[(s - s_1) u_1 + u_2]$ has a *double zero* at s_1, because Bu_1 alone is *not* zero at the pole, and Bu_2 only has a *first-order* zero at the pole. Notice these two vector components are *both* post-multiplied by the *same* transposed bimodal vector v_2^t to maintain this required scaling relationship. The second part of the residue for the multiplicity *one* pole, namely $u_2 v_1^t$, can have *any* amplitude, because Bu_2 has a first-order zero at the pole.

There are similar representations for all of the rows and columns of the transfer matrix $H(s)$, and they all have noise probability density functions analogous to the ones we have shown. In the interest of brevity, we will terminate the discussion of modal measurements with this set of examples and leave it up to the interested reader to investigate more cases.

It should be clear from this example that the correct *model* is essential in making any kind of meaningful modal measurements. There are *so* many possible cases to consider, and *so* many key interrelationships among the parameters, that an overly simplified model will often fail to adequately represent the structure. Worse than that, parameters might be found for an incorrect model, *without any effective indication* that the model might be *deficient*, in which case the measurement would be completely invalid. This type of measurement error could easily lead to serious consequences after the structure is in service. For example, if a double pole is not recognized, but is instead modeled as a single pole (or as two single poles and a zero), the *extra* negative phase shift due to the double pole might *not* be included in a control system model involving the structure, which could *mask* a potentially destructive *loop stability* problem. If the model is based on a *symmetric* system matrix, when there are rotating elements in the structure (indicating an *asymmetric* system), the *gyroscopic effects* from the rotating elements will not be properly reflected in the measured parameters.

5.5   GPS NAVIGATION SYSTEM

The Global Positioning System (GPS) uses three to five Earth-orbiting satellites to locate the position of a suitable GPS radio receiver. *Four* satellites are needed to find *three* position coordinates, but three satellites will suffice if one receiver coordinate is *known* (say the altitude above the Earth's centroid). A fifth satellite can be used to resolve any ambiguity between *two* possible solutions for the three receiver coordinates, although this is seldom necessary in practice. The *elements* of each satellite orbit and the *time of day* are continually transmitted to the receiver, along with a *pseudorandom noise sequence* that is unique to each transmitter. By measuring the *relative* time alignment between *pairs* of these signals, the receiver can calculate its location.

There are potential sources of error due to variations in the velocity of propagation of the radio waves between each transmitting satellite and the receiver (say, due to temperature gradients), but the largest error sources are generally atmospheric noise and noise generated in the receiver electronics. The net effect is to add some amount of random noise to each estimated arrival time *difference* between pairs of satellites.

We want to know *how much* some given amount of additive noise on these time differences affects the calculated position coordinates at the receiver. Each coordinate will be affected by a different amount, and this amount will depend on the geometry of the four transmitters. In addition, the coordinate errors will usually be *correlated* to a considerable extent. In this section, we will use our computer to *simulate* the measurement process, by adding known amounts of zero mean Gaussian noise to each received time difference and then calculating the resulting statistics for each receiver position coordinate. We will also determine the amount of correlation between the coordinate errors.

The two solutions to the GPS navigation equations are given in *closed form* in Appendix B, so we will not discuss those details in this section. The only caution is that the four transmitters should *not* lie in a plane, and especially should not form a *rectangle* in that plane. If the satellites *do* lie approximately in a rectangular plane, then the error in a direction perpendicular to this plane *can* be very large, especially along a plane that *bisects* the sides of the rectangle. We show an example of this situation in Figure 5–26 below.

Figure 5–24 shows a typical measurement configuration, with the four satellite transmitters (small dark spheres) above the receiver (which we will assume to be near the surface of the earth). We have chosen a coordinate system to place the receiver at the origin (except in Figure 5–26) and have plotted 500 calculated position solutions. The *rms* noise amplitude on each of the three pairs of received distance differences is chosen to be 0.001 units of distance, where one unit is half the length of each coordinate axis in this Figure. We use uncorrelated noise on each distance difference. We have also *multiplied*

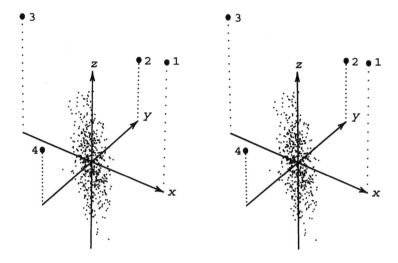

Position Errors Multiplied by 100

Figure 5–24   Typical GPS Navigation System Geometry

the position errors by a factor of 100, to make them more visible. The four satellite transmitters are located at the (x,y,z) coordinates (1,0,1.4), (0,1,0.7), (−1,0,1.3), and (0,−1,0.6).

We obtain the *error covariance matrix* by averaging all possible cross-products among the coordinate position errors. Since there are three position coordinates, this matrix will be 3×3 in size. The resulting covariance matrix (for 10,000 averages), using the geometry shown in Figure 5–24, is:

$$\text{cov}_{xyz} = \begin{bmatrix} 1.405E{-}6 & 1.750E{-}8 & -7.499E{-}8 \\ 1.750E{-}8 & 4.475E{-}7 & -1.556E{-}6 \\ -7.499E{-}8 & -1.556E{-}6 & 1.125E{-}5 \end{bmatrix} \qquad (5.81)$$

This would be a diagonal matrix if the three coordinate errors were uncorrelated. We can write the matrix of *correlation coefficients* by dividing each row and each column in the above covariance matrix by the *square root* of the *diagonal* element in that row and column. The result is:

$$\text{corr}_{xyz} = \begin{bmatrix} 1 & 0.02207 & -0.01886 \\ 0.02207 & 1 & -0.69350 \\ -0.01886 & -0.69350 & 1 \end{bmatrix} \qquad (5.82)$$

We can easily see that the y and z coordinates are highly correlated, but in a *negative* sense (−.69350), meaning a *positive z error* largely implies a *negative y error.* Note that the relative *scaling* between each coordinate error has been eliminated.

It is always possible to find an *orthonormal transformation matrix* that will *diagonalize* the covariance matrix. This means there are a set of three *orthogonal* directions along which the position errors are *uncorrelated*. The diagonal elements are the *eigenvalues* of the covariance matrix, and the *columns* of the corresponding transformation matrix are the *eigenvectors* of the covariance matrix. We can write this transformation as follows:

$$\text{cov}_{xyz} = \Phi D \Phi^t \tag{5.83}$$

where

$$\Phi = \begin{bmatrix} 0.999954 & -0.005817 & -0.007617 \\ 0.004696 & 0.990176 & -0.139750 \\ 0.008355 & 0.139708 & 0.990158 \end{bmatrix} \tag{5.84}$$

$$D = \begin{bmatrix} 1.4045E{-}6 & 0 & 0 \\ 0 & 2.2783E{-}7 & 0 \\ 0 & 0 & 1.1475E{-}5 \end{bmatrix} \tag{5.85}$$

and

$$\Phi^t \Phi = I \tag{5.86}$$

This last relation insures that the eigenvectors are *orthogonal* to one another *and* have unit magnitudes. The columns of Φ are the eigenvectors and give the directions in which the position errors are uncorrelated. The elements of D are the *variances* of the *uncorrelated* position errors in the corresponding eigenvector directions. The third element is the largest and corresponds to a direction that is approximately along the z-axis, with a small component along the negative y-axis, and a tiny component along the negative x-axis.

The three-dimensional error probability density function has an *ellipsoidal* shape around the origin, with the *axes* of the ellipsoid corresponding to the eigenvectors, and with each *semi*-axis length *proportional* to the *square root* of the eigenvalue (*standard deviation*) in that direction. In this case, these semi-axes are roughly in the ratio of 5:2:14.

Since the navigation solutions involve the roots of a quadratic equation (which is a nonlinear operation), we would expect some degree of *bias* in the results, due to noise self-rectification. This will happen for very large noise values, but in most practical cases this will not be a problem and is only a significant factor in the last example in this section.

In Figure 5–24, we have been careful to use transmitter positions that do *not* lie in a plane. In Figure 5–25, we have chosen satellites that *are* nearly in a plane to illustrate the kinds of position errors that can occur. It is apparent the position errors *perpendicular* to the approximate plane of the four transmitters are much larger than the others. In this figure, we have only multiplied the errors by a factor of 10 (instead of 100). Noise bias due to rectification can become significant in extreme cases of this sort. The transmitter coordinates for this case are (1,0,1.4), (0,1,1.3), (−1,0,0.7), and (0,−1,0.6). The resulting covariance matrix and the corresponding matrix of correlation coefficients are:

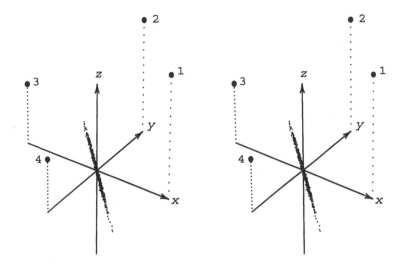

Position Errors Multiplied by 10

Figure 5–25   Satellites Approximately in a Plane

$$\text{cov}_{xyz} = \begin{bmatrix} 1.810E-5 & 2.137E-5 & -1.032E-4 \\ 2.137E-5 & 2.685E-5 & -1.286E-4 \\ -1.032E-4 & -1.286E-4 & 6.226E-4 \end{bmatrix} \qquad (5.87)$$

$$\text{corr}_{xyz} = \begin{bmatrix} 1 & 0.96955 & -0.97205 \\ 0.96955 & 1 & -0.99578 \\ -0.97205 & -0.99478 & 1 \end{bmatrix} \qquad (5.88)$$

In this case, all three coordinate errors are heavily correlated.

We can diagonalize the covariance matrix in the form of Eq. 5.83, with factors as follows:

$$\Phi = \begin{bmatrix} 0.984925 & -0.064607 & -0.160467 \\ 0.031690 & 0.979328 & -0.199783 \\ 0.170057 & 0.191686 & 0.966611 \end{bmatrix} \qquad (5.89)$$

$$D = \begin{bmatrix} 9.7182E-7 & 0 & 0 \\ 0 & 2.6520E-7 & 0 \\ 0 & 0 & 6.6630E-4 \end{bmatrix} \qquad (5.90)$$

As before, the eigenvectors are the columns of Φ. The largest error variance is the third element of D, corresponding to the third column vector in Φ. For this geometry, the standard deviations of the noise in the three eigenvector directions is in the approximate ratio of 2:1:50.

One of the *worst* transmitter configurations occurs when they all form a rectangle within a plane surface. The distance from this transmitter plane is impossible to measure if the receiver is in a plane *perpendicular* to that of the transmitters that also bisects either side of the transmitter rectangle. In this case, all of the received time and distance differences are zero for *every* distance from the transmitter plane. For other receiver locations, it is possible to obtain position data, although the accuracy of the component perpendicular to the transmitter plane may be poor. We have included Figure 5–26 to illustrate this situation. For this case, the transmitter coordinates are (1,0,1), (0,1,1), (–1,0,1), and (0,–1,1), so all of the transmitter altitudes are the *same*.

We have moved the receiver to the circle labeled "O" (for observer), whose coordinates are (0.4,0.355,0), and we have removed the error multiplication factor, so all errors are *as shown*. The cluster of position measurements has the general shape of a *hyperbola*, as we would expect if the hyperboloidal pattern for the pair of side transmitters intersects the plane through the center of, and perpendicular to, the transmitter rectangle. If we move the receiver any closer to this "forbidden" plane, these position errors become extremely large.

It is also rather obvious that there is a significant *bias* in the centroid of these 500 measurements along the *z coordinate*, due to the *nonlinear* nature of the GPS navigation equations.

Rather than running large numbers of simulations or making large numbers of physical measurements of the position errors associated with different satellite geometries, it would be helpful to have a way to *calculate* the covariance matrix of position errors from the basic GPS equations. Since we are generally interested in cases where the errors are small, we can form a linear *inverse sensitivity matrix* which relates differential changes in

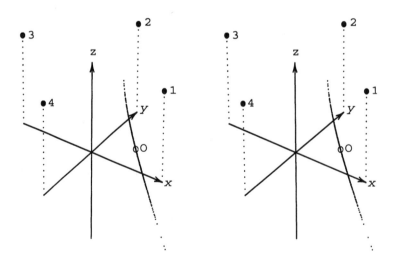

Position Errors Multiplied by 1

Figure 5–26   Satellites Exactly in a Plane Square

position to corresponding differential changes in the arrival time differences. Then, we can *invert* this matrix and use this resulting *sensitivity* matrix to calculate the approximate covariance matrix for the position errors. This will be an approximation because the derivation is based upon (infinitesimal) differential quantities, while in practice the errors are *finite*.

Note: Some books invert our definition of sensitivity, but in this case, we want the sensitivity of the *parameter values* (position coordinates) relative to changes in *observed data values* (received distance differences).

The elements of the *inverse* sensitivity matrix can be obtained by partially differentiating each of the three equations in Eq. B.2 in Appendix B, with respect to each of the receiver position coordinates. We can write the result in the form:

$$
\begin{bmatrix} dD_1 \\ dD_2 \\ dD_3 \end{bmatrix} = \begin{bmatrix} \dfrac{x_o-x_4}{L_4}-\dfrac{x_o-x_1}{L_1} & \dfrac{y_o-y_4}{L_4}-\dfrac{y_o-y_1}{L_1} & \dfrac{z_o-z_4}{L_4}-\dfrac{z_o-z_1}{L_1} \\ \dfrac{x_o-x_4}{L_4}-\dfrac{x_o-x_2}{L_2} & \dfrac{y_o-y_4}{L_4}-\dfrac{y_o-y_2}{L_2} & \dfrac{z_o-z_4}{L_4}-\dfrac{z_o-z_2}{L_2} \\ \dfrac{x_o-x_4}{L_4}-\dfrac{x_o-x_3}{L_3} & \dfrac{y_o-y_4}{L_4}-\dfrac{y_o-y_3}{L_3} & \dfrac{z_o-z_4}{L_4}-\dfrac{z_o-z_3}{L_3} \end{bmatrix} \begin{bmatrix} dx_o \\ dy_o \\ dz_o \end{bmatrix} \quad (5.91)
$$

If we call this matrix S^{-1}, then its inverse will be S. This allows us to write:

$$
\begin{bmatrix} dx_o \\ dy_o \\ dz_o \end{bmatrix} = S \begin{bmatrix} dD_1 \\ dD_2 \\ dD_3 \end{bmatrix} \quad (5.92)
$$

We form the covariance matrix of *any* vector of random variables by taking the *expected value* of the *outer* vector product of this vector times its conjugate transpose. In this case, the random variables are all *real* quantities. Our result is:

$$
\text{cov}_{xyz} = S\text{cov}_{123}S^t \quad (5.93)
$$

where cov_{xyz} is the covariance matrix of the receiver position variables x_o, y_o, z_o, and cov_{123} is the covariance matrix of the distance differences D_1, D_2, and D_3 (which are obtained from the measured arrival time differences). In this example we will assume *uncorrelated* receiver noise is added to the distance differences in *equal* amounts, so the corresponding covariance matrix will not only be *diagonal*, but will be the *common* noise power σ^2 times the *identity* matrix. Thus, we get:

$$
\text{cov}_{xyz} = \sigma^2 SS^t \quad (5.94)
$$

For the satellite geometry shown in Figure 5–24, the sensitivity matrix is:

$$
S = \begin{bmatrix} 0.804600592 & 0.035028678 & -0.873094981 \\ -0.069573761 & 0.665900570 & -0.066324772 \\ 1.978341573 & -1.976238296 & 1.885956024 \end{bmatrix} \quad (5.95)
$$

Using Eq. 5.94 we can write the *calculated* covariance matrix as:

$$\text{cov}_{xyz} = \begin{bmatrix} 1.41090397E-6 & 2.52543526E-8 & -1.24068952E-7 \\ 2.52543526E-8 & 4.52663053E-7 & -1.57870448E-6 \\ -1.24068952E-7 & -1.57870448E-6 & 1.13761833E-5 \end{bmatrix} \quad (5.96)$$

Compare this to the (simulated) *measured* covariance matrix in Eq. 5.81. Using 10,000 averages in the simulated measurement, we would only expect about two decimal digits of accuracy. The calculated form is much more accurate and much faster to obtain than either a simulated measurement or an actual physical measurement.

We can also calculate the correlation matrix, and we can *diagonalize* the covariance matrix to find directions in which the position errors are uncorrelated, just as we did for the measured covariance matrix, but we will leave that as an exercise for the reader.

For the geometry used in Figure 5–25 we find the sensitivity coefficients are considerably larger, especially for those bottom row elements that give the z-component sensitivity. We have:

$$S = \begin{bmatrix} -2.00070108 & 2.71229224 & -2.64013624 \\ -2.99955130 & 3.67840761 & -2.12815655 \\ 15.82346626 & -15.80915805 & 11.22661693 \end{bmatrix} \quad (5.97)$$

The calculated covariance matrix for Figure 5–25 is:

$$\text{cov}_{xyz} = \begin{bmatrix} 1.83296533E-5 & 2.15967451E-5 & -1.04176881E-4 \\ 2.15967451E-5 & 2.70570408E-5 & -1.29507824E-4 \\ -1.04176881E-4 & -1.29507824E-4 & 6.26348490E-4 \end{bmatrix} \quad (5.98)$$

As we mentioned in section 2.6 of chapter 2, a *good* navigation algorithm will also provide a *velocity vector* estimate and perhaps even an estimate of *acceleration*. Instead of modeling the calculated position coordinates as *constants*, we model them as *polynomials* in time, and we attach a *time tag* to each set of position coordinates. This extended model can be represented by:

$$x_{jk} = \sum_{\ell=1}^{p} b_{\ell k} t_j^{\ell-1} \quad (5.99)$$

Here, j indexes the many calculated positions x_{jk} ($1 \leq j \leq n$), each with a time tag t_j, k indexes the individual position coordinates, and ℓ indexes the polynomial coefficients $b_{\ell k}$, where $p - 1$ is the order of the polynomial. We can write this in a matrix form as:

$$X = TB \quad (5.100)$$

where X is an $n \times 3$ matrix of position coordinates x_{jk}, T is an $n \times p$ matrix of time elements $T_{j\ell} = t_j^{\ell-1}$, and B is a $p \times 3$ matrix of polynomial coefficients $b_{\ell k}$. We are *given* X and T, and we want to solve for B. As long as $n \geq p$, we can premultiply Eq. 5.100 by the *transpose* of T, and then further premultiply by the *inverse* of this product, giving:

$$B = (T'T)^{-1}T'X \quad (5.101)$$

The matrix to be inverted is $p{\times}p$ in size. For $p = 1$ we obtain only *position* coefficients b_{1k}, for $p = 2$ we get both position and *velocity* coefficients b_{1k} and b_{2k}, and for $p = 3$ we can add *acceleration* coefficients $2b_{3k}$.

The *original* parameter 3-space for this system is defined by the three equations (B.2) in Appendix B. In this *extended* model, we have a new parameter subspace of dimension $3p$, defined by p sets of equations like Eq. B.2, where the position coordinates in Eq. B.2 are augmented by a time tag and replaced by the above polynomial form.

We see the estimation of velocity and/or acceleration in addition to position is straightforward, but *more* data must be collected to obtain this new information. We can also see these new parameters will be highly *correlated*, due to the "mixing" that is indicated by Eq. 5.101. In general, the velocity parameters will have a much larger coefficient of variation (standard deviation divided by the mean value) than the position parameters, while the acceleration parameters will fare even worse.

5.6   SUMMARY OF FOUR MEASUREMENT EXAMPLES

We selected four diverse examples of measurements to help illustrate some of the theoretical topics we covered at the beginning of the book. These are *typical* measurement tasks, and have *not* been chosen for their degree of difficulty or complexity, although it may *seem* that way. Many, if not most, measurements tend to be more difficult than they first seem, especially if you really want to fully characterize the many potential sources of error in the results. Even measurements on linear systems can be fairly involved, and nonlinear systems are still more challenging.

We begin with a seemingly simple project to measure the DC resistance of a battery or power supply. This is actually a nonlinear measurement, so we quickly become involved in an *iterative* technique for estimating the resistance parameter in a best *least-squares* sense. It also provides a good opportunity to introduce the *covariance matrix,* which describes relations among the errors in the estimated parameter values.

The second example is a commonly required measurement of the parameters in a linear *closed loop control system.* However, even though the control system is linear, the solution to the best least-squares parameter estimates involves nonlinear equations, much like the first example. We use a general *curve fitting* algorithm designed to fit a *rational fraction* quotient of polynomials in the Laplace variable *s* to the *frequency response functions* of the control system along the frequency axis. Then, we convert that rational fraction into factored form, giving the *poles* and *zeros* of the system in the Laplace domain. We find it necessary to remove a bias introduced by the least-squares method, or else the pole estimates will be considerably in error.

Our third example is the measurement of the *modes of vibration* of a mechanical structure, which in this case includes a gyroscope, to illustrate the characteristics of an *asymmetric* system matrix. We have also set up the parameters to exhibit a *double* complex pole (with multiplicity two) in the Laplace domain, to illustrate how to handle this additional complexity. We introduce the concepts of *modal* and *bimodal* vectors, and we show how to represent this mechanical system in terms of these vectors, in conjunction with the Laplace domain *poles* of the system. We use the same general method of measuring these modal parameters as we used in the previous control system example, including the bias removal step.

Finally, we choose to analyze the errors in the measurement of position using the GPS satellite *navigation* system as our fourth measurement example. Again, we are faced with a nonlinear system, but we introduce a linear *parameter sensitivity matrix* that we can use to calculate an approximate covariance matrix, that describes small errors in the estimated position coordinates. We also show how to estimate velocity and/or acceleration parameters, in addition to position. We include Appendix B, which gives the details of a *closed form* solution to the GPS navigation equations.

These examples are an *essential part* of this book. Otherwise, the theory presented in the first few chapters may appear to be of only *academic* interest, with little practical value. We *need* this theoretical background to make sense out of the measurements we make on real physical systems, because these systems tend to be deceptively complicated, and are often difficult to characterize in simple terms. However, this *theory* is only as valuable as its *usefulness* in practical measurement applications. I hope these examples serve to illustrate the need for *synergism* between theory and practice.

Review of Basic Mathematical Tools

A.1 PREVIEW

Unless you are blessed with a photographic memory, you likely notice that many of the things you once learned tend to *fade* from memory, especially if they are not refreshed by continual usage. Mathematical relations and definitions are particularly susceptible to this process, since the smallest error (like a sign, for example) can invalidate an entire mathematical discourse. We have included this Appendix to help refresh your memory in a few important areas. This is not a substitute for a textbook on any topic, especially if that topic is new to you, but it *is* one step above a basic glossary of technical concepts and buzzwords.

We have chosen four subjects to review: (1) the Fourier transform, (2) the Laplace transform, (3) matrix algebra, and (4) abstract vector spaces. It is neither desirable nor possible to cover these subjects in minute detail, so in most cases we will summarize the important definitions and properties and then depend on other sources for the remaining details.

A.2 THE FOURIER TRANSFORM

A large class of events and processes that we observe in our physical world can be described by a set of partial differential equations in a rectangular coordinate system. In solving these kinds of equations, it is always best to use a coordinate system that is compatible with the shape of the boundaries, if at all possible. Each set of equations, in conjunction with its boundary conditions, has a set of related solutions, called *eigenfunctions*, each of which is indexed by an *eigenvalue*. The most general solution (for some given input excitation and initial conditions) is a weighted *sum* of all of the eigenfunctions. The eigenfunctions for a set of linear equations in *rectangular* coordinates with rectangular boundaries are *complex exponential functions*, whose exponents are the eigenvalues. The most general solution to such equations (especially when the boundaries are *not* rectangular) can be represented by an integral (which is a linear summation) of weighted eigenfunctions, using the eigenvalue as the variable of integration. If time t is the independent variable in our partial differential equations, and we define s as the associated eigenvalue (generally a complex variable), we can represent the general time domain solution $x(t)$ of our equations by:

$$x(t) = \frac{1}{i2\pi} \int X(s)e^{st}ds \qquad (A.1)$$

The eigenfunction is e^{st} and the weighting function is $X(s)/(i2\pi)$. Since we have not yet specified any contour of integration, this equation is still incomplete. The contour of integration depends on the nature of both $X(s)$ and $x(t)$ but is chosen to insure that the above integral converges to a finite time waveform over *some* useful interval of time.

If we want the allowed time interval to be unlimited (with both positive *and* negative time values allowed), then we cannot let s have a *non*-zero *real* part, or else the integrand will go to infinity. For this case, we define $s = i2\pi f$ (purely *imaginary*), and use the frequency axis (where f is the frequency in Hertz) as the contour of integration. The above integral can now be written as the *inverse Fourier transform*:

$$x(t) = \int_{-\infty}^{\infty} X(f)e^{i2\pi ft}df \qquad (A.2)$$

where we have taken the liberty of replacing $X(i2\pi f)$ with $X(f)$. All we require is that the magnitude of $X(f)$ be controlled sufficiently so this integral *exists*, at least in some sense. The forward *Fourier transform* is the inverse of this, given by:

$$X(f) = \int_{-\infty}^{\infty} x(t)e^{-i2\pi ft}dt \qquad (A.3)$$

We will introduce a shorthand notation, representing (A.3) by:

$$X(f) \leftrightarrow x(t) \qquad (A.4)$$

Notice that for each pair defined above, there is a *companion* pair obtained by replacing t by $-f$ and f by t, giving $x(-f) \leftrightarrow X(t)$, or by interchanging f and t, and conjugating both sides, giving $x^*(f) \leftrightarrow X^*(t)$. Conjugation means to change the sign of the *imaginary* part of a complex number or expression.

There are also simple scaling and shifting relations that can be derived directly from these integral definitions. For example:

$$|a| X(af) \leftrightarrow x\left(\frac{t}{a}\right) \tag{A.5}$$

$$X(f)e^{-i2\pi\tau f} \leftrightarrow x(t - \tau) \tag{A.6}$$

$$X(f - v) \leftrightarrow x(t)e^{i2\pi vt} \tag{A.7}$$

For reflections about the origin and for complex conjugation we have the relations:

$$X(-f) \leftrightarrow x(-t) \tag{A.8}$$

$$X^*(f) \leftrightarrow x^*(-t) \tag{A.9}$$

We have the *nth* derivative relations (where D is the derivative operator with respect to the appropriate independent variable):

$$D^{(n)}X(f) \leftrightarrow (-i2\pi t)^n x(t) \tag{A.10}$$

$$(i2\pi f)^n X(f) \leftrightarrow D^{(n)}x(t) \tag{A.11}$$

For the product of two functions, we get:

$$X(f)Y(f) \leftrightarrow \int_{-\infty}^{\infty} x(\tau)y(t - \tau)d\tau \tag{A.12}$$

$$\int_{-\infty}^{\infty} X(v)Y(f - v)dv \leftrightarrow x(t)y(t) \tag{A.13}$$

where the above integrals are called *convolution integrals*. Using Eq. A.9 with Eq. A.12 gives the time domain cross-correlation integral:

$$X(f)Y^*(f) \leftrightarrow \int_{-\infty}^{\infty} x(\tau)y^*(\tau - t)d\tau \tag{A.14}$$

For $Y(f) = X(f)$, we get the time domain *autocorrelation integral:*

$$|X(f)|^2 \leftrightarrow \int_{-\infty}^{\infty} x(\tau)x^*(\tau - t)d\tau \tag{A.15}$$

From Eqs. A.2 and A.3 we find the area under a function is equal to the value of its Fourier transform at the origin. Thus, we have:

$$X(0) = \int_{-\infty}^{\infty} x(t)dt \tag{A.16}$$

$$\int_{-\infty}^{\infty} X(f)df = x(0) \tag{A.17}$$

If we apply these properties to Eqs. A.14 and A.15, we get the *Power theorem* and *Rayleigh's theorem,* respectively:

$$\int_{-\infty}^{\infty} X(f)Y^*(f)df = \int_{-\infty}^{\infty} x(t)y^*(t)dt \tag{A.18}$$

$$\int_{-\infty}^{\infty} |X(f)|^2 df = \int_{-\infty}^{\infty} |x(t)|^2 dt \tag{A.19}$$

This last equation means the *total power* is the same in either the time domain or the frequency domain, which we would expect.

Next, we will show a few common Fourier transform pairs. Then, using the relations above, we can rather easily construct Fourier transforms for a large number of composite functions almost by inspection. There are many tables of transform pairs that can be consulted for more complicated functions, and there are also many general integral tables that include Fourier-type integrals. In addition, there are so called *Fast Fourier Transform* (FFT) algorithms that allow the very rapid *numerical* computation of Fourier transforms and/or their inverses. Following is a basic list of twenty Fourier transform pairs that are often useful, or that have interesting symmetry properties. Consult some of the references for these, and other more complicated pairs.

$$e^{-i2\pi f\tau} \leftrightarrow \delta(t - \tau) \tag{A.20}$$

$$\frac{1}{2}[\delta(f + \nu) + \delta(f - \nu)] \leftrightarrow \cos 2\pi\nu t \tag{A.21}$$

$$\frac{i}{2}[\delta(f + \nu) - \delta(f - \nu)] \leftrightarrow \sin 2\pi\nu t \tag{A.22}$$

$$\frac{\sin \pi f}{\pi f} \leftrightarrow \sqcap(t) \tag{A.23}$$

where $\sqcap(t)$ represents the *rectangle function*, having unit height, unit width, and unit area, centered at the time origin. Also, $\delta(f)$ is the *unit delta function,* whose area is unity over any region including the origin and zero over any region excluding the origin. The *shape* of the delta function is not defined.

$$\left[\frac{\sin \pi f}{\pi f}\right]^2 \leftrightarrow \wedge(t) \tag{A.24}$$

where $\wedge(t)$ is the *triangle function* having unit height and unit area (with width ± 1).

$$\frac{1}{1 + i2\pi f} \leftrightarrow e^{-t}, \quad \text{for } t > 0 \tag{A.25}$$

$$\frac{1}{i\pi f} \leftrightarrow \text{sgn}(t) \tag{A.26}$$

where $\text{sgn}(t)$ is the *signum function* (± 1), or sign of t. Note: sgn (0) = 0.

$$\text{III}(f) \leftrightarrow \text{III}(t) \tag{A.27}$$

where III(*) is an infinite train of unit area delta functions, spaced a unit distance apart along the abscissa. This is called the *sampling function* when used as a multiplier. Convolution with the sampling function causes *replication* along the abscissa.

$$\frac{1}{i\sinh\pi f} \leftrightarrow \tanh \pi t \tag{A.28}$$

$$\frac{\text{sgn}(f)}{i\sqrt{|f|}} \leftrightarrow \frac{\text{sgn}(t)}{\sqrt{|t|}} \tag{A.29}$$

$$-ife^{-\pi f^2} \leftrightarrow te^{-\pi t^2} \tag{A.30}$$

$$\frac{1}{1 + (\pi f)^2} \leftrightarrow e^{-2|t|} \tag{A.31}$$

$$e^{-\pi f^2} \leftrightarrow e^{-\pi t^2} \tag{A.32}$$

$$\frac{1}{\sqrt{|f|}} \leftrightarrow \frac{1}{\sqrt{|t|}} \tag{A.33}$$

$$\text{sech } \pi f \leftrightarrow \text{sech } \pi t \tag{A.34}$$

The next example shows a composite Fourier transform obtained by combining parts from the above list of transform pairs and using some of the modifying relationships discussed above. We write the frequency spectrum for an infinite train of rectangular pulses of *unit amplitude,* with a period T, a pulse width W ($W \le T$), and a delay τ of the *center* of the first pulse (from the time origin). A periodic time waveform corresponds to a sampled frequency spectrum, comprising a series of delta functions. Thus:

$$\sum_{\ell=-\infty}^{\infty} \frac{\sin\pi\ell W/T}{\pi\ell} e^{-i2\pi\ell\tau/T}\delta(f - \ell/T) \leftrightarrow \sum_{k=-\infty}^{\infty} \prod[(t - \tau - kT)/W] \tag{A.35}$$

The DC spectral line ($\ell = 0$) has an amplitude of W/T, which is the average DC level of the pulse train. The fundamental component ($\ell = 1$) is a sinusoid of peak amplitude $(2/\pi)\sin \pi W/T$, with a phase lag (relative to a cosine wave) of $2\pi\tau/T$ radians. For the ℓth harmonic, the peak amplitude is $[2/(\pi\ell)] \sin \pi\ell W/T$ with a phase lag of $2\pi\ell\tau/T$ radians. The total *power* on each side is W/T.

Next we list four Fourier transform pairs that we use in this book to obtain the *characteristic functions* for four of our probability density functions (see chapter 3). All we need to do is replace f with the appropriate random variable in the left side of the equation (giving the PDF) and replace $2\pi t$ with ω in the right side of the equation (giving the characteristic function). For a Gaussian PDF with standard deviation σ and mean value v, we have:

$$\frac{1}{\sqrt{2\pi}\,\sigma}\, e^{-\frac{1}{2\sigma^2}(f-v)^2} \;\leftrightarrow\; e^{i2\pi vt - 2(\pi\sigma t)^2} \tag{A.36}$$

This can be readily derived from Eq. A.32 using Eqs. A.5 and Eq. A.7. For the chi-squared PDF with n degrees of freedom we use the pair:

$$\frac{f^{\alpha-1}}{\Gamma(\alpha)}\, e^{-f} \;\leftrightarrow\; \frac{1}{(1 - i2\pi t)^\alpha} \;, \quad \text{for } f > 0 \tag{A.37}$$

where $\alpha = n/2$ for this application. We use Eq. A.5 to replace t by $2\sigma^2 t$ to obtain the actual PDF. A form of this pair can be found in reference [A:2], page 51, No. 524.2.

For the sum of n pairs of products of two independent zero mean Gaussian random variables, we require the pair (with $\alpha = n/2$):

$$\frac{1}{\sqrt{\pi}\,\Gamma(\alpha)}\, \left|\frac{f}{2}\right|^{\alpha-\frac{1}{2}} K_{\alpha-\frac{1}{2}}(|f|) \;\leftrightarrow\; \frac{1}{[1 + (2\pi t)^2]^\alpha} \tag{A.38}$$

where K_v is the modified Bessel function of the second kind of order v. See reference [A:2], page 61, No. 569.0.

Finally, for the discrete binomial PDF, our Fourier transform pair involves sums of delta functions, and the characteristic function becomes periodic. We have the pair (from Eq. A.7 above):

$$\sum_{k=0}^{n} \binom{n}{k} a_0^{n-k} a_1^k\, \delta(f - k\Delta f) \;\leftrightarrow\; (a_0 + a_1 z)^n \;, \quad \text{where } z = e^{i2\pi\Delta ft} \tag{A.39}$$

where the binomial coefficients are defined by:

$$\binom{n}{k} = \frac{n!}{k!\,(n-k)!} \tag{A.40}$$

In rectangular coordinates it is easy to generalize from the one-dimensional Fourier transform to multidimensional Fourier transforms by simply replacing the one-dimensional exponential kernel by the product of exponential kernels for each dimension and integrating over each dimension. It is also possible to introduce coordinate transformations, thereby getting an equivalent Fourier transform in these *new* coordinates. For example, a two-dimensional transform in polar coordinates can be obtained rather easily. If the corresponding two-dimensional function has circular symmetry, then the integral over the azimuth angle can be effected, producing a zero order Bessel function for the kernel of a *new* transform along the *radius* direction. This is called a *Hankel transform,* but it is simply a form of the Fourier transform in polar coordinates. See the references for more information.

A.3   THE LAPLACE TRANSFORM

Let's return our attention to Eq. A.1 and agree to restrict time to be *non*-negative. *Now, s* can have any real value as long as it is *finite*. Without going into the details, it turns out that if $X(s)$ is an *analytic function* in the complex plane, then a suitable integration contour is a straight line parallel to the imaginary axis and to the *right* of all singularities that appear in $X(s)$. We call the resulting integral the *inverse Laplace transform*, written as:

$$x(t) = \frac{1}{i2\pi} \int_{c-i\infty}^{c+i\infty} X(s)e^{st}ds \qquad (A.41)$$

for a suitable real constant *c*. The *forward Laplace transform* is:

$$X(s) = \int_0^\infty x(t)e^{-st}dt \qquad (A.42)$$

The Laplace and Fourier transforms are obviously very similar, especially in view of the *principle of analytic continuation*, which states that if an analytic function is defined along any line segment, or if its derivatives are all defined at any point, then the function is defined throughout the *entire* complex plane.

However, all physical systems are assumed to be *causal*, meaning we never get an output from a system *until* we apply an input excitation. If we apply our input *at* time zero, then we never encounter negative time, so the Laplace formulation is ideal. Furthermore, the characterization of linear systems (of differential equations) in the Laplace domain involves *singularities* located in the left half of the *s*-plane, generally at *complex* values of *s*, so we don't want to be restricted to the imaginary frequency axis.

Thus, we tend to associate the Fourier transform with existing signals, or with essentially continuous test signals, like random noise or sinusoids. We tend to associate the Laplace transform with transient events and with describing the response of linear systems to transient excitations. The actual characterization of a linear system can be done in *either* domain. We can even employ the Fourier transform as an intermediate step (via the *frequency response function*, and the principle of analytic continuation) in finding the parameters for the Laplace transform. However, the Laplace domain provides an efficient means for describing or *coding* linear system behavior using a minimum number of parameters.

When we apply the Laplace transform to both sides of a set of differential equations in the time domain, we get a set of polynomials in the Laplace variable *s*. The solutions to these equations can be represented by either the quotient of two polynomials in *s*, called a *rational fraction form,* or equivalently by the sum of terms involving the reciprocals of monomials in *s*, called a *partial fraction representation*. In either case, these solutions are completely defined and described either by the roots of both numerator and denominator polynomials (plus a gain factor) in the rational fraction form, or by the denominator roots (called *poles*) and the associated numerator coefficients (called *residues*) in the partial fraction form. In general, these parameters are complex numbers.

Nearly all of the modification relations described above for the Fourier transform (beginning with Eq. A.5) are also valid for the Laplace transform, *if* you replace $i2\pi f$ by s. Instead of repeating these modification relations, we instead list a few (10) useful Laplace transform pairs. Keep in mind that all these time waveforms are defined to be *zero* for *negative* values of time.

$$\frac{1}{s} \leftrightarrow 1 \tag{A.43}$$

$$\frac{n!}{s^{n+1}} \leftrightarrow t^n \tag{A.44}$$

$$\frac{1}{s+a} \leftrightarrow e^{-at} \tag{A.45}$$

$$\frac{n!}{(s+a)^{n+1}} \leftrightarrow t^n e^{-at} \tag{A.46}$$

$$e^{-\tau s} \leftrightarrow \delta(t-\tau) \tag{A.47}$$

$$\frac{a}{s^2 + a^2} \leftrightarrow \sin at \tag{A.48}$$

$$\frac{s}{s^2 + a^2} \leftrightarrow \cos at \tag{A.49}$$

$$\frac{b}{(s+a)^2 + b^2} \leftrightarrow e^{-at}\sin bt \tag{A.50}$$

$$\frac{s+a}{(s+a)^2 + b^2} \leftrightarrow e^{-at}\cos bt \tag{A.51}$$

A common composite transform pair involves a linear combination of forms Eqs. A.50 and A.51. The left side is a general representation of a pair of complex conjugate poles in the s-domain, which yields a *complex exponential function* in the time domain (beginning at time zero). The *natural frequency of oscillation* is b radians per second, and the *damping coefficient* is a radians per second. The pair of complex conjugate *poles* are located at $s = -a \pm ib$, and the *resonant frequency* is $\sqrt{a^2 + b^2}$.

As with the Fourier transform, we can use the modification rules to construct a variety of composite Laplace transforms. For example, the Laplace transform pair for a unit amplitude rectangular pulse, starting at time a and ending at time b is:

$$\frac{1}{s}(e^{-as} - e^{-bs}) \leftrightarrow \prod[(t-a)/(b-a) - .5] \tag{A.52}$$

There are numerous tables of Laplace transform pairs, just as there are of Fourier transform pairs, so there is seldom a need to actually evaluate the defining integral Eq. A.42. See the references below for more details.

Both of these transforms have two valuable properties. They convert time domain differential equations into simple *polynomials* in the transform domain and time domain convolution operations into simple *multiplication* operations in the transform domain.

A.4 MATRIX ALGEBRA

As soon as mathematicians learned to solve several linear algebraic equations simultaneously for several unknown variables, they invented matrix algebra, primarily as a shorthand notation to ease the task of manipulating such systems of equations. Matrix notation does very little to reduce the actual work involved in solving these sets of equations numerically, but it is essential in the many intermediate operations that are often required to properly modify and organize the equations so a solution can be found. Since it is basically a shorthand notation, the various rules for the manipulation of matrix quantities must be set up to produce the same answer we would have gotten from solving the equations without this notation. If some of the rules seem strange or arbitrary, remember they are simply based on the manipulations required to solve a set of simultaneous linear algebraic equations.

To keep things simple, let's use an example having only two unknown quantities. The two equations can be written as:

$$a_{11}x_1 + a_{12}x_2 = y_1 \tag{A.53}$$

$$a_{21}x_1 + a_{22}x_2 = y_2 \tag{A.54}$$

Given, the a_{jk} coefficients and the values of y, the problem is to solve for the values of x. We define a matrix and two vectors as:

$$A = \begin{bmatrix} a_{11} & a_{12} \\ a_{21} & a_{22} \end{bmatrix} \quad , \quad \text{matrix of coefficients} \tag{A.55}$$

$$X = \begin{bmatrix} x_1 \\ x_2 \end{bmatrix} \quad , \quad \text{unknown vector} \tag{A.56}$$

$$Y = \begin{bmatrix} y_1 \\ y_2 \end{bmatrix} \quad , \quad \text{known vector} \tag{A.57}$$

Vectors are written as columns of elements or components, while matrices comprise both rows and columns (a vector is also a matrix with only one column). Matrices can be square or rectangular, having any number of rows and columns. The elements in a vector or matrix can be real numbers, complex numbers, functions of some set of variables (for example, polynomials or partial fractions), or other matrices. A matrix has a *rank* and *dimensions*. The dimensions are (first) the number of rows and (second) the number of columns, while the rank is the number of *independent* rows or columns in the matrix. The dimension of a *square* matrix is called its *order*. In this current example both the order and the rank of the square matrix are two (and the dimensions are 2×2).

In these terms, we can write the *pair* of simultaneous linear equations (Eqs. A.53 and A.54) as the *single* matrix equation:

$$AX = Y \tag{A.58}$$

where AX is defined to be the *matrix product* of A times X. We can deduce the rules for performing this multiplication by looking at the original pair of equations. The first component of Y (namely y_1) is obtained by summing the products of the corresponding components of the *first row* of A with the elements of the column vector X. The second component of Y (which is y_2) is obtained by summing the products of the corresponding components of the *second row* of A with the elements of the column vector X. In any matrix product, we sum products of *rows* of the left matrix with *columns* of the right matrix. It is apparent that we generally cannot change the *order* in which the symbols are written, although there are some exceptions. In mathematical terms, matrix multiplication is usually *noncommutative*.

Since we are working with linear equations, it is possible to express the components of the solution vector X as linear combinations of the components of the known vector Y as:

$$X = BY \tag{A.59}$$

where the elements of the B matrix turn out to be:

$$B = \begin{bmatrix} b_{11} & b_{12} \\ b_{21} & b_{22} \end{bmatrix} = K \begin{bmatrix} a_{22} & -a_{12} \\ -a_{21} & a_{11} \end{bmatrix} \tag{A.60}$$

$$K = \frac{1}{a_{11}a_{22} - a_{12}a_{21}} \tag{A.61}$$

where K is a *scalar* quantity (a matrix of order *one*). Notice both matrix products AB and BA result in the diagonal identity matrix I, so we define B as the *inverse* of A (written $B = A^{-1}$). Here is a case where A and B do commute. The 2×2 identity matrix is:

$$I = \begin{bmatrix} 1 & 0 \\ 0 & 1 \end{bmatrix} \tag{A.62}$$

Multiplication by the identity matrix leaves the original matrix (or vector) unchanged. In the right hand part of Eq. A.60, the matrix in the *a* coefficients is called the *adjoint* of A (or adj A), and $1/K$ is called the *determinant* of A (or det A). In general:

$$A^{-1} = \frac{\text{adj } A}{\text{det } A} \tag{A.63}$$

The actual calculation of either the determinant or the inverse of a matrix is usually rather tedious. You can find recipes for these operations in any reference on matrix theory. In fact, we seldom *need* to calculate these quantities in practice. They are primarily of theoretical value, and we are mostly interested in their various properties and interrelationships. Here are a few properties of the determinant (for square matrices only):

$$\det(A^{-1}) = \frac{1}{\det A} \qquad\qquad (A.64)$$

$$\det(cA) = c^n \det A \qquad\qquad (A.65)$$

where c is any scalar quantity and n is the order (number of rows or columns) of the matrix.

$$\det A = \det A^t = (\det A^*)^* = (\det A^T)^* \qquad\qquad (A.66)$$

where A^t is the transpose of A (rows and columns interchanged), A^* is the complex conjugate of A, and A^T is the complex conjugate transpose of A.

$$\det(AB) = (\det A)(\det B) \qquad\qquad (A.67)$$

Many matrices are *not* square, so we need to be very careful to keep the various dimensions compatible. For example, in Eq. A.58 suppose X is an m-dimensional vector and Y is an n-dimensional vector, where $n > m$. Then, A must have dimensions $n \times m$, where the first integer is the number of rows and the second integer is the number of columns. In order to form a matrix product, the first factor must have the same number of columns as the second factor has rows. In this case, A has no unique inverse. However, if we premultiply Eq. A.58 by A^t we get:

$$A^t A X = A^t Y \qquad\qquad (A.68)$$

The dimensions of A^t are are $m \times n$, so the dimensions of $A^t A$ are $m \times m$. This is now a square matrix and can *usually* be inverted. So:

$$X = (A^t A)^{-1} A^t Y \qquad\qquad (A.69)$$

The matrix $(A^t A)^{-1} A^t$ is called the *left-handed pseudoinverse* of A because if you post-multiply it by A, you get the identity matrix. This is not a unique inverse however, because you can pre-multiply Eq. A.58 by any $n \times n$ symmetric matrix, getting a new pseudoinverse $(A^t W A)^{-1} A^t W$. There is also an analogous *right-handed pseudoinverse* for matrices that have more columns than rows ($m > n$), given by $W A^t (A W A^t)^{-1}$.

Even if a matrix *is* square, it cannot be inverted unless its *rank* is equal to its *order*, meaning all rows (or all columns) of the matrix must be linearly independent of one another. A matrix that cannot be inverted is called a *singular matrix*. You must take care to avoid using or even *implying* the inverse of a matrix whose rank is deficient relative to the order.

There are a couple of vector-vector products we don't want to overlook. The first one is the scalar *inner* vector product denoted by the sums of the conjugate products of corresponding vector elements. The other is the *outer* vector product, which is actually a matrix, but one with *unit* rank. An example of an inner vector product is:

$$X^T Y = \begin{bmatrix} x_1^* & x_2^* \end{bmatrix} \begin{bmatrix} y_1 \\ y_2 \end{bmatrix} = x_1^* y_1 + x_2^* y_2 \quad , \quad \text{(a scalar)} \qquad\qquad (A.70)$$

In contrast, the *outer* vector product is the rank 1 matrix:

$$XY^t = \begin{bmatrix} x_1 \\ x_2 \end{bmatrix} [y_1 \ y_2] = \begin{bmatrix} x_1y_1 & x_1y_2 \\ x_2y_1 & x_2y_2 \end{bmatrix} \tag{A.71}$$

The solution to a *homogeneous* matrix-vector equation is often required. For example, this is the way to calculate the eigenvectors of a matrix, once the eigenvalues have been determined. This type of equation also arises in the determination of modal vectors (see section 2.5 of chapter 2) of vibrating mechanical systems. The general form of the equation is:

$$AU = 0 \tag{A.72}$$

where A is a *singular* square matrix, and U is the *homogeneous solution vector.* This equation states that at least *one* row of the matrix is linearly *dependent* upon the other rows, so a vector must exist that is *orthogonal* to *all* of the rows of A. Vectors are defined to be orthogonal if their *inner vector product* is zero. Thus, the solution to this homogeneous equation is the vector that is orthogonal to all of the rows of the *singular* matrix. Let's emphasize that a solution of this kind cannot *exist* unless the matrix is singular.

One of the best ways to solve for this vector is by means of the *Gram-Schmidt orthogonalization procedure.* Begin with a row vector U^t of *random* elements. Then, starting with any row of A, remove that row from all *other* rows of A, *and* from U^t itself. Repeat this procedure for every remaining row of A. When you have finished, whatever is left of U^t will be orthogonal to all rows of A, because all rows of A are now orthogonal to *themselves*, as well as to the *one* possible remaining vector U^t (For an nth order square matrix there are exactly n *possible* vectors among the rows and columns, and at least one is absent when the matrix is singular). In the unlikely event that the residual of U^t is considered to be too small (if the rounding errors in the computations form a significant part of the residual vector), then simply choose a different set of starting random vector elements, and repeat the procedure.

To help clarify the Gram-Schmidt technique, we will show how to remove one vector from another, so the residual will be orthogonal to the vector removed. Let's remove as much of X as possible from Y. We need to minimize the magnitude of the vector difference $Y - aX$, by adjusting the scalar multiplier a. Thus, we minimize:

$$\epsilon = (Y - aX)^T(Y - aX) \tag{A.73}$$

We assume all of these quantities (except ϵ) are complex numbers. We simply differentiate ϵ with respect to a, and set the result to zero. We get:

$$a = \frac{X^TY}{X^TX} \tag{A.74}$$

The residual of Y (denoted by $\tilde{Y}$) becomes:

$$\tilde{Y} = Y - aX = Y - \left(\frac{X^TY}{X^TX}\right) X \tag{A.75}$$

It is easy to see that $X^T \tilde{Y} = 0$, proving the orthogonality between X and the residual of Y. This Gram-Schmidt procedure is a very useful tool in our bag of matrix-vector tricks.

We sometimes need to partition our matrices into parts, so we need to know how to manipulate such expressions. In general, matrix partitions behave just like scalar quantities as long as you do not interchange the order of any multiplications, and as long as you use matrix inversion instead of trying to divide matrices. For example:

$$\begin{bmatrix} A & B \\ C & D \end{bmatrix} \begin{bmatrix} X \\ Y \end{bmatrix} = \begin{bmatrix} AX + BY \\ CX + DY \end{bmatrix} \tag{A.76}$$

where all of these quantities are matrices. It *is* important to maintain compatibility between the dimensions of these partitions, so all indicated products and sums can be performed properly.

Suppose we want the *inverse* of a partitioned matrix, also in partitioned form. We form either of the products:

$$\begin{bmatrix} A & B \\ C & D \end{bmatrix} \begin{bmatrix} E & F \\ G & H \end{bmatrix} = \begin{bmatrix} I & 0 \\ 0 & I \end{bmatrix} = \begin{bmatrix} E & F \\ G & H \end{bmatrix} \begin{bmatrix} A & B \\ C & D \end{bmatrix} \tag{A.77}$$

We assume the A,B,C,D matrix partitions are known, and we want to calculate the parts of the E,F,G,H matrix, which by definition is the *inverse* of the first, because their product is the identity matrix. If we perform the indicated product on the left, we get four matrix equations, from which we can solve for the four unknown partitions, giving:

$$E = (A - BD^{-1}C)^{-1} \tag{A.78}$$

$$F = -A^{-1}B(D - CA^{-1}B)^{-1} \tag{A.79}$$

$$G = -D^{-1}C(A - BD^{-1}C)^{-1} \tag{A.80}$$

$$H = (D - CA^{-1}B)^{-1} \tag{A.81}$$

We can factor the above expressions to give the partitioned matrix inverse in the following form:

$$\begin{bmatrix} A & B \\ C & D \end{bmatrix}^{-1} = \begin{bmatrix} I & -A^{-1}B \\ -D^{-1}C & I \end{bmatrix} \begin{bmatrix} (A - BD^{-1}C)^{-1} & 0 \\ 0 & (D - CA^{-1}B)^{-1} \end{bmatrix} \tag{A.82}$$

It is possible to verify this result by either premultiplying or postmultiplying both sides of this expression by the inverse of the left side. An alternate form of this inverse is:

$$\begin{bmatrix} A & B \\ C & D \end{bmatrix}^{-1} = \begin{bmatrix} (A - BD^{-1}C)^{-1} & 0 \\ 0 & (D - CA^{-1}B)^{-1} \end{bmatrix} \begin{bmatrix} I & -BD^{-1} \\ -CA^{-1} & I \end{bmatrix} \tag{A.83}$$

The *Sherman-Morrison-Woodbury* matrix identity is often very useful in manipulating expressions of this type. It can be written as:

$$(A + BD^{-1}C)^{-1} = A^{-1} - A^{-1}B(D + CA^{-1}B)^{-1}CA^{-1} \tag{A.84}$$

One common matrix problem is to find a transformation that will diagonalize a square matrix. This requires the calculation of the *eigenvalues* and the *eigenvectors* of the matrix, which are defined as follows (Note: These are *not* the same eigenquantities we discussed above for differential equations):

$$AU = \lambda U \tag{A.85}$$

where U is the eigenvector corresponding to the scalar eigenvalue λ. For an *nth* order square matrix, there will be n eigenvectors and n eigenvalues. For a symmetric matrix, it is possible to show these eigenvectors are orthogonal to one another as long as each eigenvalue is different. If identical eigenvalues *do* appear, then it is still possible to *construct* a set of orthogonal eigenvectors. Also notice the scaling of each vector is arbitrary, so it is possible to define an *orthonormal* set of eigenvectors, in which the magnitude of each vector is unity. For an asymmetric matrix, the eigenvalues form an independent set of vectors that can be scaled to have unit magnitudes, but they will *not* generally be orthogonal. If we construct a matrix Θ whose columns comprise all of the orthonormal eigenvectors, and a *diagonal* matrix Λ whose elements comprise all of the eigenvalues, then we can write the square symmetric matrix A in factored form as:

$$A = \Theta \Lambda \Theta^t \ , \quad \text{where} \tag{A.86}$$

$$\Theta^t \Theta = I = \Theta \Theta^t \quad \text{(if all eigenvectors are unique)} \tag{A.87}$$

Note that det Θ is unity, as we can see from Eq. A.87. Thus, we conclude that det A = det Λ, which is the product of all the eigenvalues of A (because Λ is diagonal). The determinant of any square matrix is the product of its eigenvalues. Also note:

$$A^{-1} = \Theta \Lambda^{-1} \Theta^t \tag{A.88}$$

We see that the *inverse* of A has the same eigenvectors as A, but has eigenvalues that are the reciprocals of those of A. In this canonical form, both the inverse and the determinant of a matrix are particularly easy to calculate. Notice, if one or more eigenvalues are zero, then the matrix is singular and cannot be inverted (det $A = 0$).

In case A is square but *asymmetric*, we can write the factors as:

$$A = \Theta^{-1} \Lambda \Theta \tag{A.89}$$

$$\Theta^{-1} \Theta = I = \Theta \Theta^{-1} \quad \text{(if all eigenvectors are unique)} \tag{A.90}$$

$$A^{-1} = \Theta^{-1} \Lambda^{-1} \Theta \tag{A.91}$$

$$\det A = \det \Lambda = \prod_k \lambda_k \tag{A.92}$$

As before, we assume A is a non-singular matrix. The determinant of A is *still* the product of the eigenvalues because the determinant of Θ is canceled by the determinant of its inverse.

The references cover much more material on matrix algebra, but it is beyond the scope of this section to delve into each facet of the subject, so we will move into a discussion of some of the applications of this matrix theory in the following section.

A.5   ABSTRACT VECTOR SPACES

Most of us find a geometrical view of some of these mathematical concepts to be helpful, since our eye–brain system seems to be able to organize and comprehend vast amounts of information at a glance. The pure mathematician would like you to believe his or her world is one of theorems, proofs, and logic, with no need for visual crutches.

The head of the mathematics department at one of our major universities was once asked about this point of view, in the middle of a course in the Theory of Real Variables. The text (by Landau) comprised the statements and the proofs of something like 480 theorems, involving 101 definitions, with absolutely no figures or visual aids! When he answered, he lowered his voice, smiled just a bit, and embarrassingly admitted that professional mathematicians *sometimes* resorted to visual or graphical representations of their theories, but only in the privacy of their own homes late at night!

Since this book is not for mathematicians, we needn't have this particular hangup. A good geometrical construction can easily be worth a few equations (A picture may be worth a thousand words, but equations are more compact than words!). In this section, we will discuss ways to represent large amounts of data in a form that we can at least visualize by *analogy* with our three-dimensional spatial world.

We introduce *abstract* spaces (vector spaces), in which the coordinates of a point can be any set of numbers you choose, whether they represent something physical or not. They are not constrained to represent physical lengths or distances. However, we *will* restrict our discussion to Riemannian geometries, in which a continuous *abstract distance* measure between points is well defined. We are not restricted to *rectangular* coordinates, but allow curvilinear coordinates as well, although rectangular coordinates are often the easiest to use. Likewise, we are not restricted to flat spaces, but allow all sorts of curved spaces, although flat spaces are usually the most convenient to work with.

Our spaces can have any finite number of dimensions, starting at one. A space of zero dimension is a point, and there is nothing to say about a point except its location. A one-dimensional space is a line (generally curved) usually embedded in a space of higher dimensionality. The associated coordinate system is simply a scale of abstract "distance" along this line. Any point on this line can be indexed by a single number. A space of two dimensions is an ordinary surface, which comprises two independent sets of constant coordinate contours. Any point on this surface can be indexed by two numbers, one for each coordinate system.

Do not be confused by the fact that a two-dimensional surface (like a sphere, for example) seems to occupy some volume in a *three*-dimensional space. The surface does *not* include any of the interior or exterior regions. If any point can be described by exactly two real numbers, then that point is part of a two-dimensional surface. Additional parameters may be used to position and/or orient this subspace within the parent space (like the location of the center of a sphere, for example), but these extra parameters are not used *within* the subspace itself (which is strictly the *surface* of the sphere).

In general, an *m*-dimensional space requires exactly *m* sets of independent coordinates to index or locate any point in that space. For *each* coordinate, the entire space can be "factored" (or decomposed) into two different, but complementary, components. First, an infinite number of *coordinate lines* or threads can be defined, each of which comprises a space curve obtained by varying *that* particular coordinate, while holding all other coordinates constant. One such thread is generated for each combination of the other $m - 1$ coordinates. A ruler or scale of the value of this selected coordinate can be visualized as *marked* along each thread.

Second, orthogonal to each thread, but passing through a *common* coordinate value on each thread (as indicated by the ruler scale), is an $(m - 1)$-dimensional subspace called a *constant coordinate contour*, obtained by varying all *but* this selected coordinate over all possible ranges. Thus, the space is spanned by an infinite number of these constant coordinate contours, one for each coordinate *value* along the set of threads for *that* selected coordinate. The space is spanned by *m* distinct sets of these coordinate lines and their corresponding coordinate contours.

From another perspective, the intersection of a *j*-dimensional space with a *k*-dimensional subspace gives a space of dimensionality $j - k$. Thus, the intersection of a set of one-dimensional coordinate lines (for some coordinate value) with an *m*-dimensional space leaves an $(m - 1)$-dimensional subspace. By induction, the intersection of *m* one-dimensional sets of coordinate lines (each for a particular coordinate value) leaves a single point (zero-dimensional space), which is the point in the *m*-space selected by this particular set of coordinate values. One thread for each coordinate is selected to be called the *coordinate axis*, and is customarily the thread for which all other coordinate values are zero (although this is completely arbitrary).

A one-dimensional space is a degenerate case, since constant coordinate contours are simply points along the single coordinate line. For a two-dimensional space, the constant coordinate contours are space curves, as well as coordinate lines for the second dimension. The generality of this approach can only be fully appreciated for dimensionalities greater than two.

When discussing coordinates, it is important to be clear as to whether you are referring to constant coordinate contours (each of dimension $m - 1$), or to coordinate lines or threads, each of dimension one. This terminology often seems to be used rather loosely, and can contribute to some degree of misunderstanding.

If this is a subspace of a larger parent space of *n* dimensions (where $n \geq m$) then exactly *n* parametric equations will be needed to define the *m*-subspace, but each equation will be a function of only *m* variables. In principle, it is possible to invert *m* of these parametric equations to obtain an expression for *each* of the *m* parameter variables in terms of exactly *m* of the *n* coordinates of the parent space. Then all *m* parameter variables can be eliminated by substituting these representations into the *remaining $n - m$* parametric equations, thereby replacing the *m* parameter variables with *m* of the parent space coordinates. The result is a set of $n - m$ equations in all *n* parent space coordinates (but devoid of any references to a coordinate system in the parameter subspace). These are no longer called parametric equations, because the parameters have been eliminated. However, we *have* reduced the number of equations needed to define the parameter subspace to a minimum of $n - m$, even though we have *lost* all m of the original parameter contours, as well as all references to parameter values.

For example, we can completely describe the surface of a sphere of radius r, centered at $x = a$, $y = b$, and $z = c$, embedded in a three-dimensional space having rectangular coordinates (x, y, z) by the single equation:

$$(x - a)^2 + (y - b)^2 + (z - c)^2 = r^2 \qquad (A.93)$$

In this case, $n = 3$, and $m = 2$, so $n - m = 1$ equations are adequate. However, this does *not* reference any system of *coordinates* on the spherical surface, so we can only describe the points on this surface in terms of the original set of three parent coordinates, via this one equation. Notice, if $m = n$, we can only describe a zero dimensional space, or a single point somewhere in the n-space. This point is called the *solution* to the set of n equations in n unknowns. Similarly, a space *curve* (a one-dimensional subspace) requires two equations in (x, y, z) for its definition. However, in parametric form, all *three* of these subspaces require n equations.

In most of our applications we will use a flat n-dimensional parent space having rectangular coordinates. However, we must take whatever parameter subspace our equations dictate. These will generally be curved subspaces having curvilinear coordinates. They will often be of rather high dimensionality (equal to the number of parameters we have in the system), although we can still think *analogously* in terms of a one-dimensional or two-dimensional surface embedded in a three-dimensional space, while depending on our mathematics to handle any details resulting from this higher dimensionality.

We will represent any point in our parent n-space by an n-vector referenced to the origin of a rectangular coordinate system. The elements of this vector are its projections on each coordinate axis of the system (which pass through this origin). The parameter represented by this axis (a space curve) is indexed by the distance along the axis measured from the origin. *You* are responsible for defining the location of the origin, as well as for defining the dimensionality of the parent space. You can choose to use *non*-rectangular coordinates if you want. Ultimately, you will be writing the parametric equations for some subspace of interest using this parent coordinate system.

We will define an m-vector whose elements are the m parameter values. This vector exists wholly *within* the parameter subspace, although the geometrical interpretation is somewhat awkward unless the parameter coordinate system is rectangular, because the vector may seem to *protrude* outside of the subspace. Also, if the coordinate axes are space curves, it is hard to visualize how a component of the parameter vector can still be considered as a projection of that vector onto a parameter coordinate axis. The best way to interpret a parameter vector is simply as an *abstract vector* (having no visible size) that exists at each point in the parameter subspace and whose elements are simply those corresponding parameter values. For example, on the surface of a sphere, the parameters might be latitude and longitude angles, so the two-dimensional parameter vector has those two angles as elements at each point on the sphere.

We next introduce the notation $G(U)$ to define a subspace in parametric form. $G(U)$ is an n-vector of functions of the elements of the parameter m-vector U. Thus, each element of G is an expression involving *all* of the parameter variables, that gives *exactly one* of the coordinate values in the original n-dimensional parent system. The G vector is referenced to the origin of this system. For a rectangular coordinate system, each element of G is the projection of a particular point in the parameter subspace onto one of the coordinate axes of the original n-space. As the parameter variables range over their allowed values, they trace out the entire parameter subspace embedded in the parent space.

We would like to define the m-dimensional generalization of a tangent "plane" to our m-dimensional parameter subspace at some point. This will be a flat-space approximation to the (generally) curved parameter subspace in the infinitesimal vicinity of this point. An m-plane is defined by n *linear* equations in the m parameter variables, expressed as:

$$G_p(U) = TU + X_c \qquad (A.94)$$

where T is an $n \times m$ matrix whose columns are tangent vectors, and X_c is a constant offset n-vector. The offset vector can be eliminated by making the origin of the coordinates in the parent space the same as the origin for the parameters in the parameter subspace. Here, the elements of U enter into each of the n parametric equations linearly. The matrix T of m tangent vectors to this plane is given by:

$$T = \frac{\partial G(U)}{\partial U} \qquad (A.95)$$

In this formulation, the tangent plane *changes* as a function of U. $G_p(\mathrm{U})$ and X_c are both n-vectors, and U is an m-vector.

If we want to find *all* vectors that are orthogonal to the tangent plane, we simply solve for the $n - m$ possible n-vectors X (say, using the Gram-Schmidt procedure) that satisfy the homogeneous equation:

$$\left[\frac{\partial G(U)}{\partial U} \right]^t X = 0 \qquad (A.96)$$

If we want to find the orthogonal vector that exactly passes *through* a point X_o (which is *not* in the parameter subspace) we solve the equation:

$$\left[\frac{\partial G(U)}{\partial U} \right]^t [G(U) - X_o] = 0 \qquad (A.97)$$

for the parameter vector U. Unfortunately, this is generally a nonlinear equation and must usually be solved in an iterative fashion. If $G(U)$ is actually linear, or if we choose a local linear approximation to $G(U)$, then we can use Eq. A.94, giving:

$$T^t[TU + X_c - X_o] = 0 \qquad (A.98)$$

We can now solve this linearized equation explicitly for U, giving:

$$U = (T'T)^{-1}T'(X_o - X_c) \tag{A.99}$$

You can begin with a starting approximation for U, substitute these *newly* calculated elements of U back into Eqs. A.95 and A.99 and repeat this iteration until the answer converges.

There are times when we need to *integrate* a function over some region of our parameter space. An example would be the integration of the joint probability density function (PDF) over m random parameter variables. We need to know the infinitesimal m-volume element in our parameter subspace to use in this integration.

The problem is, each parameter is measured in its *own* units, so they are related to one another like apples and oranges. One parameter might be an angle and another might be a frequency or a damping coefficient. Some parameters might have *no* units at all. However, they are all related to the parent coordinate system in n-space by the definition of the parameter subspace $G(U)$. Thus, we need a way to translate between infinitesimal changes in *each* individual parameter value, and the corresponding infinitesimal vector changes in the n-vector $G(U)$. Referring to Eq. A.95 above, we see that each column of T represents the tangent n-vector to one of the parameter coordinate lines. If we post-multiply T by a *diagonal* matrix comprising the differentials of each parameter, we get a matrix of *differential tangent vectors*. Thus, each column is *now* a differential basis vector representing one parameter in the parameter coordinate system, *but* is expressed in the n-space coordinates of the *parent* system.

We can determine all possible *interrelations* between these vectors, by projecting each one onto all members of the set, resulting in an $m \times m$ symmetric matrix that no longer involves n. We can then use an eigenvector/eigenvalue decomposition to obtain the square root of the result, giving a matrix of m differential basis m-vectors that lie *solely* within the parameter subspace. The new vectors have the same interrelations among themselves as the original ones. Let's define the diagonal matrix of parameter differentials as:

$$\delta U = \begin{bmatrix} du_1 & & & 0 \\ & \cdot & & \\ & & \cdot & \\ & & & \cdot \\ 0 & & & du_m \end{bmatrix} \tag{A.100}$$

The corresponding differential n-vector components in G are:

$$\delta G = T \delta U \tag{A.101}$$

All possible interrelations between column vectors are given by:

$$(\delta G)^t \delta G = \delta U \, (T'T) \, \delta U \tag{A.102}$$

However, we would like the square root of this matrix, to obtain an expression involving only first-order differentials. We can do this by finding the eigenvalues and the orthonormal eigenvectors of $T'T$, as we indicated above in Eqs. A.86 and A.87. Let's define:

$$T'T = \Theta \Lambda \Theta^t \tag{A.103}$$

Now we can write the square root of this matrix as:

$$\sqrt{T'T} = \Theta \sqrt{\Lambda} \, \Theta^t \tag{A.104}$$

To prove this is correct, $T'T = \Theta \sqrt{\Lambda} \, \Theta^t \Theta \sqrt{\Lambda} \, \Theta^t = \Theta \sqrt{\Lambda}\sqrt{\Lambda} \, \Theta^t = \Theta \Lambda \Theta^t$. Recall, Λ is a diagonal matrix, so its square root is well defined (except for sign). Now we can write the square root of Eq. A.102 as:

$$\delta \widetilde{G} = \sqrt{(\delta G)'\delta G} = \Theta \sqrt{\Lambda} \, \Theta' \delta U = \sqrt{T'T} \, \delta U \tag{A.105}$$

If we premultiply this by its own transpose, we get Eq. A.102 back again. The distinction between δG and $\delta \widetilde{G}$ is, the first is a set of m basis n-vectors and the second is a set of m basis m-vectors, but they comprise the *same* vectors, namely the differential tangents to each of the parameter coordinate lines *in* the parameter subspace. In the formulation in Eq. A.105, we describe these tangent vectors without any reference to the parent n-space. Yet, these tangent vectors have the *units* of the parent coordinate system (which are carried by the T matrix) and thereby provide a common way to represent the effects of the various parameter changes, no matter what *their* respective units might be. This T matrix serves to convert the *units* of the parameters to those of the parent vector space in much the same way the *conditional* probability density function performs this task in Bayes theorem for the estimation of parameter vectors (see Sec. 4.6 of Chap. 4).

In any dimensionality, the set of orthonormal eigenvectors of a symmetric matrix form the boundaries of a multidimensional unit cube (a hypercube), and each eigenvalue multiplies the length of one side of the cube, so the multidimensional volume of the resulting rectangular parallelepiped (called an orthotope) is simply the product of the eigenvalues. This is also the value of the *determinant* of the original matrix, so we do not really need to calculate the eigenvalues to get the volume, after all.

Even more generally, the multidimensional volume of the parallelotope, defined by *any* set of (at least partially) independent tangent vectors is equal to the determinant of the matrix whose columns comprise those vectors. So, given any $m \times m$ non-singular matrix, the m-parallelotope formed by all of the column vectors (or all of the transposed row vectors) has an m-volume given by the determinant of the matrix.

One consequence of this relation is a *zero* determinant value when any vector becomes a linear combination of the others, because the m-parallelotope collapses into an $(m-1)$-parallelotope, hence the *volume* of the original goes to zero. The matrix becomes singular and *non*invertible when this occurs.

Returning to Eq. A.105 we can write the $m \times m$ matrix of tangent vector differentials for any given diagonal matrix of parameter differentials δU as:

$$\delta \widetilde{G} = \sqrt{T'T} \, \delta U \tag{A.106}$$

and the m-volume differential element becomes:

$$\det(\delta \widetilde{G}) = \sqrt{\det(T'T)} \, (du_1 du_2 du_3 \ldots \ldots du_m) \tag{A.107}$$

where the du_v are the elements of δU, which are the differentials of the individual parameters.

For some examples of the determinant representation of area or volume, consider a two-vector representation of a parallelogram, spanned by the pair of vectors $[x_1 \; y_1]^t$ and $[x_2 \; y_2]^t$. The determinant of the 2×2 matrix of which these two vectors are the columns is:

$$\det \begin{bmatrix} x_1 & x_2 \\ y_1 & y_2 \end{bmatrix} = x_1 y_2 - x_2 y_1 \tag{A.108}$$

It is easy to show this is the 2-volume or area of the parallelogram. We should mention that the two vectors must be translated until they intersect at one corner of the parallelogram.

In 3-space we have a normal parallelepiped defined by the three vectors that comprise the columns of a 3×3 matrix, and that all intersect at a corner of the parallelepiped. The volume is:

$$\det \begin{bmatrix} x_1 & x_2 & x_3 \\ y_1 & y_2 & y_3 \\ z_1 & z_2 & z_3 \end{bmatrix} = x_1(y_2 z_3 - y_3 z_2) + x_2(y_3 z_1 - y_1 z_3) + x_3(y_1 z_2 - y_2 z_1) \tag{A.109}$$

As an interesting sidebar, if we join the ends of a pair of intersecting vectors in two-space, we get a triangle whose two-volume (area) is $1/2!$ of that for the corresponding parallelogram. If we join the ends of a triplet of intersecting vectors in three-space, we get a tetrahedron, whose three-volume is $1/3!$ of the associated parallelepiped volume. In general, in m-space, an m-dimensional version of the tetrahedron (called an m-simplex) has $1/m!$ of the m-volume of the related m-parallelotope.

As an example of the area (or volume) element of integration over a subspace, consider a sphere of fixed radius (centered at the origin) as our two-dimensional parameter subspace, in which the parameters are latitude θ and longitude φ. The matrix $G(U)$, defining this sphere in terms of the parent (x, y, z) three-space and the two parameters is given by:

$$G(U) = r \begin{bmatrix} \cos\theta \, \cos\varphi \\ \cos\theta \, \sin\varphi \\ \sin\theta \end{bmatrix}, \quad \text{where} \tag{A.110}$$

$$U = \begin{bmatrix} \theta \\ \varphi \end{bmatrix} \tag{A.111}$$

and r is the constant radius of the sphere. Note that the three elements of G are the (x, y, z) coordinates of the sphere in the parent three-space.

We can immediately write the elements of the matrix of tangent vectors in the θ and φ directions as:

$$\frac{\partial G(U)}{\partial U} = T = r \begin{bmatrix} -\sin\theta\,\cos\varphi & -\cos\theta\,\sin\varphi \\ -\sin\theta\,\sin\varphi & \cos\theta\,\cos\varphi \\ \cos\theta & 0 \end{bmatrix} \qquad \text{(A.112)}$$

The corresponding diagonal matrix of parameter differentials is:

$$\delta U = \begin{bmatrix} d\theta & 0 \\ 0 & d\varphi \end{bmatrix} \qquad \text{(A.113)}$$

Next we form:

$$T'T = r^2 \begin{bmatrix} 1 & 0 \\ 0 & \cos^2\theta \end{bmatrix} \ , \ \ \text{giving} \qquad \text{(A.114)}$$

$$\sqrt{T'T} = r \begin{bmatrix} 1 & 0 \\ 0 & \cos\theta \end{bmatrix} \qquad \text{(A.115)}$$

These last two matrices will only be diagonal if the tangent vectors are orthogonal. Finally, we get:

$$\delta \widetilde{G} = r \begin{bmatrix} d\theta & 0 \\ 0 & \cos\theta\,d\varphi \end{bmatrix} \qquad \text{(A.116)}$$

The required area element is:

$$\det(\delta \widetilde{G}) = r^2 \cos\theta\,d\theta\,d\varphi \qquad \text{(A.117)}$$

As a check, we integrate this area element over the entire surface of the sphere, giving:

$$\int_0^{2\pi} \int_{-\pi/2}^{\pi/2} r^2 \cos\theta\,d\theta\,d\varphi = 4\pi r^2 \qquad \text{(A.118)}$$

which is the correct area of a sphere with radius r.

This concludes our review of some of the basic mathematical tools needed in making measurements. We discussed the Fourier transform, the Laplace transform, matrix algebra, and abstract vector spaces. Of course, there are numerous other topics that we could have included, but we should leave some of these "fun" activities for the reader. There are numerous good references to consult for further information.

BIBLIOGRAPHY ON MATHEMATICAL TOOLS

[A:1] Bracewell, Ronald N. *The Fourier Transform and Its Applications,* McGraw-Hill, 1986. An excellent book on all aspects of the Fourier transform. Very readable.

[A:2] Campbell, George A., and Foster, Ronald M., *Fourier Integrals for Practical Applications,* D. Van Nostrand Co., 1948. This book is an excellent table of Fourier transform pairs, especially for higher transcendental functions.

[A:3]   Coxeter, H.S.M., *Regular Polytopes,* Dover Publications, 1973. Covers *m*-dimensional volume elements, including the *m*-parallelepiped (*m*-parallelotope) and the *m*-simplex (which is a general *m*-dimensional tetrahedron).

[A:4]   Gantmacher, F.R., *The Theory of Matrices,* Chelsea Publishing Co., volume 1, 1960. One of the standard references on matrix theory. Includes a discussion of the volume of *m*-parallelepipeds.

[A:5]   Golub, Gene H. and Van Loan, Charles F., *Matrix Computations,* Johns Hopkins University Press, 1984. Good general reference on matrix theory and on practical methods of matrix computation.

[A:6]   Householder, Alston S., *The Theory of Matrices in Numerical Analysis,* Dover Publications, 1964. A standard reference on matrix theory and applications.

[A:7]   Johnson, Lee W., Riess, R. Dean, and Arnold, Jimmy T., *Introduction to Linear Algebra,* 3rd ed., Addison-Wesley, 1993. A general introduction to matrix algebra.

[A:8]   Lass, Harry, *Elements of Pure and Applied Mathematics,* McGraw-Hill, 1957. An old book, but a good review of many of the topics we discuss in this appendix.

[A:9]   Roberts, G.E., and Kaufman, H., *Table of Laplace Transforms,* W.B. Saunders Co., 1966. A very extensive compilation of Laplace transform pairs.

[A:10] Walker, James S., *Fourier Analysis,* Oxford University Press, 1988. Includes both theory and applications.

[A:11] Whittaker, E.T., and Watson, G.N., *A Course of Modern Analysis,* Cambridge University Press, a 1992 reprint of the 4th edition, originally published in 1927. The first edition was published in 1902. It must be good to have survived that long (and it is).

B

Derivation of (Closed Form) GPS Navigation Equations

Given the three *distance differences* from an observer to a set of four Earth-orbiting satellites, it is possible to derive the three position coordinates of the observer in a *closed form* (non-iterative) manner, *if* the positions of all of the satellites are known. We will derive these solutions in this appendix, using a rectangular coordinate system. It is straightforward to convert to and from a spherical coordinate system, but that conversion will not be discussed here.

We assume transmitter coordinates (x_k, y_k, z_k) for $k = 1,2,3,4$, and observer (or receiver) coordinates (x_o, y_o, z_o). The distances between the observer and the kth transmitter are:

$$L_k = \sqrt{(x_o - x_k)^2 + (y_o - y_k)^2 + (z_o - z_k)^2} \tag{B.1}$$

The formulation of the distance differences is somewhat arbitrary, but for this derivation we will subtract the other three distances from L_4, giving:

$$D_k = L_4 - L_k \quad , \quad \text{for } k = 1, 2, 3 \tag{B.2}$$

If we multiply this by $L_4 + L_k$, we can obtain two other forms:

$$2D_k L_k = L_4^2 - L_k^2 - D_k^2 \quad , \quad \text{for } k = 1, 2, 3 \tag{B.3}$$

$$2D_k L_4 = L_4^2 - L_k^2 + D_k^2 \quad , \quad \text{for } k = 1, 2, 3 \tag{B.4}$$

These forms are useful because they are *linear* expressions in the receiver coordinates. In particular:

$$L_4^2 - L_k^2 = 2(x_k - x_4)x_o + 2(y_k - y_4)y_o + 2(z_k - z_4)z_o + R_4^2 - R_k^2 \quad \text{(B.5)}$$

where

$$R_k^2 = x_k^2 + y_k^2 + z_k^2 \quad , \quad \text{for } k = 1, 2, 3, 4 \quad \text{(B.6)}$$

We can express *all* of the distances L_k between the satellites and the receiver *linearly* in terms of the receiver coordinates. We can subtract any one of the equations in B.3 from the other two, giving *two* linear equations relating the receiver coordinates in terms of the measured distance *differences*. Then, we can use one of the equations in B.4 along with the corresponding equation in B.1 to get a *quadratic* expression in the receiver coordinates. We can use the two linear expressions to eliminate *two* of the receiver coordinates, thereby getting a quadratic in the *remaining* coordinate. The linear equations can be written as:

$$D_j D_k (D_k - D_j) = D_k(L_4^2 - L_j^2) - D_j (L_4^2 - L_k^2) \quad , \quad \text{or} \quad \text{(B.7)}$$

$$K_{jk} = A_{jk} x_o + B_{jk} y_o + C_{jk} z_o \quad , \quad \text{for } j \neq k = 1, 2, 3 \quad , \quad \text{where} \quad \text{(B.8)}$$

$$A_{jk} = 2 \left[D_k(x_j - x_4) - D_j (x_k - x_4) \right] \quad \text{(B.9)}$$

$$B_{jk} = 2 \left[D_k (y_j - y_4) - D_j (y_k - y_4) \right] \quad \text{(B.10)}$$

$$C_{jk} = 2 \left[D_k (z_j - z_4) - D_j (z_k - z_4) \right] \quad \text{(B.11)}$$

$$K_{jk} = (D_j D_k - R_4^2) (D_k - D_j) + D_k R_j^2 - D_j R_k^2 \quad \text{(B.12)}$$

The remaining *quadratic* equation is obtained by squaring both Eqs. B.1 and B.4, substituting Eq. B.5 into Eq. B.4, and then equating the resulting two expressions for $4D_k^2 L_4^2$, giving:

$$[2x_o(x_k - x_4) + 2y_o(y_k - y_4) + 2z_o (z_k - z_4) + R_4^2 - R_k^2 + D_k^2]^2$$
$$= 4D_k^2[(x_o - x_4)^2 + (y_o - y_4)^2 + (z_o - z_4)^2] = 4D_k^2 L_4^2 \quad \text{(B.13)}$$

There are three possible choices of pairs of linear equations from Eq. B.8, for indices $(j, k) = (2,1)$; $(3,1)$, $(1,2)$; $(3,2)$, or $(1,3)$; $(2,3)$, depending on which coefficients are zero. Then, there are three choices as to which pair of receiver coordinates to eliminate using these two linear equations. Finally, there are three possible choices for the quadratic equation from Eq. B.13.

In some cases, one set of coefficients in Eq. B.8 (say the C_{jk}) are all zero, so one of the receiver coordinates (say z_o) cannot be represented in terms of the other two. In these cases, we get explicit solutions for the other two coordinates (say x_o and y_o) from the two linear equations in B.8, and we can try to solve for the third coordinate using the quadratic equation B.13.

There are some cases when *no* solutions are possible, or at least not practical. For example, imagine the four satellites forming the corners of a rectangle within a plane. If the receiver is located anywhere along a line perpendicular to the transmitter plane and passing through the center of the rectangle, then all distance differences are equal (namely *zero*) everywhere on this line, and the equations cannot predict the receiver *position* along this line. There are other configurations that pose similar problems, and there are many configurations in which the calculated position has large errors in at least one direction.

Once we choose the best pair of *jk* values in Eq. B.8, we can write the resulting pair of linear equations as:

$$A_1 x_o + B_1 y_o + C_1 z_o = K_1 \tag{B.14}$$

$$A_2 x_o + B_2 y_o + C_2 z_o = K_2 \tag{B.15}$$

where these coefficient subscripts (1,2) represent the two *jk* subscript choices from Eq. B.8.

In general, we can eliminate any two receiver coordinates by expressing them in terms of the third coordinate by means of Eqs. B.14 and B.15. However, we do not want to *divide* by any of these coefficients, in case they are zero (or very small). We define the following six quantities:

$$F_1 = B_1 C_2 - B_2 C_1 \qquad F_2 = A_1 C_2 - A_2 C_1 \qquad F_3 = A_1 B_2 - A_2 B_1$$

$$G_1 = K_1 A_2 - K_2 A_1 \qquad G_2 = K_1 B_2 - K_2 B_1 \qquad G_3 = K_1 C_2 - K_2 C_1$$

We can now represent the three possible linear equations for the removal of *any two* of the receiver coordinates as follows:

$$F_2 x_o + F_1 y_o = G_3 \tag{B.16}$$

$$F_3 x_o - F_1 z_o = G_2 \tag{B.17}$$

$$F_3 y_o + F_2 z_o = -G_1 \tag{B.18}$$

We expected three *pairs* of these equations, but it turns out *half* of the six equations are redundant, so we are left with three *equations* instead of three pairs. Actually, only two of these three equations are linearly independent.

If either *one* or *two* of the F coefficients are zero, then we can immediately solve for one or two of the receiver coordinates using these linear equations. For example, let $F_1 = 0$. We get two possible solutions for x_o, namely $x_{o1} = G_3/F_2$, and $x_{o2} = G_2/F_3$. We can still use Eq. B.17 to eliminate either y_o or z_o, and then we can use the quadratic equation B.13 to solve for the remaining value. If *both* F_1 and F_2 are zero, we can write $x_o = G_2/F_3$ and $y_o = -G_1/F_3$, and then use the quadratic form to get z_o. Similar arguments apply for the other F coefficients.

Next, we will derive expressions for the three possible quadratic equations indicated in B.13, in terms of either x_o, y_o, or z_o. For the first case, we will use Eqs. B.16 and B.17 to remove y_o and z_o, giving a quadratic in x_o. First, multiply Eq. B.13 by F_1^2 and then replace y_o and z_o. We can write Eq. B.13 in the two forms:

$$(H_k x_o + E_{xk})^2 - 4D_k^2(P x_o^2 + Q_x x_o + S_x) = 0 \tag{B.19}$$

$$(H_k^2 - 4D_k^2 P)x_o^2 + (2E_{xk}H_k - 4D_k^2 Q_x)x_o + (E_{xk}^2 - 4D_k^2 S_x) = 0 \tag{B.20}$$

where

$$H_k = 2[F_1(x_k - x_4) - F_2(y_k - y_4) + F_3(z_k - z_4)] \tag{B.21}$$

$$E_{xk} = 2[G_3(y_k - y_4) - G_2(z_k - z_4)] + F_1(R_4^2 - R_k^2 + D_k^2) \tag{B.22}$$

$$P = F_1^2 + F_2^2 + F_3^2 \tag{B.23}$$

$$Q_x = -2[F_1(F_1 x_4 - F_2 y_4 + F_3 z_4) + F_2 G_3 + F_3 G_2] \tag{B.24}$$

$$S_x = F_1^2 x_4^2 + (F_1 y_4 - G_3)^2 + (F_1 z_4 + G_2)^2 \tag{B.25}$$

With one more set of substitutions we can write the quadratic Eq. B.20, along with its two solutions as:

$$T_{2k} x_o^2 + T_{1xk} x_o + T_{oxk} = 0 \tag{B.26}$$

$$x_{o1} = -\frac{T_{1xk}}{2T_{2k}} + \sqrt{\left(\frac{T_{1xk}}{2T_{2k}}\right)^2 - \frac{T_{oxk}}{T_{2k}}} \tag{B.27}$$

$$x_{o2} = -\frac{T_{1xk}}{2T_{2k}} - \sqrt{\left(\frac{T_{1xk}}{2T_{2k}}\right)^2 - \frac{T_{oxk}}{T_{2k}}} \tag{B.28}$$

where

$$T_{2k} = H_k^2 - 4D_k^2 P \tag{B.29}$$

$$T_{1xk} = 2E_{xk}H_k - 4D_k^2 Q_x \tag{B.30}$$

$$T_{oxk} = E_{xk}^2 - 4D_k^2 S_x \tag{B.31}$$

In case $T_{2k} = 0$, then x_o is given by:

$$x_o = -\frac{T_{oxk}}{T_{1xk}} \tag{B.32}$$

If $T_{1xk} = T_{2k} = 0$, then there is no solution for x_o. Likewise, since we require that x_o be a real number, there is no solution if the radical in Eqs. B.27 and B.28 is imaginary. Thus, we require that $T_{1xk}^2 \geq 4T_{2k}T_{oxk}$.

To form a similar quadratic equation in y_o, we multiply Eq. B.13 by F_2^2 and replace x_o and z_o using Eqs. B.16 and B.18. We get:

$$(H_k y_o + E_{yk})^2 - 4D_k^2(P y_o^2 + Q_y y_o + S_y) = 0 \tag{B.33}$$

where H_k and P are the same as above, and:

$$E_{yk} = 2[-G_3(x_k - x_4) + G_1(z_k - z_4)] - F_2(R_4^2 - R_k^2 + D_k^2) \tag{B.34}$$

$$Q_y = -2[F_2(-F_1x_4 + F_2y_4 - F_3z_4) + F_1G_3 - F_3G_1] \tag{B.35}$$

$$S_y = (F_2x_4 - G_3)^2 + F_2^2y_4^2 + (F_2z_4 + G_1)^2 \tag{B.36}$$

Our two solutions are similar to the previous case:

$$T_{2k}y_o^2 + T_{1yk}y_o + T_{oyk} = 0 \tag{B.37}$$

$$y_{o1} = -\frac{T_{1yk}}{2T_{2k}} + \sqrt{\left(\frac{T_{1yk}}{2T_{2k}}\right)^2 - \frac{T_{oyk}}{T_{2k}}} \tag{B.38}$$

$$y_{o2} = -\frac{T_{1yk}}{2T_{2k}} - \sqrt{\left(\frac{T_{1yk}}{2T_{2k}}\right)^2 - \frac{T_{oyk}}{T_{2k}}} \tag{B.39}$$

where

$$T_{2k} = H_k^2 - 4D_k^2P \tag{B.40}$$

$$T_{1yk} = 2E_{yk}H_k - 4D_k^2Q_y \tag{B.41}$$

$$T_{oyk} = E_{yk}^2 - 4D_k^2S_y \tag{B.42}$$

Finally, we will repeat this process to get a quadratic in z_o by multiplying Eq. B.13 by F_3^2 and using Eqs. B.17 and B.18 to replace the variables x_o and y_o. We have:

$$E_{zk} = 2[G_2(x_k - x_4) - G_1(y_k - y_4)] + F_3(R_4^2 - R_k^2 + D_k^2) \tag{B.43}$$

$$Q_z = -2[F_3(F_1x_4 - F_2y_4 + F_3z_4) - F_1G_2 - F_2G_1] \tag{B.44}$$

$$S_z = (F_3x_4 - G_2)^2 + (F_3y_4 + G_1)^2 + F_3^2z_4^2 \tag{B.45}$$

Our two solutions are similar to the previous two cases:

$$T_{2k}z_o^2 + T_{1zk}z_o + T_{ozk} = 0 \tag{B.46}$$

$$z_{o1} = -\frac{T_{1zk}}{2T_{2k}} + \sqrt{\left(\frac{T_{1zk}}{2T_{2k}}\right)^2 - \frac{T_{ozk}}{T_{2k}}} \tag{B.47}$$

$$z_{o2} = -\frac{T_{1zk}}{2T_{2k}} - \sqrt{\left(\frac{T_{1zk}}{2T_{2k}}\right)^2 - \frac{T_{ozk}}{T_{2k}}} \tag{B.48}$$

where

$$T_{2k} = H_k^2 - 4D_k^2P \tag{B.49}$$

$$T_{1zk} = 2E_{zk}H_k - 4D_k^2Q_z \tag{B.50}$$

$$T_{ozk} = E_{zk}^2 - 4D_k^2 S_z \qquad (B.51)$$

If there are degenerate solutions in these last two cases, they can be determined in the same manner as the values for x_o in the first case.

Notice that the coefficient T_{2k} on the squared coordinate is the same for all three cases, so if this coefficient is zero, then we will have degenerate solutions for all cases. However, there are three choices for k (1,2,3), so they may not all be zero.

We need some criteria by which we can make the optimum choices among all of the coefficient options that are inherent in these equations. You might be tempted to think the final results are independent of these choices, but this turns out to be false. Nearly any of the choices work fine in most cases, but there are degenerate configurations in which many options fail. Of course, sometimes all options fail! Our goal is to try to maximize the accuracy of the position solutions under the greatest number of transmitter and receiver configurations.

Our first choice is among the coefficients in the linear equations that are indexed by the k subscript in Eq. B.8. These are ultimately used to derive equations B.16 through B.18, which we use to eliminate two of the three receiver coordinates, so we are left with a single quadratic in the remaining coordinate. We want at least *one* nonzero F coefficient, and we would prefer they *all* be nonzero. Thus, a reasonable criterion for selecting these coefficients might be to choose the set having the *largest* of the *least* or smallest (but *nonzero*) magnitudes. This should give us the best chance to use these linear equations.

The next choice is which variable to assign to the quadratic equation. This really depends on the F coefficients in Eqs. B.16 through B.18. Notice that to eliminate variables y_o and z_o via these linear equations, we need a substantial F_1 coefficient. Then we would use a quadratic in x_o for the remainder of the solution. Thus, we select the quadratic coordinate x_o, y_o, or z_o, depending on the largest of the coefficients F_1, F_2, or F_3.

Finally, we still have a choice of coefficients within the selected quadratic, as indexed by the k subscript in Eq. B.13. Our main concern is to avoid imaginary or complex roots, because we know our receiver coordinates are real numbers. Thus, we might choose the set of coefficients to maximize the algebraic value of the discriminant of the quadratic (the part involving the square root operation). This would improve our chances of getting real answers, and it would also be a good strategy if the quadratic degenerated into a linear equation.

These choices work well in computer simulations of various transmitter/receiver geometries, although there are still many cases when at least one receiver coordinate is of poor quality. There are also some degenerate cases in which no solution is possible without another transmitter.

Glossary of Technical Words and Concepts

a posteriori: Determined or defined *after* an event or observation has occurred and thus partly derived from *observed* facts.

a priori: Determined or defined *before* an event or observation has occurred and thus derived from basic principles *without* supporting observations.

abscissa: The coordinate or axis (usually drawn horizontally) of the *independent variable* in a mathematical expression.

algorithm: A precise, step-by-step, procedure or recipe for solving a problem or for implementing some mathematical function or process.

analytic function: A function of a complex variable having a unique single *value* at each point in a region and also having a unique single value for each *derivative* at each point in the region. This is a *continuous* function and *excludes* branch points, singular points, and points with multiple values.

angular frequency: A frequency measured in *radians per second*, as opposed to *cycles* per second, or Hertz.

asymmetric matrix: A matrix *without* any significant symmetry properties. A matrix where the elements *mirrored* across the diagonal are *not* all equal.

bandwidth: The *width* of a particular frequency interval of interest, usually expressed in *Hertz* or cycles per second.

basis functions: Complete sets of functions that can be *linearly* combined to represent any other *arbitrary* function. Examples are: *powers* of the independent variable (Taylor's expansion), *sinusoids* (Fourier series), and various *orthogonal polynomials* (such as Chebyshev polynomials).

basis vectors: Any *linearly independent* set of vectors that span the *entire* space in question. Any other arbitrary vector in this space can be represented as a linear *sum* of these basis vectors.

Bayes theorem: The factorization of a *joint* probability density function (PDF) into the *product* of an *ordinary* PDF and a *conditional* PDF. For two random variables x and y, the conditional PDF of x *given* y times the PDF of y is the same as the conditional PDF of y *given* x times the PDF of x.

bias: The difference between a *measured* or *estimated* mean value of a probability density function and the *true* mean value.

bimodal vectors: A set of homogeneous solutions to the equations describing an *asymmetric* linear system. If the asymmetric matrix B represents a linear physical system, then $B^t v = 0$ is the homogeneous equation whose solutions v are bimodal vectors.

Central Limit Theorem: The probability density function (PDF) of the *sum* of several random variables approaches a Gaussian form as the number of variables approaches *infinity*, independent of the *shape* of each individual PDF, for a large class of PDFs.

central moment of PDF: A moment of a probability density function (PDF) *centered* at the *mean value* of the PDF. The definition for the mth central moment is:

$$E[(x - \mu_x)^m] = \int_{-\infty}^{\infty} (x - \mu_x)^m p_x(x)\, dx \qquad (G.1)$$

where μ_x is the mean value, and $p_x(x)$ is the PDF of x.

characteristic function: The inverse Fourier transform of the probability density function of a random variable. Also, one of a set of homogeneous solutions to a differential equation.

chirp: A sinusoid that is frequency modulated with a linear ramp. A sinusoid whose frequency is linearly "swept" between two limits in a *short* period of time.

closed loop: A closed loop control system is one where the *difference* between a reference signal and some version of the output signal becomes the composite *input* signal, thereby forming a closed signal path or loop.

coefficient of variation: The *standard deviation* (the square root of the variance) divided by the *mean value* of a random variable.

complex conjugate: A new complex number obtained by changing the *sign* of the *imaginary part* of an original complex number.

complex exponential: An exponential function whose exponent is a complex coefficient multiplied by time. This is also called a *decaying* sinusoid.

complex number: The sum of an ordinary *real* number and $i = \sqrt{-1}$ times a second real number $(a + ib)$. This latter part is called the *imaginary part* of the complex number. Without these complex numbers, the results of certain arithmetic operations on *real numbers* could not be defined.

condition number: The product of the *norm* of a matrix times the norm of the *inverse* of that matrix. The norm of a matrix is a measure of the "magnitude" of the matrix. The condition number is greater than (or equal to) *unity* and goes to infinity as the matrix becomes singular (meaning the matrix is *not* invertible).

conditional PDF: A joint probability density function in which some "random variables" are held *constant*.

confidence interval: An interval along the *abscissa* of a probability density function, within which the *area* under the function has some preassigned value, called the confidence *level*.

confidence level: A preassigned *area* (less than unity) under a portion of a probability density function used to define a confidence *interval* for that random variable.

conjugate transpose: The *interchange* of rows and columns of a matrix, where all complex element values are conjugated (the sign of the imaginary part is changed) *as* they are interchanged.

control system: A physical system comprising various electrical and/or mechanical parts connected in a way such that some *output* quantity (say position or voltage) is "forced" to follow some prescribed input *reference* quantity, at least as closely as possible. Most control systems use *negative feedback* to compare some form of the output quantity to the input reference quantity, and then *use* this *difference* to try to *correct* the output.

convolution: A process in which *translated* replicas of some *reference* function are *summed* together in accordance with the *values* of a *second* "weighting" function. The *same* result is obtained when these two functions are *interchanged*. The convolution $z(t)$ between $x(t)$ and $y(t)$ is defined as:

$$z(t) = \int_{-\infty}^{\infty} x(t - \tau)y(\tau)d\tau = \int_{-\infty}^{\infty} y(t - \tau)x(\tau)d\tau \qquad \text{(G.2)}$$

correlation coefficient: The *expected* (or average) value of the *product* of two random variables *after* each of their *mean values* have been removed, divided by *each* of their standard deviations. The correlation coefficient between x and y is:

$$\rho_{xy} = \frac{E[(x - \mu_x)(y - \mu_y)]}{\sigma_x \sigma_y} \qquad \text{(G.3)}$$

where μ_x and μ_y and are the mean values, and σ_x and σ_y are the standard deviations of x and y, respectively.

covariance matrix: The *expected* value of the *outer vector product* of a zero mean value random vector times its *complex conjugate*. This will be a square symmetric matrix. The definition is:

$$\text{cov}(X) = E[(X - E[X])\,(X - E[X])^T] \tag{G.4}$$

critical damping: The damping of a resonant system when two conjugate poles of the Laplace transform coalesce to produce a *double* pole on the negative real *s*-axis.

cross-diagonal elements: The elements of a matrix along the cross-diagonal from the *lower left* corner to the *upper right* corner.

cumulative probability distribution: The *integral* of a probability density function from *negative infinity* to some finite value of the random variable. The definition is:

$$P_x(x) = \int_{-\infty}^{x} p_x(u)\,du \tag{G.5}$$

damping coefficient: The negative of the real part of a pair of complex conjugate poles in the Laplace domain, associated with a resonant system.

damping factor: The damping coefficient divided by the resonant frequency in radians per second. The resonant frequency is the *distance* of each pole from the origin. The damping factor is also the cosine of the *angle* of each pole relative to the negative real axis.

determinant: A *scalar* quantity that appears in the denominator of *each* element of the *inverse* of a matrix. This can be considered as an indicator of the *linear independence* between the rows or columns of a square matrix. The determinant will be *zero* if any row or column is *linearly dependent* on the others. The determinant is also the "*n*-volume" within the *n*-parallelotope formed by its *n* column vectors or transposed row vectors.

direction cosines: The direction cosines are the *projections* of a given *unit* vector onto a set of *unit basis vectors* that span the entire vector space. These direction cosines define the *direction* of the given vector relative to the basis set.

discrete random variable: A random variable that *only* takes on *discrete* numerical values (say the integers, for example).

double pole: A double pole occurs in a system if two of the roots of the denominator of the Laplace transform of that system *coincide*, forming a pole of *multiplicity two* at that point.

double precision numbers: By current custom, single precision floating point numbers comprise 24 bits (about 7 decimal digits) for the mantissa, and double precision floating point numbers comprise around 53 mantissa bits (about 16 decimal digits).

eigenvalues: When a matrix is post-multiplied by one of its eigenvectors, the result is the (same) eigenvector, but *scaled* by the corresponding *eigenvalue*. When a matrix is *diagonalized*, the diagonal *elements* are the eigenvalues.

eigenvectors: For a *given square* matrix, there is a unique set of vectors for which the product of the *matrix* times one of these vectors produces a *scaled* version of that *same* vector. These are called *eigenvectors*. They can be used to transform the given matrix into a *diagonal* form.

ergodic process: Any random process where the *statistics* (probability density function, moments, etc.) are the *same,* whether collected on *one* signal along the *time axis,* or collected at *one time* from an *ensemble* of "identical" signals.

estimation theory: A set of mathematical procedures that can help you decide on the "best" parameter values (called *estimates* or *measurements*) to assign to a physical system, based on some set of *observations* of the behavior of that system under *given* conditions. This theory helps you make an *educated guess* as to each optimum parameter value, rather than a *random* guess.

expected value: The *expected* value of a random variable (or of a *function* of a random variable) is *conceptually* the same as the *average* of an *infinite* number of samples of this random variable (or function). Mathematically, it is the *integral* of the *product* of the function *times* the probability density function of that random variable, over *all* possible values of the variable, as indicated by:

$$E[g(x)] = \int_{-\infty}^{\infty} g(x)p_x(x)dx \qquad (G.6)$$

Fourier transform: An integral that *transforms time* domain data into *frequency* domain data without *any* loss of information (meaning the process is *reversible*). It is also used to obtain the *probability density function* from the *characteristic function* of a random variable, in addition to a number of other applications. The Fourier transform $X(f)$ of the function $x(t)$ is given by:

$$X(f) = \int_{-\infty}^{\infty} x(t)e^{-i2\pi ft}dt \qquad (G.7)$$

frequency: The number of cycles per second of a sinusoidal time waveform (the units are called Hertz).

frequency response: The *response* (comprising both a *magnitude* and a *phase* angle) of a linear system to a *sinusoidal* excitation of known amplitude, phase, and frequency over a range of frequencies.

Gaussian PDF: The probability density function (PDF) of the *sum* of an *infinite* number of ordinary random variables (see the Central Limit Theorem). The equation is:

$$p_x(x) = \frac{1}{\sqrt{2\pi}\,\sigma_x} e^{-\frac{(x-\mu_x)^2}{2\sigma_x^2}} \qquad (G.8)$$

where μ_x is the *mean value* and σ_x is the *standard deviation* of x.

Gram-Schmidt orthogonalization: Given a set of vectors that *span* some space, this is a method for finding a set of *orthogonal* vectors that span the *same* space. The procedure is to begin with *any one* of the original vectors and successively remove *each* vector from *all* other vectors in a least-squares sense. There is *no unique* set of such orthogonal vectors.

Hermitian symmetry: For a complex function (say a frequency response function), Hermitian symmetry means the *real* part is an *even* function of frequency about the origin, and the *imaginary* part is as *odd* function of frequency about the origin. For a square matrix, Hermitian symmetry means that elements *mirrored* about the *diagonal* are complex conjugates of one another.

homogeneous solution: The solution to a differential equation or a matrix-vector equation that is set to *zero*.

identity matrix: A diagonal matrix, with unity for each element. Multiplication by the identity matrix leaves the original matrix unchanged.

imaginary number: A real number multiplied by $i = \sqrt{-1}$.

impulse response: The response of a linear system to an impulse shape (also called a *delta* function), comprising a pulse having a *finite area*, but *zero width*.

infinitesimal: The inverse of infinite. A quantity that becomes arbitrarily small.

inner vector product: A *scalar* quantity that equals the *product* of the magnitude of one vector times the magnitude of the *projection* of a second vector upon the first. It is given by the sum of the conjugate products of the *corresponding* elements of the two vectors.

invariant: A quantity that does *not* change under any coordinate transformation and is therefore characterized by *new* coordinate values that are *dictated* by the transformation *equations*, independent of the quantity itself. In geometry, these are called "tensors."

joint PDF: A multidimensional probability density function of more than one random variable, *all* of which occur simultaneously.

Laplace transform: An integral transformation between the time domain and the Laplace domain (indexed by s). This transform converts time domain differentiation into Laplace domain multiplication by s. It also converts time domain convolution into Laplace domain multiplication. The Laplace transform $X(s)$ of $x(t)$ is defined by the relation:

$$X(s) = \int_0^\infty x(t)e^{-st}dt \qquad (G.9)$$

least-squares: The *minimum* of the *sum* of the squares of the *differences* between corresponding elements of two vectors or sequences of numbers having the same number of elements.

linearity: A relationship described by *first*-order polynomials.

magnitude: The positive square root of the sum of the squares of the real part and the imaginary part of a complex number.

marginal PDF: A probability density function (PDF) obtained from a *joint* PDF by integrating over the entire range of *one or more* of the associated random variables.

matrix: A rectangular *array* of numbers, or expressions that are associated in *some* manner. A matrix is generally used to represent the coefficients of a set of simultaneous linear equations.

matrix inverse: A square matrix multiplied by its inverse (in either order) yields the *identity* matrix.

matrix pseudoinverse: This is a *nonunique* inverse of a *nonsquare* matrix. If A is a rectangular matrix having dimensions $m \times n$, where $m > n$, then $(A^t A)^{-1} A^t$ is a left-handed pseudoinverse of A. If $m < n$, then $A^t (AA^t)^{-1}$ is a right-handed pseudoinverse of A. In *both* cases the dimensions of the pseudoinverse are $n \times m$.

matrix rank: The number of *linearly independent* rows or columns in a matrix.

matrix transpose: A matrix obtained by *interchanging* the rows and the columns of an original matrix.

maximum likelihood estimate (MLE):   Given an appropriate probability density function (PDF) with its *local origin* at a point in the observation space corresponding to a set of parameter values, the *most likely* set of parameter values are those that place the *mode* (maximum or peak value) of the PDF at the (single) *observation point*.

maximum a posteriori (MAP) estimate: The *mode* (maximum point) of the *conditional* PDF of the parameters, given a *single* observation.

mean value: This is the value obtained after an *infinite* number of averages of a random variable. More precisely, the mean value μ_x of a random variable x is defined by:

$$\mu_x = \int_{-\infty}^{\infty} x p_x(x)\,dx \qquad (G.10)$$

where $p_x(x)$ is the probability density function of the random variable x.

measurement model: A set of equations that define a *mathematical model* of a physical system, including all possible sources of noise and interference, in terms of a set of parameters whose subsequent estimates will comprise the measurements of the system.

median of PDF: The *abscissa* value that divides a probability density function into two halves with *equal area*. The probability of finding a random variable *above* the median is the same as the probability of finding it *below* the median (namely 0.5).

modal vectors: The *homogeneous* solutions to the equations describing a linear system. For example, if the matrix B represents a linear physical system, then $Bu = 0$ is the homogeneous equation whose solutions u are *modal vectors*.

mode of PDF: The abscissa of the *maximum* point on a probability density function of a random variable. This is the most *probable* value of the variable.

modes of vibration: Any mechanical structure tends to vibrate at certain *discrete frequencies*, and the collection of complex amplitudes of the motion at each point on the structure at one of these discrete frequencies is called a mode of vibration.

moment of PDF: The mth moment of a probability density function (PDF) is the *expected value* of the random variable raised to the mth power. If $p_x(x)$ is the PDF, the precise definition is:

$$E[x^n] = \int_{-\infty}^{\infty} x^m p_x(x) dx \qquad \text{(G.11)}$$

Monte Carlo simulation: A computer *simulation* of a random process in which the required random numbers are generated by a *numerical* algorithm designed to produce the desired probability density functions for *each* random variable.

multiplicity: The *order* of a pole in the transfer function (Laplace domain) of a physical system. This is the *exponent* on the denominator of a partial fraction representation of a transfer function. For example, the partial fraction term representing a pole of multiplicity p at s_o is $a/(s - s_o)^p$.

multiple pole: A pole having a multiplicity greater than one.

noise: Any *random perturbations* on signals or waveforms within a physical system, or on the *observations* of that system.

nonlinear: A relationship or process that *cannot* be described by polynomials of *first* order.

observations: The "raw" data collected by monitoring the signals or waveforms of a physical system, to be subsequently used in *measuring* or *estimating* the *parameter* values for that system.

observation space: An *abstract* multidimensional space defined such that *each* related *set* of observations on a physical system corresponds to exactly *one point* in the observation space.

observation vector: A vector in the observation space drawn from the origin to an observation point.

orbital elements: The orbit of a satellite around the Earth is an *ellipse* lying in some orbital *plane*. The elements of the orbit are the parameters of the ellipse *within* the orbital plane, along with the parameters describing this plane *relative* to the Earth.

orthogonal: Two *vectors* are orthogonal if the *projection* of one vector upon the other is *zero*. Two *functions* are orthogonal if the integral of the *product* of the functions over some prescribed range is *zero*.

outer vector product: The outer product of an m-vector and an n-vector is the $m \times n$ *matrix* obtained by multiplying the m-vector times the transpose of the n-vector, element by element.

parameters: Quantities within a physical system or within an equation that determine the properties of that system or equation.

parameter space: The abstract *subspace* of a multidimensional observation space that is obtained from the model of a physical system with *all noise sources set to zero*, as *all* of the parameters of the system are *varied* throughout their allowed ranges.

parameter vector: A vector *within* the parameter subspace whose *elements* are the parameters of the system.

partial fraction: A *sum* of terms of the form $a/(s - s_o)^p$. The quotient of two polynomials in s can always be written in this form, where s_o is a pth order root of the original denominator polynomial, and a is a scalar.

phase angle: The angle of a sinusoid at the origin. The angle of a complex number, written in polar form, relative to the positive real axis.

physical system: A system comprising *real physical* components, rather than *abstract* mathematical components.

pole: A *characteristic value* associated with the *homogeneous* solution of a time domain differential equation. A *root* of the *denominator* of a transfer function in the Laplace domain. A pole is often a complex number, and the *real part* is always *negative* for a stable system.

power spectral density: A function of frequency in which the *area* within a given *frequency interval* is equal to the *power* in that interval. This is the amount of *power per unit of frequency*, where frequency is usually measured in cycles per second (or Hertz).

probability density function: The *area* under this function within any given *abscissa interval* is equal to the *probability* of finding the random variable *within* that interval. Thus, the *total area* under this function is defined to be *unity*, because it is *certain* the random variable will be found *somewhere* along the abscissa.

probability theory: A theory that is designed to "quantify" the properties and interrelationships of quantities that seem to vary in a random and unpredictable manner.

pseudorandom noise: Noise that *appears* to be random, but which is actually generated by a computer algorithm that is *completely predictable* and therefore *not* random at all.

quantize: The conversion of a *continuous* variable into a set of *discrete* quantities separated by some *quantization interval*.

random variable: Any quantity that seems to vary in a random and unpredictable manner.

rational fraction: The *quotient* of two polynomials in some variable.

repeated mode: A mode of vibration that has the *same frequency and damping coefficient* (same pole value) as another mode, but has a *different spatial distribution* of motion.

residue: *Strictly* defined as the (scalar) numerator coefficient on *each* of the terms having *unit* multiplicity in a partial fraction representation of a function. More *loosely* defined as the numerator coefficient on *each* term (*independent* of multiplicity).

residue matrix: In the representation of a transfer *matrix* (for a multidimensional system), the numerator coefficient on each term in a partial fraction expansion is a residue *matrix*, rather than a scalar residue quantity.

resonant frequency: The *magnitude* of each pole of a *pair* of complex conjugate poles in the transfer function of a linear physical system. This frequency corresponds to the *peak value* of the associated frequency response function near that pole.

root-mean-square (rms): The square root of the sum of the squares.

rounding error: A computational *error* that is introduced after various arithmetic operations between numbers, in order to keep the number of digits used to *represent* each number constant.

self-rectification: When a signal or noise waveform with zero mean value is passed through an *even order* nonlinearity (like a quadratic shape, for example), the nonlinearity adds a bias (or DC value) to the waveform.

sensitivity coefficients: As used in this book, the *ratio* of the changes in parameter values to *small* changes in the observations. The matrix of *partial derivatives* of all parameters relative to all observations.

singular matrix: A square matrix whose rank is *less than* its order (thereby making its determinant *zero*), so it cannot be *inverted*.

***s*-plane:** The complex plane defined by the Laplace variable *s*.

stability margin: A control system becomes *unstable* when its loop gain is equal to −1. The *stability margin* is the *minimum distance* between the loop gain contour (as a function of frequency) and this point of instability.

standard deviation: A measure of the width of a probability density function (PDF). This is the square root of the variance (second central moment) of the PDF.

stationary process: A random process in which the statistics (probability density function and its moments) are independent of time.

swept sinusoid: A sinusoid whose frequency is changed linearly with time, slowly enough to generate negligible spurious (or new) frequencies.

symmetric matrix: A square matrix that remains the same if the rows and columns are interchanged.

system matrix: A square matrix comprising the coefficients of the set of linear equations in the Laplace variable *s* that describe a linear physical system. These are the same coefficients found in the time domain differential equations that describe the system.

tensor: Geometrical quantities that describe *invariants* that are inherent in any particular geometry. The coordinates of invariant quantities must change in a well defined manner as coordinate systems are changed. There are both covariant and contravariant tensors, of any order from 0 (scalars), 1 (vectors), and 2 (some square matrices), to any higher order.

topology: The way components in a system are interconnected.

transfer function: The ratio of the output of a physical system to *any* applied input, in the Laplace domain. This becomes the ratio between two polynomials in the Laplace variable *s*, which can also be written in either factored or partial fraction form.

uncertainty principle: Whenever two domains (like time and frequency) are *related* by the Fourier transform, the *product* of the *attainable abscissa resolutions* in the two domains is a *constant*. The *more* certain you are of the abscissa value of a quantity in *one* domain, the *less* certain you are of the abscissa value of the transformed quantity in the *other* domain.

variance: A measure of the *power* in a random variable. More precisely, the second central moment σ_x^2 of the probability density function (PDF) for a random variable, as defined by:

$$\sigma_x^2 = \int_{-\infty}^{\infty} (x - \mu_x)^2 p_x(x) dx \qquad \text{(G.12)}$$

where μ_x is the mean value of x, and $p_x(x)$ is the PDF of x.

vector: An invariant first-order tensor, comprising a set of n numbers spanning an n-dimensional space.

weighting matrix: A *diagonal* matrix used in the *weighted least-squares* estimation procedure. The elements of this matrix are arbitrary, but one *common* choice is the *reciprocal of the variance* of the random variable corresponding to that element.

Index